Kurozumi Shinto

The Main Shrine (*Daikyōden*) of Kurozumi-kyō at Shintozan near Okayama. Photo courtesy of Kurozumi-kyō.

# Kurozumi Shinto

## An American Dialogue

Edited by

## Willis Stoesz

Anima Books

LIBRARY OF CONGRESS
Library of Congress Cataloging-in-Publication Data

Kurozumi Shinto / edited by Willis Stoesz.
p.    cm.
Bibliography: p.
Includes index.
ISBN 0-89012-049-X
1. Kurozumi (Sect) — Congresses.  I. Stoesz, Willis.
BL2222.K884K87  1988
299'.5619—dc19                                              88-503
                                                              CIP

Anima Publications is a subdivision of Conococheague Associates, Inc. 1053 Wilson Avenue, Chambersburg, Pennsylvania 17201. Printed in U.S.A.

To D
in
sincere gratitude

The drawing and writing on the front cover are by Kurozumi Munetada, founder of Kurozumi-kyō. It was part of a message he sent to a follower, and includes a poem (dōka; "song of the way") written as a parting gift as the follower was leaving for Edo as a samurai attending his feudal lord. Within the sun, the visible manifestation of her presence, the founder has inscribed *kokoro*, the mind (or heart) of Amaterasu. A line joins two other (human) hearts with the heart in the sun; other lines run outward but without "heart" being explicitly written there. Though Edo is far from Okayama, those whose hearts share in the same true faith remain united in that spirit. The distance does not matter since Amaterasu, in whom each heart is present, is everywhere. The poem appears as number 38 in chapter 6.

The four *kanji* (the calligraphy that divides each part) are from the hand of Kurozumi Muneharu, current Chief Patriarch of Kurozumi-kyō. In *romaji* script (roman letters) they may be given as *makoto, sei, michi,* and *wa* respectively. Each is a protean concept in Kurozumi teaching, as elsewhere in Japanese religion, used in combination with other characters. "Sincerity," "fidelity," "(the) way", and "harmony" roughly translate them. Used emblematically, as here, they draw attention to basic concerns of Kurozumi-kyō.

# Contents

**Preface**

## Part I. Backgrounds

Definition of Shinto • Historical Formation and Development. Early
Shinto; Medieval Shinto; Recent and contemporary Shinto • Shinto as a
Religious System • The Vitality of Shinto Today

Introduction • The Founder's Early Career. The aspiration to become a
kami; Kurozumi's concept of divinity; Healing; Healing and the Great
Purification Prayer; Early followers • Seclusion. Meetings of the followers; Proselytizing through village headmen; The High Disciples •
The Late Phase

## Part II. Kurozumi Teaching

The Mind of Amaterasu: Source of All • Munetada's "Direct Acceptance
of Divine Mission" • Subsequent Development of Kurozumi-kyō • The
Spread of the Teaching • The Basic Message of Munetada • The Unity
of Kami and Humans • The All-Encompassing Divine Virtue • Health
and The Mind of Kami • Religious Practice in Kurozumi-kyō

First Lecture. We should practice *Ōharai*; Receiving *yōki*; The presence
of *bunshin*; To cultivate *bunshin* • Second Lecture. Watch your mental
condition; The importance of greetings; Thanks and apologies; To forgive people; The basis of the human mind; About those who have died
(*mitama*) • Third Lecture. Joy in giving and in offering

Origins in Japanese History • Kurozumi Munetada, Founder of Kurozumi-kyō • Ethical Results of The Fundamental Experience • Inner
Relation to Kami • Conclusion

## Part III. Perspectives on Kurozumi-kyō

# Preface

*This book originated in the initiative of The Reverend Muneharu Kurozumi, Chief Patriarch of Kurozumi-kyō, to introduce Shinto to English-speaking audiences, and in several scholarly moves to put this religion into perspective.*

The close look we get at Japanese religious values by considering the Kurozumi-kyō[1] sect of Shinto, the oldest of the official thirteen sects of Meiji times, lets us see this tradition in a more concrete way than is often possible from general studies of Shinto. We gain a view of Kurozumi spirituality that gives us a direct, fresh approach to the broader Japanese tradition. Seeing the distinctive emphases of this group also provides new insight into the diversity of that tradition. Here, for instance, is Japanese religion with a sense of mission and outreach stemming from its Edo period beginnings.

Moreover, since Kurozumi-kyō took its basic shape in the late Edo period, it affords insight into a kind of Shinto sheltered from Meiji-period efforts to establish a "purified" national religion divorced from "non-native" aspects. We see a more overtly syncretistic form of Shinto than is often visible in studies of contemporary expressions of this basic strand of Japanese life.

Kurozumi-kyō is unquestionably a form of Shinto, drawing its fundamental religious energies both from the worship of Amaterasu, Kami ("Goddess") of the Sun, and from the spirit of its founder, Kurozumi Munetada, known to his followers as Munetada Kami.[2] Yet, as our studies show, the Confucian and Buddhist strands of the founder's faith also inform his worldview and that of his group. The Shinto of Kurozumi-kyō is closer to the "seamless web" of Japanese religious tradition than are more modern manifestations of Shinto.

## Kurozumi-kyō: A Brief Introduction

Kurozumi-kyō owes its origins to the religious experience and mission of its founder, Kurozumi Munetada (1780-1850).[3] Munetada spent his life in and around Okayama in western Honshu, halfway between Osaka and Hiroshima, except for a number of pilgrimages to Ise. He was a quietly charismatic Shinto priest who formulated a way for others to live which gave them inner serenity and family concord in socially and politically troubled times. His religious powers were drawn from his own inner experience of Amaterasu from whom he received physical healing, an abiding mood of joy and confidence, and charisma to heal others. His daily morning sun worship (*nippai*) became a kind of sacrament practiced until today by members of his group. Through his sermons, his poetry, his letters, and his personal example he guided them to an inner selflessness and an unpretentious service to others that still mark the piety of Kurozumi-kyō members.

The most rapid spread of his movement was in western Japan, radiating outward from Okayama. This city was at that time the seat of Bizen, domain of the Ikeda clan prominent among the lords (*daimyō*) of western Japan. A secondary but crucial center of the movement was Kyoto, where a follower was able to secure support in highly placed official circles during the closing years of the Tokugawa shogunate. Though Kurozumi-kyō has no overt political expression, its close reliance on Amaterasu, divine ancestor of the imperial line, accorded well with the thinking of many who in the last years of the shogunate wished to restore the official role of the emperor in Japanese political life. Later, during the Meiji period when the development of State Shinto was a priority of the national government, it became one of the so-called "Thirteen Sects" of Shinto under some government influence but with a measure of independence.

Today Kurozumi-kyō has about 220,000 members, though it is difficult — perhaps impossible — to be exact. Many descendants of former members still live near churches[4] of the denomination, often treating them somewhat as ordinary Shinto parish (*uji*) shrines. The number of people who identify with it as an aspect of their local community are thus many more than the estimated number of active members. Since Kurozumi teaching in many ways represents an intensified and focused expression of ways of thinking fundamental to Japanese culture, the boundaries of its influence and significance cannot be estimated only in terms of membership statistics.

The members are predominantly rural, concentrated in western Japan. Life patterns among them are quite traditional and families quite stable. Extremes of poverty and wealth are absent. Comparatively few have more than basic formal education, although talented leaders in education and medicine have emerged and its own leaders are forward-looking.

Membership in the denomination is ordinarily expressed as the participation of families in congregations. There are about 371 branch churches (branches of the central headquarters in Okayama) and preaching stations throughout Japan. Local leadership, both male and female, places heavy emphasis on pastoral care, and churches are strongest where this care, most often given by women, is most attentive. Ritual and festival activities are conscientiously maintained, chiefly by the male leadership.

Kurozumi-kyō displays both "main-line" Shinto characteristics and its own distinctive emphases. The kami of Shinto — especially the 800 million kami summarizing the spiritual heritage of ethnic Japan and Amaterasu, patron Kami of the nation — are held in high regard. In Kurozumi shrines traditional prayers and offerings are performed in traditional vestments and furnishings.

At the same time, the founder is also a principal Kami for Kurozumi-kyō. His example in initiating a special relationship with Amaterasu remains in members' minds as they also draw upon her power. His distinctive way of worshiping before the rising sun (*nippai*) is the central ritual by which access to transforming power in people's lives is made available. Beyond this, members rely on his mediation for assistance in finding well-being in their lives. The practice of extensive repetitions of the traditional *Ōharai* prayer as the means by which inner purification is achieved is, Professor Hardacre shows, his innovation. His explanation of how the inner divine presence is to be cultivated provides the rationale of the Kurozumi cultus.

In Okayama Kurozumi-kyō is quite visible. In spring its annual *Go-Shinkō* festival procession moves, banners flying, a number of miles from the original shrine of the founder through downtown streets of the city to Korakuen, a park-like public garden near the castle of the former lords of the area. Its headquarters at Shintōzan may be seen up on a high hill, flag waving, from a right-hand window as one leaves the city westward on the *shinkansen*, Japan's "bullet train." Its members support the work of local hospitals and of a medical research center. Handicapped people, especially children, are a special object of concern. Stories about the founder are part of local Okayama lore.

During the annual *Go-shinkō* festival, the portable shrine (*mikoshi*) passes the train station in downtown Okayama. Photo courtesy of Kurozumi-kyō.

The current head of Kurozumi-kyō is the sixth in direct descent from the founder. He is a vigorous and cordial man who has been to the United States several times, twice as head of his denomination. In 1979 he participated in a World Conference on Religion and Peace held at Princeton University. At that time he preached a sermon in English in St. Patrick's Cathedral in New York. In 1981 he visited New Zealand as head of a cultural delegation, and he has also visited Australia several times. In 1985 he came to Dayton, Ohio as the main speaker at a conference on Kurozumi Shinto sponsored by Wright State University in cooperation with other local institutions.

## Materials of This Book

Four sections of this book are written by Kurozumi Muneharu. Two chapters (3 and 4) were written originally for Japanese audiences, and two (chapter 5 and part of chapter 12) were prepared for

American conference audiences in Dayton. They represent, respectively, views "from the inside" of the Kurozumi circle of religious experience prepared "for the inside," and views "from the inside" prepared for people outside that immediate circle.[5]. Chapter 3, an introduction to Kurozumi Munetada's religion, was originally written for a general Japanese audience, but a draft translation was distributed at the conference. Chapter 4 was made available subsequently, as the Chief Patriarch responded to the interest shown by the audience by providing closer and more intimate information. It is a unique document in giving us the lectures he presented to large numbers of Kurozumi congregations in their own church buildings throughout Japan for the instruction of local members in their own faith and practice. The heart of Kurozumi religion, as summarized in simple terms for its members needing encouragement in basics, is opened for inspection and understanding.

Chapter 6 is a translation of poetry of the founder, presenting about a fifth of his total production as preserved in the written canon of Kurozumi-kyō. Harold Wright's translation — really a transcreation as English poetry — carries forward much of the spirit as well as the verbal content of the original.[6] Here we see the sophistication of the founder's insight. When taken together with the present Patriarch's lectures to church members, we see the character of his pastoral effort in their behalf and the reserves of spirituality on which he can draw in giving leadership.

The remaining chapters are background and analysis, providing "outsider's" perspectives in several ways. Byron Earhart's contribution (chapter 1) was presented at the Dayton conference with members of the community/academic audience who knew little about Shinto in mind, and it serves that same purpose for readers of this book. Specialists in Japanese religion may wish to skip over it, though as a succinct summary of the broad tradition of Shinto (and baseline of comparison for seeing the distinctiveness of Kurozumi-kyō) it will be useful to students and to many with only general knowledge. Chapter 2 is also a chapter in Helen Hardacre's book on Kurozumi-kyō, slightly shortened by her for presentation to the conference audience. We are enabled by her account of the founder's development to move from Earhart's broad picture of Shinto to the discussions of Kurozumi faith presented by its Chief Patriarch.

A certain amount of repetition occurs as several chapters (3, 7, and 8) give accounts of the life of the founder in addition to that in chapter 2, and to references elsewhere. The differences in perspective brought to these retellings are part of the subject matter of this book, taken up again in the concluding part of chapter 12. Chapter 3 is the view from inside the Kurozumi-kyō circle of faith, showing its basis in the life of its founder. The others are outsiders' accounts. Chapter 2 provides a historical summation; chapter 7 carries out a phenomenological analysis focusing on the developing intention of the founder; chapter 8 is concerned with typological and comparative analysis.

Five scholarly chapters (7-11) were prepared after the conference. My own study, in chapter 7, draws on concepts developed by Robert Lifton and Ninian Smart to show how the founder's personal religious development led to his universal point of view. His ecstatic union with Amaterasu was his charter as founder, providing him a source of insight to formulate teachings and to live a life that serves as a paradigm for his group. The founder's universal attitude is a valuable resource for understanding how Japanese religious tradition may approach the contemporary global interaction of cultures.

Some of our stimulus to investigate Kurozumi religion derives from the Chief Patriarch's remark (chapter 3) that his group's official recognition as a Shinto sect by the Meiji government was slowed by the Buddhist affinities they noted in it. Responding to an invitation to identify those affinities, Alan Miller (chapter 8) applies typological analysis to show the importance of the bodhisattva theme in the founder's self-understanding.

Intriguing also in the Chief Patriarch's presentations is his use of the founder's poetry. In chapter 9, Gary L. Ebersole shows how Munetada's poetry is continuous with the larger Japanese religio-aesthetic tradition. Harold Wright continues the discussion of this poetry in chapter 10, emphasizing its didactic uses in comparison to other ways the *tanka* form is employed in Japanese culture. Apparent in both chapters is the importance of Buddhist themes in Munetada's work. Eugene Swanger's contribution follows in chapter 11, enabling us to see how charms and amulets, so much a part of Japanese popular religion, may in Kurozumi hands become a form of far-sighted pastoral guidance.

Taken together, these five chapters are by no means a fully systematic study of Kurozumi-kyō. On the analogy of an archaeological dig, they may be considered exploratory trenches cut across a site that shows promise of further rewarding study. Yet, taken together with Hardacre's description of the founder's development, especially of his Neo-Confucian dimension, and with Kurozumi Muneharu's own exposition of Kurozumi faith, we are enabled to see how this form of Shinto religion is both many-faceted in its inner resources and personally rewarding to its followers.

The dialogue that is presented in chapter 12 adds a dimension that brings all of this into closer range for many readers than might otherwise be possible. An inevitable abstraction goes with scholarly studies, and a certain distance attends presentations from within a faith — or a cultural perspective — other than the reader's own. The dialogue setting in which The Reverend Muneharu Kurozumi and Father Bertrand Buby gave their presentations personalizes Japanese and Christian points of view, enabling us to see something of the "power of presence" behind the words on the page.

My summary in chapter 13 starts from a scholarly appreciation of that dialogue setting, and moves toward making the insights presented from within the Kurozumi circle of faith available to readers' understanding whose assumptions about the nature of religion grow from their western and Christian backgrounds. In doing so it has been possible to achieve some correlation of our several studies — both the "insider's view" and the several "outsider" accounts — of Kurozumi Shinto. Key to this appreciation is the recognition we gain of the distinctive religion of its founder, Kurozumi Munetada.

## Thanks and Acknowledgements

Numerous individuals contributed to the making of this book beyond those named in various notes. Most of them, though much deserving of thanks, shall for avoidance of readers' tedium, go unmentioned. We must, however, say that our conference was a necessary stage in bringing out these materials. That we had a conference on Shinto in Dayton, Ohio was an outgrowth of an exchange program between Wright State University and Okayama University of Science, two institutions whose leaders' commitment to international understanding has borne this tangible fruit among many others.[7]

The expenses of the conference were paid partly by a regrant from the Ohio Humanities Council and partly by the College of Liberal Arts of Wright State. The Program's requirement that lay and scholarly audiences should be brought together, so as to promote broad understanding of how humanities scholars work, guided us in planning the conference, and suggests the range of audience to which this book is directed. The headquarters office of Kurozumi-kyō bore travel expenses for the Chief Patriarch and his companions.[8]

Helen Hardacre's participation, advising us as we planned the conference and serving as interpreter for the Reverend Kurozumi's main presentation, was indispensable. Harold Wright's contribution also was indispensable and is only partly visible on the printed page. As part of the small team hosting our visitors he fluently served as a facilitator of understanding, both during their stay in Dayton and subsequently in Japan during his two-year residence in Kyoto while engaged in translation projects. His attentive, committed participation and that of the conference presenters made it possible to consider developing the book. A person whose indispensable contribution would not ever be known if not mentioned here is Professor Yoshihiko Murashima of the Okayama University of Science, who first introduced me to Kurozumi-kyō, arranging my visit to *nippai* on a chilly February morning in 1983. It was with this graceful contact, far-reaching in its potential effects, that this effort in intercultural understanding began. I am deeply grateful also to Professors Joseph Kitagawa and Byron Earhart for their criticisms of a first draft of these materials, though I do not hold them responsible for what I have done in response. Harry Buck and Barbara Rotz have been both pointed and patient in their help: *arigatō gozaimasu.*

Principally, thanks are due to The Reverend Muneharu Kurozumi, Chief Patriarch of Kurozumi-kyō. His keen interest in having Shinto be understood and his confidence in an American scholar visiting Shintōzan (supported by various patient explanations!) bear testimony to the depth of his faith.

Thanks are due also to Princeton University Press for permission to use Helen Hardacre's contribution which was first published (appearing after the conference took place) in her *Kurozumikyō and the New Religions of Japan* (1986), to Harper and Row for permission to use a quotation in chapter 1, to Overlook Press to use translations by Harold Wright, and to Unwin Hyman for permission to use a quotation in chapter 8.[9]

# Part I

# Backgrounds

# 1

# The Modern Vitality of Shinto

H. Byron Earhart

The purpose of this chapter is to introduce Shinto to those who have had relatively little contact with it or knowledge about it, and also to contribute to a discussion with those for whom Shinto is a living faith. There may be a difference of approach and outcome between my "outside" view as a historian of religion and the "inside" view held by representatives of Kurozumi-kyō. Writing about Shinto taking both of these points of view into consideration is a considerable challenge. In attempting to make good on my intention I shall discuss four aspects of Shinto: the definition of Shinto, an overview of the historical formation of Shinto, the general nature of Shinto as a religious system, and the vitality of Shinto as a religious tradition today.

## Definition of Shinto

It is best to begin with some aspects of this religious tradition which are so well known that they might be taken for granted and forgotten in the process of analyzing details of Shinto history and practice. Especially for westerners first approaching Shinto, it is well to remember that Shinto is strikingly different from the more familiar religions such as Christianity, Islam, and Buddhism. Several characteristics shared by these religions set them apart from Shinto:

a) they are founded religions, started at particular times by specific historical persons, or "founders": Jesus, Muhammad, and Buddha;

b) they are missionary religions, which have eagerly and energetically spread their respective messages over vast geographic areas;

c) they are religions shared by many cultures and nations.

Shinto presents a sharp contrast with each of these characteristics. Shinto is not a "founded religion," since it was not founded at a particular time by a specific person. Rather, it developed gradually, almost naturally, out of prehistoric Japanese culture. Shinto is not a missionary religion, and it has not sought to convert non-Japanese people to its message and practice. It is tied very closely to the cultural and national experience of Japan, and to no other culture or nation.

In defining Shinto it is important to identify it as Japan's distinctive "homegrown" religious tradition. This feature is expressed in the very name Shinto, which can also be pronounced "*kami no michi.*" In either case it literally means "the way of the kami."

Kami are the spiritual beings or "divinities" worshiped in Japan from prehistoric times; thus, Shinto is the religious practice — and more widely, the way of life as a whole — transmitted from ancient Japan that centers around kami. Through history Shinto has, of course, come into contact with other traditions and has become broader than just a "native tradition," but this much at least has remained true.

Our initial definition of Shinto, then, is "the highly distinctive Japanese religious tradition of worship and way of life centering around kami."

It is always easy to stereotype the religion of other cultures and peoples, and there is the danger that this initial definition could lead to such stereotyping, as if Shinto were simply or merely the distinctive Japanese tradition, in contrast to other world religions. This would be far from the truth. Shinto is a complex tradition, and it should be clear from the outset that this initial definition only prepares us for a closer examination of its various aspects. In order to appreciate its complexity and richness, it is essential to recognize at least five aspects within the tradition: shrine Shinto, imperial Shinto, national Shinto, folk Shinto, and sect Shinto.

Each of these aspects deserves brief identification. The worship of kami once took place in the midst of nature, but the major setting of Shinto worship is within buildings known as *miya* or *jinja*. These may be tiny structures (*hokora*) on raised pedestals, local parish shrines, or imposing regional and national shrines. The ritual life associated with these shrines can be called shrine Shinto.

In the mythic traditions of ancient Japan it is believed that the kami created the Japanese islands and that the emperor is descended from the kami, especially from the Sun Goddess, Amaterasu Ōmikami. Traditionally this has meant that the emperor is a kind of "manifest kami" and is responsible for special annual ceremonies such as the harvest festival. The enthronement of the emperor is an elaborate ceremony. The ritual life of the imperial household, still practiced today, quite separate from the local shrines, can be called "imperial Shinto."

Some values that derive from ancient Shinto belief and practice are shared by the Japanese nation as a whole, implicit within both shrine Shinto and imperial Shinto. For example, there is the general understanding that Japan is a sacred land created by the kami, that Japan is guided by an imperial line descended from the kami, and that the Japanese people have a common destiny provided by kami. Before and during World War II these values were interpreted in a rather narrow nationalistic fashion and were part of compulsory education in schools as "national Shinto." Many Shinto scholars and some Japanese people, while disavowing the nationalistic and militaristic dimensions of national Shinto, still see it as an important part of the Shinto tradition.

There is a wealth of religious practices handed down from ancient and prehistoric Japan that are observed by individuals, families, and villages, either in conjunction with or apart from institutional Shinto. These range from seasonal rites such as rice transplanting festivals to decoration of house gates with pine branches at New Year's. In recent centuries it has even been the custom for most families to have a miniature Shinto style altar (*kamidana*) in the home and to present prayers and offerings before this altar. Such practices have sometimes been labeled "folk Shinto."

In the late nineteenth century the Japanese government created another category of Shinto when it attempted the double feat of proclaiming freedom of religion and at the same time declaring Shinto "non-religious." The government wanted to use Shinto values as an integral part of the new national education system in order to unify and mobilize the country, and in effect required all citizens to profess values such as loyalty and service to the nation.

However, from the eighteenth century on there had been some religious movements related to Shinto, but founded by specific historical persons who set forth systems of teaching and spread their messages in the attempt to draw in members. Obviously, such movements could not be called "non-religious," so the government separated them from the "non-religious" shrine Shinto. It labelled them "sect Shinto," and eventually recognized thirteen movements in this category. This is no longer an official legal concept, but scholars still refer to the thirteen — which exist today as independent religious movements — as sect Shinto.

These five aspects or categories of Shinto by no means cover all of this religious tradition. There is considerable disagreement about how many key aspects it has and how they should be distinguished. But if we keep in mind these five aspects we will have a much broader appreciation of Shinto than can be gained from the minimal or initial definition.

## Historical Formation and Development

Shinto, like any religious tradition, is not a static entity but a living, changing force in the life of a people and its culture. Although it is not possible to deal completely with the entire range of Shinto history, a general overview of the historical formation and development of Shinto can be gained by oversimplifying this history into three major periods:

a) *early Shinto*, from the emergence of the earliest Japanese culture in prehistoric times to the formation of Shinto as an identifiable tradition from about the seventh or eighth century A.D.;

b) *medieval Shinto*, from the early Shinto of about the eighth century to the elaboration of more widespread shrines throughout the countryside and more highly developed theories up until about the seventeenth century;

c) *recent and contemporary Shinto*, from the elaborate shrine system of about the seventeenth century to the dramatic changes establishing Shinto in the life of the nation from 1868 to 1945 and its disestablishment after 1945.

### Early Shinto

Shinto did not begin with one founder or one set of doctrines or even one code of conduct. It emerged out of Japan's prehistoric heritage of a mixture of cultures and peoples which eventually came to form the identity of the Japanese people and Japanese culture. In prehistoric times many elements entered Japan from the north and the south. From the south came elements such as the distinctive shrine architectural style of a raised building on pillars with cross-pieces at the ends of the roof lines. Some mythical themes from the South Pacific are similar to those found in the Japanese written mythologies *Kojiki* and *Nihon Shoki* (also known as *Nihongi*). From the north came the notion of kami as hovering over the earth and temporarily descending to the earth by way of trees. The Ainu, who lived in northern Honshu and Hokkaido, worshiped deities called *kamui*, and this term may be related to the Japanese kami. For centuries these elements intermingled within local cultures that shared many features but remained separate from one another.

Some features that were shared by these local cultures from about the middle of the first millennium B.C. were religious themes related to rice agriculture, especially concern for fertility of the rice crop and veneration of ancestors. The family was the primary religious unit, with family ancestors major objects of worship. In southwest Honshu one leading family came to be revered as the ritual and political head of the people as a whole. There were specialized rituals and traditions around this leading family, antecedent of the imperial line, as well as local legends and practices. But there was still no official name for its set of beliefs and practices.

About the middle of the first millennium A.D., when there was still no written language or centralized government in Japan, an influx of Chinese cultural influence brought to Japan all the riches of Chinese language, thought, and government as well as the Indian treasures of Buddhism and the Chinese tradition of Taoism and Confucianism. Japan's response was both enthusiastic reception of the continental culture and also retention of the prehistoric heritage. The long tradition of Japanese religious beliefs and practices was retained at the same time that Buddhism was being adopted. One explanation for the creation of the name "Shinto" for the Japanese heritage of religion is that since Buddhism was called the "way of the Buddha" the native religion was called the "way of the kami." A good example of the way religious traditions interacted in early Japan is seen in the so-called Constitution of Prince Shōtoku in the early seventh century. He urged his countrymen to value the social harmony of Confucianism, to revere the three treasures of Buddhism, and to obey the commands of the emperor (as in Shinto).

This process of interaction shows how Japanese culture and Shinto are open to other religious traditions. Shinto readily accepted Confucian notions of loyalty and Buddhist rituals and theories. In the adoption of a writing system, the oral traditions and prayers of prehistoric Japan were written down for the first time. One of the objectives in compiling the mythologies of *Kojiki* and *Nihon Shoki* was to unify the many local legends into one national tradition. This unified tradition presented the creation of the Japanese islands and the descent of the imperial family through one lineage of kami traced through the Sun Goddess (Amaterasu Ōmikami). By about the eighth century Shinto had assumed the status of an identifiable Japanese tradition coexisting with the "foreign" traditions which were rapidly being naturalized.

### Medieval Shinto

From the eighth century onward Shinto coexisted with Buddhism and other traditions in a process of mutual influence. In some ways Buddhism, as the major organized religion of the Chinese cultural heritage, tended to overwhelm Japanese culture and dominate Shinto. But the native heritage was resilient as well as flexible and tolerant, and Shinto retained its position as the only indigenous Japanese religious tradition. Buddhist statues and scriptures were featured in Shinto shrines and worship services; at the same time Shinto also preserved and practiced ancient Japanese customs. Mutual borrowing by both Shinto and Buddhism brought these traditions very close together. For example, one traditional account has it that when the Sun Buddha (Dainichi) was to be installed in the large central imperial Buddhist temple, the Todaiji in Nara, a messenger was sent to the Ise Shrine. Ise is the most important Shinto shrine because the Sun Goddess Amaterasu Ōmikami is enshrined there. The messenger requested an answer by oracle on whether it was proper to install the Sun Buddha at Todaiji. The response was that since the Sun Buddha and the Sun Goddess are identical, it was proper to install the Sun Buddha there. This is but one example of the many equivalences between Buddhist and Shinto objects of worship.

At the same time that Shinto absorbed features of Buddhism it also became more highly codified and systematic. One major achievement of the tenth century was the writing down of the Codes of the Engi era, recording local shrines and prayers. From about this time the shrines of southwest Honshu spread to the northeast, often in conjunction with Buddhist temples. As shrines spread throughout the country, they became closely related to elaborate local support systems. Originally many shrines were established as the family or clan shrines of the leading families, and the kami of these shrines were worshiped as a kind of clan ancestor or deity. Eventually these shrines and their kami were seen as the protective tutelary agencies for the local residents, and systems of belief and practice developed around thousands of local shrines.

These systems included both annual rituals and rites of passage in which people participated more as members of families and villages than as individuals. Buddhism contributed to these rituals. Shortly after Buddhism entered Japan it emphasized funeral and memorial rites, and from the seventeenth century the government required families to belong to local Buddhist parish temples and to have rites for the dead performed by temples. Thus, there came to be a pattern of families belonging to Buddhist temples through hereditary family affiliation. At the same time, it increasingly became the custom for families to participate in local Shinto shrines according to the residential pattern of where the family lived. Thus, it was common for many families, especially the "main" first-son family of the larger extended family, to have both a Buddhist altar and Shinto altar within the home.

During this period Buddhism tended to dominate the life of the country and Shinto scholars came to resent this domination. They responded in numerous ways seeking to strengthen and "restore" Shinto to its primary place in Japanese life. Some scholars associated Shinto and the emperor as the combined source and mainstay of Japanese life; other scholars developed more complex systems of thought to purify Shinto of Buddhist influence and to express the ritual life of Shinto. Partly as a result of their Confucian interest in classics, some Japanese scholars became interested in Japanese classics and developed "national learning" as an attempt to revitalize Shinto. Eventually they argued that Shinto was superior to Buddhism.

### Recent and contemporary Shinto

Two important dates in Japanese history are crucial for understanding recent and contemporary Shinto. The first is 1868, the beginning of the Meiji Restoration that marked the transition of a feudal country to a nation-state. The second is 1945, the end of World War II and a watershed for many religious changes such as complete freedom of religion. Shinto helped bring about the momentous changes of the Meiji Restoration, in the sense that Shinto ideas were used to force the Tokugawa *shōgun* out of power and

Morning prayer (*nippai*) at the Wright Brothers Memorial.
Ōharai is being prayed. Photo by Willis Stoesz.

"restore" the emperor to at least symbolic leadership of the country.
At the same time the ancient Department of Shinto was "restored"
as the centerpiece of this new government.

From 1868 until 1945 Shinto played a crucial role in the government's plan to unify and mobilize the people. For about two centuries prior to 1868 Buddhism had been practically an arm of the
government and almost an established religion, with every family
required to belong to a local parish temple. After 1868 Buddhism
lost favor and Shinto gained favor with the government. In effect
Shinto became an established religion, but only after the government tried a number of abortive programs aimed at requiring or
persuading universal participation in Shinto.

The eventual solution was not to make Shinto the universal
religion but to declare Shinto "non-religious," and to require school
children and citizens to express patriotism and loyalty to the state
through Shinto ceremonies. By declaring Shinto non-religious, the
government could maintain the Meiji constitution's guarantee of
freedom of religion and at the same time require the "patriotic"
teachings of Shinto in public schools. By the 1930s rather strict in-
doctrination in patriotism and loyalty was the rule, especially
through the ultranationalistic textbook *Kokutai no Hongi*. This

text maligned western individualism and praised Confucian loyalty and Shinto patriotism. It taught absolute loyalty to the emperor as a descendent of the kami and absolute commitment to Japan as a superior country founded by the kami. From the early 1900s the government had assumed much control over local shrines, eliminating some smaller shrines and merging others for purposes of more efficient administration. Control was exercised by appointing priests and by giving some shrines financial support. This phenomenon has sometimes been called "state Shinto."

Not included in this state Shinto were a number of religious movements which had arisen in the eighteenth and nineteenth centuries around popular leaders. These individuals gathered followers into voluntary organizations which gradually developed larger memberships over wide geographical areas. These movements shared many beliefs and practices with Shinto, but because they had their own founders and teachings they were not included in state Shinto and were classified by the government as "sect Shinto." In this way they were allowed to operate as religions only within narrowly defined limits. Some of the sect Shinto movements, as well as many of the other religious movements that arose during the same time, were persecuted or suppressed by the government.

The years 1945 and 1946 are critical for contemporary Shinto, because at the end of World War II the Allied Forces required the disestablishment of Shinto and other measures such as the renunciation of divinity by the emperor. This meant a wider separation of religion and state, such that no religion was sponsored or financed by the government and none was allowed to interfere with the government. People could not be required to attend or financially support any religion, nor would any religion (including Shinto) be disseminated in public schools. Westerners may think that this is a simple matter, but actually some aspects of this "separation" are still not completely resolved. For example, the emperor is still a symbolic head of state, and even if he does not wield real power he does perform rituals that theoretically benefit the entire country; however, according to the separation of religion and state these are "personal" rituals and he has to use his personal funds to perform them. Even more problematic are the issues of using public funds for the Ise Shrine, which is seen as a kind of national monument, and using public funds for the Yasukuni Shrine, the national monument for the war dead. There is still a small but active minority in

Japan that would like to see both a greater role for the emperor and state support for some shrines such as Ise and Yasukuni.

Shinto shrines continue to exist today just as other religious institutions do, which means they are quite different than they were before World War II. Before the war, the local parish shrine (*uji*) system was rather strong, and all homes within the territory of a parish shrine were expected to contribute money and participate in shrine ceremonies. Today all contributions and participation are voluntary, with no state support. This has meant hard times for many small rural shrines, but ironically many large shrines in cities and in famous tourist spots have profited from holiday visits and vacation travel.

## Shinto as a Religious System

To lay down a foundation for assessing the vitality of Shinto today it has been necessary to sketch an overview of Shinto's historical formation. However, it is equally important to view Shinto as a systematic unity, an interrelated pattern of beliefs and practices that forms a worldview. It is potentially misleading to reduce a living religious tradition to a succinct worldview, because being alive it is always much richer and more complex than any interpretation that attempts to represent it. Nevertheless, whenever we talk about Shinto we are making some assumptions about its basic beliefs, organization, and practices, and we need to make them clear.

Systematic views of Shinto should grasp essential features of this tradition across time, rather than be limited to a specific historical period. If in simple terms we think of a religious worldview as including a system of beliefs, social organization, and ritual practices, the crucial aspects of Shinto are kami, shrines, and worship and festivals.

The belief system of Shinto is centered around the many Japanese kami. These kami include the deities of the mythic age who created the Japanese islands and established the imperial line, as well as kami within the natural realm today. They also include the emperor and, to a lesser extent, extraordinary human beings such as revered family ancestors and great religious leaders. Generally Shinto has not focused on a western-style monotheistic form of theology concerned with questioning and demonstrating the existence and nature of deity. Rather, in Japan existence of kami has been "naturally" assumed as part and parcel of the processes of nature, from the creation of life in the age of the mythic kami to the regeneration of life in the flow of the seasons and of the vegetative cycle. In other words, Shinto assumes that at the beginning of life and at the heart of life is the kami's providential power of creation and re-creation. The imperative that is inherent in this belief system is the notion that humans should accept gratefully the blessings of kami, especially by living pure, "bright" lives in harmony with the kami.

The social organization of Shinto ranges from the individual and the family, continues through the village or parish unit, and culminates in the nation. Individuals have always had access to kami through personal visits to shrines for special petitions or thanks, but usually participation in Shinto has been through groups — especially families and villages. It is not an individual but a family that purchases a Shinto altar for a home, for the family as a whole to be blessed. The customary manner of participating in Shinto ceremonies has been for families to worship in the home or for villages to hold a festival. At the highest level there is an ideal and implicit unity of all Japanese worshiping the kami, a nation observing the providential protection of the kami who created the nation. Families may express this national religious sentiment by annually enshrining in the home an amulet of the Ise Shrine, and much of the country together observes the seasonal celebrations such as New Year's. The emperor performs annual rituals that commemorate and celebrate this providential protection by the kami.

A great deal of the social organization related to Shinto is at the local level or implicit. There is a minimum of the ecclesiastical structure found in the Catholic Church and Protestant denominations. However, the fact that it is not expressed as a tightly organized ecclesiastical body does not mean that its role in Japanese life is any less important. The notion of the unity of all Japanese people is a very important part of the Japanese national consciousness. It includes a strong sense of having a venerable culture and a conviction of possessing a common destiny. This notion of Shinto unity is implicit, in sharp contrast to the explicit notions in Christianity and Islam of the brotherhood of all believers.

Ritual practice in Shinto, obviously, focuses on worship of kami. But where, when, and how does this take place? The two most important sites for worshiping kami are the small *kamidana* in the home and the local Shinto shrine. Each constitutes a sacred place where the kami temporarily reside. Simple offerings and individual or family prayers before the home altar or in the shrine call down the kami and bring humans into contact with the kami, providing protection and blessing. Other sacred palces are the national shrines such as Ise and large regional shrines.

There are daily occasions for worship, an ideal for the home, and annual celebrations at local shrines, such as New Year's, in the spring, and in the fall. An individual may pay regular visits to a shrine for special devotions or for thanksgiving. For example, it is the custom for students — and for mothers of students — to visit special shrines praying for help with examinations. Another custom is the age-old rite of passage when parents bring an infant to a local shrine for blessing.

One of the prerequisities for all such ritual practices, and one of the hallmarks of Shinto, is purification. All Shinto shrines provide water, preferably running water, for rinsing of hands and mouth. Ritual purity is essential before contact with kami. Impurity is directly associated with sickness, open wounds, or death. All of these traditionally required a lapse of time and a special rite to remove the impurity before a person could again come into the presence of kami. A state of purity is not simply a physical condition but also means an inner purity or sincerity when approaching kami.

From ancient times special ritual prayers, or *norito*, have been recited as part of the worship of kami. After purification, offerings are made and the kami are invoked or called down. The kami partake of the spirit of the offering and then are "sent off." The priests who recite the prayers and make the offerings, sometimes joined by parishioners, may then eat the offerings. This is an abbreviated description of festival (*matsuri*). Some scholars see it as the heart of Shinto and of Japanese religion generally.

This festival may be rather quiet and sedate, but often it entails crowded shrine grounds with a carnival atmosphere, with booths and vendors all around the shrine selling food and souvenirs. The many people who throng a shrine during a popular festival usually take home not only souvenirs but also a shrine paper with the name of the shrine and a protective phrase. This shrine paper will be installed in the home, perhaps in the *kamidana*. Especially at New Year's time old shrine papers from the previous year are discarded or burned, and new shrine papers are brought home.

## The Vitality of Shinto Today

We are now in position to consider the modern vitality of Shinto. There are at least three prerequisites for interpreting questions such as the vitality of a religious tradition: first, knowledge of the historical development and transformation of the tradition; second, an understanding of the tradition as a religious system; and third, an assessment of the contemporary situation of the tradition with a reasonable model of interpretation. The first two areas have been sketched, even if all too briefly. What remains is to make clear a model of interpretation and to apply it to the present situation in the light of the historical and systematic material.

The question of the relation of traditional to modern culture or religion is a matter that has plagued scholarship in the West at least since the Enlightenment. It has been especially prominent in the various modernization theories that have proliferated in the past decades.

A major premise of much modernization theory is that what is traditional is a hindrance to development of what is new or modern or scientific. In this light, modernization theory has not just given a description or analysis of the decline of the traditional, but actually has tried to hurry the process along. Even when such scholars have not openly advocated the demise of tradition, they have phrased the question in terms of how tradition can survive in the face of modernity, implying that the two are incompatible.

The following approach to the question borrows from several scholars, especially Edward Shils and Jaroslav Pelikan, who have questioned these assumptions about modernization.[1] This view states that the traditional is not necessarily a hindrance to the future, but is, in fact, an enabling factor in transmitting to the future a culture's or a people's identity. This means that there is no necessary disjuncture between tradition and whatever we call the present: "modern" or "contemporary." One of the major benefits of such an approach is that it is a shift in viewpoint. Rather than looking backward at tradition as a relic of the past, it looks at tradition in a forward sense as a progression into the future.

However, this "forward-looking" view of tradition does not mean that assessing vitality is a simple process. For tradition never marches into the future in the exact shape in which it existed in the past. A tradition is transmitted by previous generations, accepted in part and modified by the present generation, and then handed down to subsequent generations. Each in turn accepts it in part and modifies it. What is left out is lost, what is added is gained, and there are always changes. Jaroslav Pelikan has used an apt phrase to characterize this process with regard to Christianity: "Tradition is the living faith of the dead; traditionalism is the dead faith of the living."[2] In other words, every generation accepts beliefs and practices from a previous generation, and as this becomes a living faith for the new generation it lives on and becomes the new tradition. Traditionalism, on the other hand, is the attempt to cling to elements of the previous generation which no longer are viable in the present and fail to gain acceptance into the future.

This set of assumptions is the basis of a model for interpreting the vitality of Shinto today. The question then is what aspects of Shinto are being handed down as a living faith, and what aspects of Shinto seem to be passing out of existence?

Perhaps the single most significant aspect of Shinto's vitality today is what is quite obvious, and yet easily and often overlooked: the vitality of Shinto is directly related to the vitality of Japanese culture and the Japanese nation. Shinto is closely related to all aspects of Japanese life, from the birth of the nation in its own self-conception to the identity of the people as sharing a common destiny in this island country. In fact, we may assume that so long as Japan exists, it is likely that Shinto will be vital to this existence.

However, even if Shinto is central to the continuation of things Japanese it does not mean that Shinto will take exactly the same shape as in the past. Indeed, its history shows that it has assumed many forms, from the rather loose heritage of prehistoric times to a more organized form as Japanese culture became more highly organized. Shinto experienced geographical expansion even at a time when Buddhism tended to dominate it, and in later times it traded places with Buddhism as the religion favored by the government.

Historical insight enables us to say that Shinto does not now and perhaps never again can have the loose structure of prehistoric times. Shinto is too highly organized, and Japanese society is too pluralistic today, for a return to Shinto's ancient role as the keystone of a unified religious and political order. In fact, it may be safe to say that some of the Meiji attempts to restore the Department of Shinto as the centerpiece of a unified religious and political Japanese government were instances of traditionalism, in the sense of unsuccessfully trying to revive dead features of a tradition that could not be resuscitated. This is a delicate issue, and one which some Shinto scholars may well see quite differently. From an "inside" viewpoint, a religious thinker may wish to hold to a past ideal, trying to revive it and change the social scene, at the same time that others may use the social situation as a basis for arguing that religious ideals should be changed. This tension between religious ideals and social circumstances is found in every religious tradition.

In whatever way followers of Shinto may prefer to balance past ideals with present situations, it remains true that social circumstances have changed and Shinto has changed too. For example, Shinto arose in an agricultural setting and its ritual life was very closely attuned to agricultural and seasonal rhythms. But Japan already began moving several centuries ago to an urban and industrial society, and this means that Shinto's agricultural-seasonal emphasis is more a reflection of past conditions than of the actual lifestyle of contemporary Japanese. One aspect of Shinto's ability to change is seen in the fact that as Japan shifted to an urban culture, urban shrines developed and became quite popular for the blessing of business enterprises. Shinto, like Buddhism, has been innovative in the midst of modern times: probably the most important blessing bought at Shinto shrines and Buddhist temples is for traffic safety. These are just a few indications of how Shinto can and has changed through time. What would be impossible and almost unthinkable is for Shinto to attempt a return to a preindustrial, agricultural setting. What is possible and indeed likely is that concern for environmental and ecological issues may be informed by the living Shinto heritage of respect for nature as the providential creation of kami.

Some dimensions of the current scene tend to place limits on how Shinto may be socially organized. Instances of two of these dimensions are tendencies toward the formation of nuclear families rather than extended families and toward residential mobility rather than long-term residences. Both are directly related to changes in how Shinto is — and is not — practiced. The tendency toward nuclear families and apartment living has been accompanied by a sharp decrease in the number of family units with Shinto altars. More families possess a Buddhist altar than a Shinto altar. With migration of people from countryside to the city, many smaller country shrines lose their parishioners but the people who move into cities do not always develop a parish relationship with a local shrine. These new city residents may participate in Shinto, but they do so more as individuals, and on occasions of interest to them such as the blessing of an infant or a visit at New Year's to a large, famous shrine. Kiyomi Morioka, a sociologist of religion, has called this phenomenon "the delocalization of the Shinto belief and behavior," showing that recent residents in large cities participate less in local parish shrines and their group activities, and more in large shrines where they go as individuals rather than as parish members. He calls this a change to diffuseness, and "diffuseness is born of the delocalization of Shinto belief and practice."[3]

These observations make several comments possible. Some people, including Shinto leaders, may deplore the weakening of local parish ties. However, this does not necessarily mean a loss of vitality. In fact the change demonstrates some degree of vitality because Shinto has taken new form. One blind spot scholars of religion have had in interpreting questions such as the vitality of a tradition is to assume that the opposite of vitality is a changed set of circumstances rather absence of the tradition. So long as Shinto continues to exist, even if in changed form within different social circumstances, it demonstrates vitality.

The vitality of Shinto is its ability to preserve, modify, and transmit its message of kami, shrines, and festivals. The fact that these beliefs and practices are being transmitted in changed form shows that it is a "living faith." I conclude by quoting from the life history of a member of a new religion, Gedatsu-kai, which I recorded several years ago. This man was talking about his experience as a member of Gedatsu-kai and was not asked to mention Shinto, but for that very reason his comments about Shinto are fresh and candid. This fifty-one year old man, a college graduate whose family had long resided in Tokyo, was explaining the relationship between his "traditional" upbringing of respect for kami and the practice of Gedatsu-kai.

> There were many people who didn't go on the first and fifteenth of the month to the local Shinto shrine of the tutelary kami, but my family was a shrine parish representative. And my family went not only on the first and fifteenth of the month, but every day. From my youth, I went every day. My family is still parish representative. I myself don't participate that much as parish representative, but my mother, who is seventy-eight and healthy now, goes to the shrine as parish representative.

I go to the local shrine of the tutelary kami for "good morning" and "good night." ... In the morning, my "good morning" greeting is, "Again today your favor-blessing"; in the evening, my "good night" is, "Thank you for another safe day." I did this every day, as a custom, just as if I were greeting my parents.[4]

The religious commitment of this one member of Gedatsu-kai certainly should not be considered as typical of the Japanese population as a whole or of Shinto generally. In Japan, as well as in most highly developed countries such as the United States, economic commitment is probably much higher than religious commitment, and indifference to religion is a major competitor to religious commitment. The faith this person professes may not be typical of Japanese culture today.

However, it does indicate the depth of vitality that Shinto holds for some people, not only as a heritage of the past, but also as a possibility for the future, especially in changed forms such as new religions.

# 2

# Kurozumi Munetada, Founder of Kurozumi-kyō

Helen Hardacre

## Introduction

This chapter considers the life of the founder of Kurozumi-kyō, Kurozumi Munetada (1780-1850), the development of his thought, and the early history of his religion. We begin with a brief consideration of Japan in the time of the founder.

Tokugawa Japan was governed by a central administration called the *bakufu* ("tent government") and by local domains, or *han*. The *shōgun* headed the *bakufu* and ruled as the emperor's military deputy. The *shōgun* controlled lands amounting to about one-fourth of the whole, and other members of the Tokugawa family and their direct retainers (*fudai daimyō*) held another thirty-six percent. A little less than forty percent was held by about one hundred *tozama daimyō* (those who surrendered to the Tokugawa after 1600). The remainder was allocated to the imperial court and to a number of temples and shrines.[1]

The *han* or domains were ruled by *daimyō*, and the *han's* revenue was measured in rice, by units called *koku* (about five bushels). A rice tax was collected from peasant cultivators and then redistributed by the *daimyō* for his own use and that of this retainers. A fixed system of classes ranked samurai, peasants, artisans, and merchants in a hierarchy. Samurai received fixed stipends in rice, which made them especially vulnerable to fluctuations in the market value of rice as a cash economy inexorably gained ascendancy over the agrarian ideal.[2] In addition to the four classes, there were elaborate distinctions within each, in the case of samurai representing differences in stipends and ceremonial privileges in relation to the *daimyō*. As the period drew to a close, greater mobility and status differences were to be seen in both commoner and samurai society.[3]

By 1800 Tokugawa society differed greatly from the situation in the seventeenth century. Mutual interest drew lower samurai and rich peasants together across class lines, and the realities of interest, influence, and power diverged widely from the traditional ideal. An important cause of these changes was fiscal mismanagement at the top. From 1750 on, the *bakufu's* expenditures rose while rice revenue fell, and the result was a growing annual deficit which by 1840 had reached half a million *ryō* of gold.[4] To redress the deficit the *bakufu* debased the currency and exacted forced loans from merchants, which predictably played havoc with the entire economy.[5] Simultaneously, it soberly lectured the people on the necessity of frugality, diligence, and thrift through sumptuary laws. The Tempō Reforms (1831-1843) represented a concerted effort to reduce the deficits, but they produced no lasting results.[6] There were increasing numbers of people who were under the direct control of no authority and who were easily drawn into a rising tide of peasant unrest.[7]

Between the years 1813 and 1868 there were no less than 400 peasant revolts of varying scale. One of the most alarming to the *bakufu* was led by one of its own officials, Oshio Heihachiro, in Osaka in 1837.[8] News of this uprising spread throughout Japan. No area of Japan was free of revolt, and the *bakufu* had reason to fear for its preservation and safety. Although these revolts were not "revolutionary" in the sense of seeking to replace the entire system with another, they clearly expressed the varied discontents of the people with their rulers.[9] Often the *bakufu* and *han* authorities responded to these uprisings with educational programs designed to raise village morale and secure allegiance to the status quo. Local authorities sponsored lecture tours by men representing a variety of creeds, incorporating Shinto, "national learning" (*kokugaku*), and "Learning of the Heart-Mind" (*Shingaku*) concepts to convey to peasants a sense of place and purpose. Their theological differences aside, all espoused the values of filial piety, obedience to authority, thrift, and diligence: the so-called core values of the age.[10]

A popular movement which exerted great influence on the growth of new religions was Ise pilgrimage.[11] Because of the Grand

Shrine's national status, it was easier for commoners to secure permission to travel there on pilgrimage than anywhere else, and by the end of the era there was a popular, explicit understanding that all persons, male or female, had a patriotic duty to make the pilgrimage at least once. It fact, pilgrimage became associated with coming-of-age rites and acquired an air of custom and duty rather than individual faith. Pilgrimage was surrounded with many secular amusements in the towns of Ise and Yamada, which sported baths, hotels, brothels and similar accoutrements of a "tourist trap."[12] The pilgrimage played an important role in creating widespread, popular awareness of the entire nation in what was otherwise a highly localized society. Pilgrimage brought village people into contact with the tastes, accents, and customs of other areas of Japan, and the shrine became a symbolic vehicle for expressing a sense of common identity. Appropriately, the notion of Ise as the seat of the ancestral gods (kami) of the imperial house was superseded in popular consciousness by the idea of Ise as enshrining the highest gods of the Japanese people.[13] Thus Ise pilgrimage was instrumental in casting a growing sense of national identity in a Shinto idiom.

Tokugawa popular religions involved a Confucian conception of society as a hierarchy of complementary functions, regulated by proper conduct in the five relations governing social life. As long as the relations of human society are in order, society will be harmonious, and the human world will be in accord with the cosmos. Humanity is the recipient of countless blessings (on) from superiors and beneficence from superordinate entities such as Heaven, the Buddhas, and the kami. These must be repaid, and the repayment of obligation (hō-on) became a primary religious action.

In addition to (but not in competition with) superordinate entities was the idea of an underlying principle of the universe (Neo-Confucian li, the Buddha-nature, kami-nature), and of humanity's need to seek union with this principle. This idea is found in Confucian, Shinto, and Buddhist idioms, expressed as the quest to become a sage, to become a kami, or to attain Buddhahood. Towards this end, humanity must practice spiritual cultivation. The means to true cultivation was one of the enduring questions of the age, receiving a variety of answers from founders of new religions at the end of the period. Because egotism prevents unity with cosmic principle, moral cultivation is a sustained struggle against selfish desire. Virtually all popular religions of the nineteenth centuries originate in this matrix of ideas.[14]

The cult of sagehood was a central ideal in Neo-Confucian thought, in Japan as well as in China. The aspect of sagehood most congenial to the Japanese was the sage neither as an ideal ruler nor as an original source of authority and orthodoxy, but instead as an individual perfected in self-cultivation.[15] Japanese thinkers such as Yamaga Sokō (1622-1685) recorded their self-cultivation in autobiographical works, and from these we learn what the central questions of the pursuit of sagehood are. There must first be an awakening to the need of self-cultivation and a resolution to pursue it.[16] But in what does self-cultivation consist? Is it to be attained through "quiet sitting"? Must the formal codes of behavior prescribed in Confucian writings be strictly followed? Is the object of these disciplines a repression of physical nature and a curbing of desire? Or should self-cultivation instead have the aim of nurturing the human spirit, originally one with the principle underlying the entire cosmos? All these were questions inevitably involved in the quest for sagehood as Japanese thinkers in the Tokugawa period understood that ideal.[17]

As appropriated by Japanese thinkers such as Yamazaki Ansai (1611-1682),[18] Kaibara Ekken (1603-1714),[19] and Nakae Tōju (1608-1648),[20] Neo-Confucian thought took on a theistic emphasis that bore deep affinities with Shinto. Although each of these thinkers was quite different and founded a separate school of thought, they all believed in the perfectability of human beings, a tenet that made the quest for sagehood plausible. Each saw in principle (li) a unity between humanity and the universe, and each idealized an experience of absolute oneness with the cosmos. It was on this last point in particular that they perceived a similar ethos in Shinto. In fact, it was shortly after a pilgrimage to the Ise Shrine that Nakae Tōju abandoned a formalistic insistence on observance of rites and codes of behavior. Instead he came to uphold the view that humanity is naturally in harmony with universal principle and must not be so preoccupied with observance of rites and rules that the spontaneity of the spirit is stifled.

> For a long time I have acted according to the formal codes of conduct. I have recently come to understand that such codes are wrong ... Abandon the ... desire which causes you to adhere to formal codes, have faith in your own essential mind, do not be attached to mere convention.[21]

The variety of Neo-Confucian thought that probably influenced Kurozumi most directly was the Shingaku ("Learning of the Heart-Mind") of Ishida Baigan (1685-1744).[22] While appropriating the notion of the heart-mind (the *kokoro, shin*), Baigan emphasized its ethical and affective dimensions, paying less attention to the rationalist side developed by other Japanese Neo-Confucians. Baigan's Shingaku was less a philosophical system than "a type and method of spirituality"[23] especially directed to townsmen and merchants. The basis of Shingaku was Mencius' concept of nature according to which the "innermost temperament" of humanity is originally good. Failure and misfortune result from lack of cultivation of *kokoro*, and it is the aim of Shingaku to "promote the recovery and cultivation of original, innate nature."[24] Daily cultivation consisted of introspection and self-examination in order to develop awareness of original nature. Because selfish desire obstructs the individual's progress toward perfection and prevents the experience of all-prevading unity, another aim of self-cultivation is to be rid of egoism and to nurture a state of egolessness, *ware nashi*.[25] Although Kurozumi states these ideas in a Shinto idiom, he incorporated the basic Shingaku framework virtually intact.

## The Founder's Early Career

Kurozumi Munetada was born on December 21, 1780, the third son of a low-ranking priest of the Imamura Shrine, a tutelary shrine of the Okayama domain.[26] In secular matters, Kurozumi held the samurai rank.[27] As a child the founder considered filial piety the highest good, and many incidents of his filial behavior are related. One which is often retold in contemporary Kurozumi-kyō churches has it that Gonkichi, as the child Kurozumi was called, was told by one parent on a rainy day to wear straw sandals and by the other to wear wooden clogs. Loathe to disobey either, he set out with a sandal on one foot and a clog on the other. At the age of nineteen he resolved to honor his parents further by becoming a kami in his own lifetime and this remained the central goal of his life.[28]

Of the founder's early education little is known, but there is no evidence to suggest that it surpassed that of the average priest of his day, which is to say that he knew such classical works as the *Kojiki*, the poetry collection *Man'yōshū*, the *Kokinshū*, the Chinese classics to a certain extent, and the writings attributed to Lao Tzu and Chuang Tzu. In addition, he studied divination by the hexagrams and had a knowledge of Chinese medicine. He was familiar with the Shingaku thought of Ishida Baigan, and he must have been acquainted with the writers of the National Learning (*kokugaku*) school. And, although he surely had some knowledge of Buddhism, it was probably not of a specialist nature.[29]

### The aspiration to become a kami

Munetada grieved desperately when his parents died of dysentery within a week of each other in 1812. This sorrow probably contributed to his contraction of tuberculosis. He weakened until late in 1813, when the end was pronounced near. Believing he would not live to fulfill the dream of becoming a kami in this life, he vowed to heal the sickness of the living after passing into the other world, there to become a healing deity, or *reijin*.[30] He had his pallet carried to the veranda to worship the sun for the last time. This was the first of three occasions of sun worship (*nippai*) prior to his revelation.[31] The first took place around January 19, 1814. Two months later he had recovered enough to rise, bathe, and put on fresh clothes. Again he worshiped the sun, this time in gratitude for the restoration of health. This occurred around March 19, 1814.

By November of that year he had completely recovered, and he worshiped the sun on the winter solstice (also his birthday) of his thirty-fifth year by the traditional method of counting age.[32] Facing the east at dawn, he inhaled the sun's rays deeply, and as he did so the sun seemed to come down out of the sky, enter his mouth, and pervade his entire body as if he had swallowed it. In this mystical experience he became one with the sun. This experience of unity with divinity, called the Direct Receipt of the Heavenly Mission (*tenmei jikiju*) constituted the inspiration of the remainder of his life.[33]

The Direct Receipt of the Heavenly Mission was an experience of absolute unity with the one god of the universe. Kurozumi referred to the deity both by Sinified pronunciations (Tensho Daijin, Tenshōkōtaijin) and by the Japanese readings (Amaterasu or Amaterasu Ōmikami).[34] He believed Amaterasu to be the creator of all the universe and hence the parent of all living beings.[35] In their common origion, heaven and earth are one, and all the earth is governed by a single, divine rule. Amaterasu is the source of all life, and each separate life represents a portion of the life soul (or spirit) of the universe, a microcosm of that vital source, the "small soul" (*bunshin, wake-mitama*).

Believing sickness to be a result of a lack of harmony with deity, Munetada attributed his illness to excessive grief for his parents' loss. Filling his heart with sorrow, he had injured the small soul, depriving it of the joy (*yōki*) on which it alone can thrive. Thus the bright, joyous, vital character which is the natural state of humanity gave way to gloom and despair, sapping the small soul of its vital essence. Put in other terms, *yang* gave way to *yin*, and a state of purity degenerated to a state of pollution bringing about his illness.

### Kurozumi's concept of divinity

Kurozumi's view of Amaterasu amounts to henotheism in that the existence of myriad kami (*yaoyorōzu no kami*), the eight million gods, is accepted, and it is said that human beings are kami or become so upon death. But worship singling others out only rarely played a part in Kurozumi's post-revelation experience. This was unlike the Imamura Shrine where Kurozumi continued to serve, for there the deities Kasuga Myōjin and Hachiman were enshrined in addition to Tenshō Daijin.

Kurozumi saw all existence pervaded with a vital principle which he called *yōki*, "*yang* essence." As he used this term, it was equivalent to kami-nature, and it could also mean "joy" or "joyous." The world is pulsing with *yōki*, with divine life, and while it takes many forms, all depend upon a single source.[36] Alternately stressing the many forms or the unique origin, Kurozumi sought continual unity with divinity, the absence of any separation between human and divine will (*shinjin fuji*). Because the grace of Amaterasu falls upon all without distinction, life united with her is open to all without respect to social station. This note of equality was vastly different from the contemporary practice of established religions of any stripe, which underwrote existing social stratification.[37] Kurozumi's characteristic statements on the rewards of union with divinity include a doctrine of immortality. For example, "Those who dwell within the precincts of the shrine of Amaterasu, [i.e., those with faith in Amaterasu] shall have eternal life," and "The heart of Amaterasu is our heart; when they are undivided, there is no death."[38]

Kurozumi's concept of divinity differed greatly from others of his day with which he was probably familiar. Conspicuous in its absence was any special link between Amaterasu and the Imperial House. The theory holding that Amaterasu is the apical ancestress of the imperial line was prominent in the myth compilations and in the *Jinnō shōtoki* of Kitabatake Chikafusa (1293-1354). Kurozumi did not explicity deny this theory, but neither did he choose to incorporate it in his own teaching. Nor did he appropriate Motoori Norinaga's (1730-1801) theory of Amaterasu as the sun or that of Hirata Atsutane (1776-1843) calling her the ruler of the sun. Kurozumi viewed the solar body as a symbol of Amaterasu, but not identical with divinity.[39] Thus it is somewhat inaccurate to speak of sun worship *per se:* it is not a question of worshiping the sun itself, but of the sun as symbol of divinity. Amaterasu is a superordinate entity whose vital essence, *yōki,* is the ground principle of all being.

## Healing

Soon after the Direct Receipt of the Heavenly Mission, Kurozumi began to preach, and his first converts were made by faith healing. Early in 1815 a maidservant in his household was seized with fierce abdominal pains, and Kurozumi cured her by applying his hand to her abdomen and blowing upon the area. This method of curing, called *majinai* or *toritsugi,* was accompanied by recitation of the Great Purification Prayer. *Majinai* was believed to cure by inspiring the sick one with an abundance of *yōki,* directly transferred by hand and breath. That *yōki* in turn was acquired by Kurozumi through daily worship of the rising sun, inhaling its rays and reciting the prayer daily.[40]

Kurozumi unknowingly encroached on carefully guarded turf by healing. Physicians, (*yamabushi*) ascetics of the cult of sacred mountains, and Nichiren-school prayer-healers (*kitōshi, norikura*), stood to lose much from any new competition in the field of healing, and they were quick to protest. It is related in the *Tales of the Founder (Kyōso sama no oitsuwa)* that one morning Munetada awoke to find seven scars on his roof where an arsonist had tried to set it ablaze. The torch was found, and this Munetada enshrined upon his domestic altar, thinking it no ordinary event. Three weeks later the incendiary came forth and confessed, begging for forgiveness. He was a faith healer frustrated by loss of his erstwhile patients to Munetada.[41] The date of this event is not recorded, but in 1822 there were protests to domain authorities from Nichiren-school priests and from physicians complaining that Munetada was interfering with their practice of medicine.[42] These and similar incidents, which were repeated throughout Munetada's life, testify to the enmity with which he was regarded by physicians and secular healers.

Physicians, priests, and healers associated with the mountain cult Shugendo all practiced medicine as a trade, holding customary title to a clearly defined group of people.[43] The news of Munetada's healing power spread rapidly, taking no account of the customary prerogatives of local healers nor of the economic loss his successes spelled for them. The attraction of Munetada's healing was greater for the fact that he accepted no fees. He regarded healing as an expression of his mission and not as a trade.[44] Moreover, he made no distinction among those he healed regarding their social position or prior affiliation with his shrine.

Kurozumi's was an age in which medical treatment consisted of Chinese and native herbal medicine, moxa cautery, and massage, in combination with religious ritual, except in the case of those few secular physicians ministering to the upper strata of samurai society. Poor conditions of sanitation and the ravages of epidemic disease took a heavy toll. In these circumstances, a charismatic healer was no less than a living god, and many were drawn to Kurozumi just to be healed, inquiring only later into the content of his doctrine.[45]

Believing healing to be no more than the natural expression of unity with divinity, Kurozumi wrote as follows:

> (1) The heart is the master, and the body the servant. When we awaken, the heart commands the body, but when we are confused, the body commands the heart.[46]
>
> (2) The heart of Amaterasu is the heart of humanity, and when they are united, life is eternal.[47]
>
> (3) The heart of the ancients had no form, nor has ours today. When we forget the body and dwell in the heart, now is the age of the gods; the age of the gods is now![48]

### Healing and the Great Purification Prayer

The significance of Kurozumi's use of the Great Purification Prayer in healing is a complicated matter. At the most obvious level, use of that prayer in this context amounts to a purification of pollution. Conceiving of disease as a sort of pollution (*kegare*), it makes sense that healing would consist of a purification. However, for Kurozumi, pollution was only symptomatic of the more general problem of inharmony with divinity.

The Prayer's original use as specified in the *Engi Shiki* (A.D. 927) was a biannual rite of exorcism at the Heian capital on the last days of the sixth and twelfth months. Later, under Buddhist influence, the prayer in its several versions came to be recited much more frequently. In Kurozumi's shrine, priests probably recited this and other *norito* on prescribed occasions for a set fee. Kurozumi's innovations lay in frequent, daily repetitions, in reciting the prayer for all and sundry regardless of whether they were parishioners, and reciting it gratis. Furthermore, he urged his followers to recite it as the nucleus of their own self-cultivation, without priestly mediation. Recitation by followers at their meetings became a central congregational observance.

### Early followers

In 1847 the High Disciple Tokio Katsutarō began compiling a registry of members from 1815, and for the years 1815-1825 a total of seventy-nine names are recorded,[49] all from Bizen or adjacent Bitchu. This fact seems to be contradicted by information that beginning in 1825 a group of disciples (the beginning of the group's ministry) was kept busy day and night in many locales, holding meetings for preaching and healing. It seems likely that, in line with later practice, only those who received a personal certificate of fellowship (*jinmon*) in Kurozumi's hand were actually recorded, while in fact many more attended meetings. Most members of the inner circle were samurai and members of their families who resided in the castle-town of the domain. Kurozumi wrote regularly to samurai followers[50] while they were in Edo for the obligatory period of alternate attendance (*sankin kōtai*).[51]

At first, Kurozumi's followers were a confraternity of the Imamura Shrine. Kurozumi continued to serve as a priest there, but his relation to the shrine was severely strained by his new activities. A document of 1816 from the head priest directed him to cease healing and distributing talismans of the shrine to all comers. He was told to send those who came for healing to other shrine priests for performance of rites. Healing by charisma was beyond the scope of a priest's duties in traditional conception, and distribution of charms suggested that the shrine endorsed Kurozumi's activities.[52]

### Seclusion

The second major period of Kurozumi's career (1825-1843) alternated between proselytizing and strict seclusion. This "seclusion" meant primarily sleeping at the shrine; it did not mean that he never left the shrine. He confined himself to the Imamura Shrine for a total of a thousand days and nights during the period from September 1825 to May 1828. This seclusion was a traditional discipline called *sanrō* or *okomori*. While in seclusion Kurozumi practiced sexual abstinence, recited prayers in astronomical numbers, and gave a course of lectures on the Ise Shrine. He continued to receive those seeking healing, to conduct meetings, and to distribute tens of thousands of talismans.[53] Here Kurozumi was experimenting with purification and abstinence as a type of self-cultivation. However, his seclusion was less strict than originally intended and he gave up the disciplines before the time he originally set for himself.

Seclusion, purification, and abstinences are traditional forms of self-discipline and cultivation in Shrine Shinto. These are the disciplines of the professional priest which set him apart from the layman and give him a greater religious authority.[54] In rejecting these disciplines, Kurozumi asserted that self-cultivation is not incompatible with the lay life.

Rejecting Shinto's traditional purifications and abstinences, Kurozumi established a unique form of self-cultivation. Still pursuing the goal of becoming a kami, he practiced worship of the sun (*nippai*) daily. As in his original healing, he worshiped by kneeling, facing the east, and opening his mouth wide, breathing in deeply and swallowing the sun's rays to receive its *yōki. Nippai* was accompanied by recitation of the Great Purification Prayer. These observances were made the nucleus of daily individual self-cultivation as well as the core of group ritual. In addition, Kurozumi recommended a spirit of egolessness (*ware nashi, ware o hanareru,* and other terms) and cultivation of an attitude of joy (*yōki*). When these attitudes become pervasive, the spirit of joy and gratitude express unity with divinity.

Even in seclusion Kurozumi was active in proselytizing throughout Bizen and Bitchu while his disciples proselytized further afield. Between 1828 and 1833 some two hundred merchants were converted, and Kurozumi apparently paid them special attention.[55] Also, he frequently lent money to samurai followers or acted as guarantor of their loans. Okayama samurai, like their fellows all over Japan, were living ever more meagerly in the final years of the shogunate.[56]

Throughout his life Kurozumi practiced divination[57] by the hexagrams, based on the *I Ching.* At first glance this practice seems to be at odds with the doctrine of individual responsibility and the dependence of all things on the state of one's individual heart and mind (*kokoro*). However, it would be mistaken to think that Kurozumi sought deterministic prognostication from the hexagrams. It is more likely that he used divination to know the general direction of change so that he could prepare himself and be in harmony with it.[58]

### Meetings of the followers

Nominally a confraternity of the Imamura Shrine, Kurozumi's followers met in *kōshaku*, a term applied both to meetings held in Kurozumi's house and to meetings hosted by followers in their own homes. Meeting days (*kaijitsu*) were held six times monthly at Kurozumi's home and the followers, called *michizure*, assembled to hear Kurozumi preach, to recite the Great Purification Prayer together and to receive healing rites. Kurozumi spoke without notes of any kind, and the meetings lasted as long as eight hours.

Followers themselves hosted periodic meetings on a rotating basis, called *kōseki*, beginning in 1815.[59] Most were in southern Bizen and Bitchu in the area around Okayama. For example, there was one meeting hosted by seven samurai but also including merchant members, and when they held a meeting, Kurozumi would attend, conduct recitation of the Great Purification Prayer, preach a sermon, and perform *majinai* for those seeking healing. *Kōseki* were named in various ways, generally after the locale; or in the case of merchants, after the shop where they held meetings.[60]

### Proselytizing through village headmen

Kurozumi and his disciples developed the important practice of using the mediation of *shōya*, village headmen, to gain access to new followers.[61] Village headmen held a pivotal position in Tokugawa society. They represented the lowest rank of domain control and were commoners, not samurai. Except for serious crime, they held the "powers of justice and police" and they collected the rice tax. They represented the pinnacle of village organization and were the best spokesmen of local, rural interests.[62] *Kōseki* were held in temples, shrines, and houses of village headmen. Meetings were advertised with the call for all the sick to come and be healed.[63]

Why should village headmen have been willing, even eager, to have Kurozumi preach to peasants in their charge? In spite of the hierarchy of the four classes and the assumption that class status

acquired at birth was unchangeable, there was by the end of the
Tokugawa period considerable mobility in the lower strata of the
peasant class.[64] Their mobility weakened the authority of village
headmen, putting the latter in the position of trying to defend and
strengthen the normative order. This was particularly true of the
"rich peasant" group (gōnō).[65] In defending traditional prerogatives,
the interests of the gōnō and of domain authorities were identical
insofar as both strove to maintain a peaceful, orderly peasantry.
The threat of peasant revolt and uprising was an ever-present
spectre at the end of the period, and education in traditional values
was seen as one preventative measure.

Long a leader in education, the Okayama domain had an im-
pressive institution for gōnō and headmen's education, the Shizu-
tani School (est. 1675).[66] Attached to it was a less formal school for
commoners, staffed mainly by gōnō and samurai teachers, called
the Tenshinkō (est. 1782).[67] Actually, the school was modeled on a
religious confraternity (kō), and was convened periodically for
study of the Classic of Filial Piety and other Confucian writings.
During the eighteenth century the fortunes of this Okayama school
rose and fell, but by the century's end the Tenshinkō was flourish-
ing and continued to do so until the Meiji Restoration.

Contemporary reports by the headmen to the domain voice
the fear that the peasants have departed from the ways of their
fathers, are worshiping strange gods, and are using these observances as an excuse to take holidays. Whereas previously village
officials had complete authority over religious holidays and the
work schedule, by about 1780 their control was crumbling, and
they sought to employ the Tenshinkō to bring their charges back to
tradition by preaching the values of obedience and filial piety. By
the end of the eighteenth century there were men and women students, including both gōnō and ordinary peasants. Throughout the
latter days of the Tokugawa period, village officials tried to instruct
the peasantry in values congenial to the traditional order, and their
efforts included sponsoring both religious and secular preachers.
The Shingaku thought of Ishida Baigan was viewed as a popular
version of Confucian thought, the official orthodoxy, and these
Shingaku preachers were frequently invited by village headmen to
speak to the peasantry.

When Kurozumi's disciples approached village headmen in
Okayama, they followed in the footsteps of Tenshinkō lecturers.

In fact, one word for Kurozumi-kyō Laymen's Meetings used throughout Okayama today is Tenshinkō. While Kurozumi's doctrines represented to him the path to sagehood, they doubtless appeared to local leaders anxious to shore up their own authority a serendipitous recommendation to preserve the status quo.[68]

### The High Disciples

Kurozumi's closest disciples are known as the High Disciples. There were seven in all, not all of whom became significant leaders during Kurozumi's lifetime. Furuta Masanaga was a high-ranking samurai of the Okayama *han*, who received a *jinmon* in 1819 and thereafter continued to promote Kurozumi's teaching.[69] In 1821 Ishio Kansuke, originally a parishioner of the Imamura shrine, joined Kurozumi. He held laymen's meetings in his home and wrote frequently to Kurozumi when he was in Edo (Tokyo) for alternate attendance. About one-quarter of Kurozumi's total correspondence is addressed to Ishio, who promoted Kurozumi's teaching by proselytizing on the road to Edo. Of the early High Disciples, Ishio was the most active in proselytization.[70]

The third High Disciple, Hishikawa Ginzaburō, better known as Ginjibe, was the son of a Buddhist priest who converted to Kurozumi's teaching. He was Kurozumi's personal attendant, following him everywhere, but not becoming active in proselytization.[71] The fourth High Disciple was Kawakami Tadaaki, a Wang Yang Ming scholar in the employ of the Bizen domain who joined in 1822. He wrote a book in Chinese on Kurozumi's teaching, apparently intending to use it in proselytization. The conversion of a scholar of Chinese thought seems an unlikely event, and in fact it was precipitated by rather extraordinary circumstances. Kawakami's mother was cured by Kurozumi of an eye ailment, and she persuaded her son to join.

Later Kurozumi was joined by others numbered among the High Disciples, most notably by Akagi Tadaharu (1816-1867), who was most influential in the period immediately following the founder's death, and Tokio Katsutarō, (1817-1862) mentioned above. Upon Munetada's death, the high disciples divided proselytization territories among themselves to advance the group in Western Japan.[72]

It should also be noted that there were important women disciples from an early date, including Kawakami Tsuyako, mother of the High Disciple Kawakami Tadaaki. After her healing she was constantly at the Kurozumi house to assist in meetings. She was close to Kurozumi's wife, Iku, who must also be counted an important disciple. Although convention did not permit samurai women to preach and proselytize, they were influential in spreading Kurozumi's teaching through contacts with other women.[73]

The presence of one high-ranking samurai among the High Disciples, Furuta, and at least two others of relative consequence, Kawakami and Ishio, probably account for the Imamura Shrine's toleration of Kurozumi's violation of the 1816 order to stop healing and using the shrine as a base from which to launch a religious association. Had Kurozumi not had this protection the shrine could easily have forced him to its will.

The formation of the "Daily Observances," or the Seven Household Principles, was the most important event of Kurozumi's middle period. They are Kurozumi's prescription for correct self-cultivation.

1. Born in the Land of the Gods, you shall not fail to cultivate faith.
2. You shall neither become angry nor do harm.
3. You shall not give way to conceit nor look down upon others.
4. You shall not fix upon another's evil while increasing the evil in your own heart.
5. You shall not malinger in the work of your house except in illness.
6. While pledged to the Way of Sincerity, you shall not lack sincerity in your own heart.
7. You must never stray from the spirit of gratitude.

These rules must never be forgotten. The hearts of all you encounter shall be as mirrors to you, reflecting the face you have presented to them.[74]

These Principles stress faith (1), harmony with other people (3, 4) and with the existing social order so that there is no interior resistance to full absorption in duty (2, 5), resulting in a total commitment (6, 7).

## The Late Phase

In the last phase of Kurozumi's career (1843-1850) his movement made strides to independence. In 1843 he resigned from his post as *negi* of the Imamura Shrine and passed it on to his first son,

Munenobu. We can see from the registry of followers that numbers increased rapidly after this time, particularly of commoners, while samurai stopped joining after 1846. This shift is due to a perception of Kurozumi and his followers as constituting a new religion and hence a phenomenon unsuited to samurai involvement.[75]

In relinquishing the post of *negi*, Kurozumi cast off the limitations the job imposed on his activities and freed himself to devote his life entirely to proselytizing. However, it was no longer possible to regard the group as a confraternity of the shrine. In 1846 a document called the Rules of 1846 (*Kōka sannen goteisho*), drafted by his disciples and authorized by Kurozumi, established the independent status of Kurozumi Kyōdan, the Kurozumi Church.[76] As a *kyōdan* had no legal status, its members were in effect "outside the law." The six articles of the Rules grant authority to Kurozumi's disciples to minister in his stead and to perform all rites in his name.

The ceremony of joining the ranks of the followers had until that time consisted of making a personal vow to Kurozumi to uphold the Seven Household Principles, and thus membership had been directly linked to the person of the Founder. However, when the group expanded to further regions a new method had to be found. Delegating authority to the disciples made it possible to perpetuate the group after the founder's death. The Rules specify that certificates, talismans, and healing of ministers carry the same validity as if given by the founder. Followers were urged to regard ministers' words as the founder's, and the Rules were promulgated to all followers by the ministers.[77]

The membership register by 1835 contained 1,117 names by date of entry and place of residence. Of these 317 (28.4%) were from Bizen, while Mimasaka in northern present-day Okayama prefecture accounted for 503 (45%). There was a large influx of commoners from the Southern Okayama area (Akasaka and Oku counties in Bizen) from 1840 to 1850. These had mostly been recruited by village headmen of the area. The Akasaka headman was particularly devout and had Kurozumi come and preach there twice monthly, a distance of twenty-five kilometers each way.[78]

Most samurai who joined Kurozumi did so between 1836 and 1846. Until the promulgation of the Rules of 1846 and the Membership Register of 1847 there was no particular significance attached by domain authorities to samurai receiving a certificate of membership from Kurozumi or to their pledge to obey the ... Household

Principles. Residence in the castle town made many parishioners of the Imamura Shrine, and under this umbrella they could attend Kurozumi's meetings without attracting domain attention.

However, the matter was put on a different footing with the publication of these documents and Kurozumi's retirement from the shrine. Their leader was no longer acting as a priest but as a private individual. To be listed in the Membership Register thereafter identified a person as a follower of Kurozumi, not in his capacity as shrine priest but as the author of an independent creed; in short, as the founder of a new religion.

Moreover, the presence of one's name upon the register implied acceptance of the Rules. Implied was a possible subordination of samurai to the ministers, not all of whom were of samurai rank, to say nothing of the further niceties of rank within the samurai category. In brief, then, a samurai who followed Kurozumi after 1846 stood open to charges that he might put his allegiance to Kurozumi Kyōdan before his allegiance to the domain lord, and that he was willing to countenance a person of lesser secular rank being above him in religious matters. None of this harmonized well with the prevailing status ethic, and as a result we find that samurai ceased to join after this time, though there is no evidence of a formal proscription originating with the domain at this time.[79]

Another tangible proof of the independence of Kurozumi Kyōdan was the creation of preaching halls (sekkyōsho). That is, in addition to occasional meetings, we now find structures whose only function was to accommodate meetings and which had no connection with temples or shrines.[80]

A treatment of the last phase of Kurozumi's career is appropriately concluded with a contemporary account of meetings as they were held in the late 1840s and as perceived by a commoner follower.

> The meetings on the twenty-seventh were very well attended, and we nearly always went; but there were others who came from even greater distances, only to return on the same day. In those days there was a sword-rack in the entry way, and there were many swords placed there [indicating that samurai were in attendance]. Everything was quite dignified, and as we left our umbrellas there and entered the house, there was a great crowd come to worship. Among them were such distinguished samurai as Lord Ishida, Lord

Furuta and others. However, they didn't receive seats of honor just because they were samurai while farmers sat in the back. There were no such distinctions. Merchants, artisans, whoever came first, sat in the front. Some prominent people had to kneel on the ground all day while lowborn women and children took the best seats. Even though those were days when the samurai held high status, they could neither see [to the front of the room] nor move about.

Once the meeting began there was silence. The only sound was an occasional clap.[81] No one so much as moved — not even the women and children. You might suppose that a stiff air of formality prevailed, but it wasn't that. Our Founder's voice seemed to penetrate into our very bones, and quite naturally our heads became heavy and we knew nothing but the sense of gratitude. Once the meeting was over, I forgot entirely what had been said. I have such a good memory for other things that I have been called a "living calendar," and until I turned sixty or so I could remember events of the past down to the hour they happened. But I have never been able to recall the content of a sermon. I never tried to — I was simply grateful.

After the sermon people requested healing, also in the order of first-come-first-served. There were some who had been carried in to receive healing. After these healings we took supper, and it was about [ten at night] when the meeting broke up.

All the followers were kind and treated each other warmly, taking special care of the sick. Thus, whenever we met followers it was like meeting a relative, and we had an unaccountable affection for each other. Once when I was returning home from a meeting I chanced to meet five or six samurai ahead of me on the road. I was following along behind when they asked me politely how far I was going. When I replied that I was going to Shimo Yamada in Oku county [about twenty kilometers away], they apologized for detaining me when I had so far to go and bid me go on before them. When they stood aside and let me pass, I knew they had acted this way because they were followers, and I was filled with gratitude.[82]

Believing that all humanity are children of Amaterasu, possessing small souls that mirror her own, Kurozumi countenanced no class distinctions. While he did not denounce the pervasive obsession with hierarchy, his own conduct and that of the group constituted an implicit denial. Similarly, in relations between the sexes, he recommended a spirit of "mutual reverence" (*ogamiai*). Incidents from his life describing his love for his wife are numerous and are often retold today.[83] The theme of human equality evoked a strong, positive response from commoner followers.

Kurozumi developed a distinctive form of self-cultivation, centering on daily sun worship and recitation of the Great Purification Prayer. These practices also became major congregational observances. The incompatibility of Kurozumi's doctrine with Shrine Shinto was signaled in the founding of a separate organization. Kurozumi and his followers found support and a means of access to the peasantry by proselytizing among the village headmen. By the time of the founder's death, the ministry had achieved a secure position and was able to consolidate doctrine and ritual.

Contemporary Kurozumi-kyō is one of the smaller of Japan's modern religions, but it retains considerable vitality. This vitality derives in no small measure from Kurozumi Munetada, its founder.

# Part II
# Kurozumi Teaching

# 3

# The Teaching of
# Kurozumi-kyō

### The Reverend Muneharu Kurozumi

When Kurozumi-kyō was founded at the end of the Tokugawa period, it was at first known simply as "the Way" (*Omichi*). As Munetada explained it, "the Way is the Way of Nature (*shizen*)," and "the Way is the Way of Heaven (*ten*)." It is the Way of Amaterasu Ōmikami he meant, not the way of Munetada. It was, however, Munetada who conceived and experienced the Way, and it was he who propagated it.

Though Kurozumi-kyō was called by the name "*Omichi*," this was not intended to set it apart from other teachings. Its precepts did not conflict with other religions, and it was not taught to people to the exclusion of other religions. It was not unusual to find Buddhist priests present when Munetada was preaching, and often he even preached at Buddhist temples. Many of these priests gained spiritual awakening in Buddhism because of his preaching. Though some of them accepted the teaching of Munetada, Kurozumi-kyō was presented to people as the Way of Heaven and Earth rather than as a denomination of religion. It was only later, as a result of the Meiji government's efforts to regulate religious groups, that it came to be regarded in a sectarian manner.

The early years were marked by enthusiasm and spirit. For instance, in the early 1870s there was a government officer in Oita prefecture named Morishita Keitan, who was one of the seven high disciples of Munetada. He did his missionary work enthusiastically in that prefecture, building more than fifty meeting places and preaching to many believers. When he employed people to work as government officials he gave priority to those who had converted to Kurozumi-Kyō. People criticized him, but he said, "I'm not doing this to propagate Kurozumi-kyō. The Teacher's preaching is the Way of Amaterasu Ōmikami, and it is the Way to follow as a human being and as a Japanese. Therefore, I want everybody to understand this Way in order to be happy."

As we look back on this now, we see that he was doing too much to force people. However, his knowledge and his attitude were excellent, and he was a highly spirited disciple. The Teacher and other disciples worked hard at missionary work with this kind of spirit and belief.

### The Mind of Amaterasu: Source of All

Kurozumi-kyō is one of the thirteen sects of Shinto of the pre-war period. It is based in the fundamental ideas of Shinto; however, it built its doctrine (*kyōgi*) in a way based distinctively on the personal characteristics and experiences of Kurozumi Munetada. It developed in its own way, independently from the other sects. This is similar to the way Christianity started from Judaism and developed its thinking through the character and experiences of Jesus Christ. It is natural for religions to develop their ideas through ethnic beliefs, and Kurozumi-kyō developed in such a way.

Because Kurozumi-kyō is based on the character and experiences of a single person, it is in a narrow sense a personal religion. In a broader sense, however, it has the characteristics of a universal religion.

This universality may be shown by naming the kami worshiped by Kurozumi-kyō. These are (1) the *yaoyorōzu no kami* (8 million kami), (2) Amaterasu Ōmikami as the leading kami, and (3) the Teacher Munetada as kami. Amaterasu Ōmikami is the kami from whom Munetada directly accepted his divine mission, and Kurozumi-kyō worships her as the High Kami of the universe, of heaven and earth. This is fundamental to the practice (*shugyō*) of Kurozumi-kyō.

Amaterasu Ōmikami is the kami who created the world. She is Almighty Kami. She is a universal kami, the Kami for everybody. People should not have the concept "my kami." Her way of thinking is universal, and all humanity can understand this because we are all a part of the Kami. The poems of Munetada are our resource to understand it. For instance, he wrote:

Interior of Main Shrine (*Daikyōden*). The central altar is to Amaterasu Ōmikami. At the left is the altar to ancestors and to the myriads of kami. To the right is the altar to the Founder as Kami, and to the spirits of the previous Chief Patriarchs. Photo courtesy of Kurozumi-kyō.

> The divine virtue
> of Amaterasu
> fills Heaven and Earth;
> Ah, in such abundance
> is this limitless grace.[2]*

This poem makes it clear that her divine virtue can be found everywhere in the world. Another of his poems says:

> It is in our hearts
> that the kami and Buddha
> are found to dwell;
> Indeed to pray elsewhere
> would be truly a pity.[8]

*Numbers in square brackets after *waka* indicate their location in chapter 6, where the original text is also given.

We must understand the standpoint from which this should be read. The concept of kami was in the past based on the idea of their existence apart from people, interpreted as a supernatural presence. The first part of the poem is very important, emphasizing the existence of kami within people. Humanity should not forget that Kami exists inside of them and they are one part (*bunshin*) of Kami. The mind of human beings is but a portion of Amaterasu Ōmikami. This mind of human beings *is* Amaterasu Ōmikami.

Everything in this world comes from one mind, the mind of Amaterasu Ōmikami. One poem says,

> Although the moon
>      dwells in every drop of dew,
>           in the sky above
> The moon of True Sincerity
>      certainly remains as one.[16]

Some people think that Kurozumi-kyō regards Amaterasu Ōmikami as the sun itself, and that it worships the sun as kami. However, Munetada says "The sun, the moon and myself come from Amaterasu Ōmikami." We should see that she is the source from which these come.

## Munetada's "Direct Acceptance of Divine Mission"

The purpose of Kurozumi-Kyō teaching is summarized in two sayings: "Propagation of the Way" (*taidō senpu*) and "Save Everyone" (*bannin no kyūsai*). "Propagation of the Way" means delivering the mind of the great Amaterasu Ōmikami to the world. It propagates this teaching in order to lead the people who are suffering to enlightenment and in order to save them. This is the main reason Kurozumi-kyō was established.

The teacher Munetada composed the poem:

> That vast treasure
>      here within Heaven and Earth
>           continues to glow;
> Having now accepted it,
>      my heart indeed knows joy.[3]

It is said that he wrote this poem just after he experienced the Direct Acceptance of the Divine Mission[1] when he was 35 years old. In it he expresses his pleasure at his own enlightenment (*kaigen*). Enlightenment and mission belong together in Kurozumi-kyō.

To understand this better, let us, again look briefly at the course of Munetada's life as seen from inside the Kurozumi-kyō circle of faith. He was born on November 26, 1780.[2] This date, as well as the date of his acceptance of divine mission in 1814, fell during the winter solstice season. His family were hereditary Shinto priests at the Imamura Shrine in Okayama. He was the 9th priest in his family's history. Before that, one of his ancestors was a samurai of Nancho who moved to Bizen and settled in Okayama.

He was a person who was dutiful to his parents. There are many stories about his filial piety. But, as he was growing up, he could not satisfy his strong desire to be dutiful to his parents simply by obeying them. He began to seek a deeper way. Finally, when he was about 20 years old he reached the conclusion that the best way to fulfill filial duty was to become a living kami and to save people in this world.

Munetada sought how to become a living kami, looking in books, asking his teachers, and questioning himself repeatedly. He reached the conclusion that he could become a kami in this life by eliminating evil from his heart. Senior disciples later explained this with the sayings: "To be a humane human being is the way to be a kami" and "To be a perfect human leads you on the way to be a kami."

He enumerated attitudes to be avoided in five articles and put them up wherever he could see them. He committed himself to obey them. Later these five articles were made the basis of the "Seven [Household] Principles," known as "golden principles" by his followers. At first, however, they were for himself and he endeavored for ten years to follow them daily.

However, his parents' deaths in 1812 caused him unbearable suffering, particularly because all the motivation of his life came from his devotion to them. As a result, he came down with tuberculosis and at the beginning of 1814 he himself was about to pass away. As he faced his own death, he resolved to become a kami in the life after death, since he had not been able to complete the mission he had chosen for himself to be a living kami and to save people.

After he accepted the fact that his death was coming he was no longer frightened, and he could look back on his life more calmly. He realized then that he had made a big mistake, and that his illness was caused by his grief. He was about to destroy the body his parents had given him. He knew they would be sad if they saw his misery, and he regretted what he had done.

However, believing that his death was coming soon, he decided to concentrate all his efforts on living the rest of his life in the way that would have pleased his parents. He asked his wife to move his bed to the veranda in order to worship the rising sun. This occasion is called "Munetada's first sun worship." He prayed for his ancestors' spirits, especially for his parents' spirits, telling them his thankfulness for the gift of life.

Because of this "first sun worship," Munetada changed. Until then he was in a state of sadness and depression, frustrated with the world; after this act of worship he regretted his mistake even more and realized that the best way he could observe his filial duty was to get rid of his frustration. He became a cheerful and happy person, and he was thankful to the world. The things which used to bring him sadness did not make him sad any longer; rather, they even brought him happiness. His health began improving because of his great gratitude to the world and to his life. He performed "the second sun worship" on March 19, and recovered from his illness. These changes in him enlightened him and brought him new life.

During the winter solstice later that year he carried out "the third sun worship," in gratitude for his recovery and for receiving new life. It was at the time of this third sun worship that he experienced the Direct Acceptance of Divine Mission. It was then that he decided to propagate the Way. At first he did not tell other people about it. However, a month later, his housemaid had a severe stomach ache which caused her suffering, and he cured her of it. He did not expect this to happen, but it was his first step toward saving others. People who heard this story began coming to his place asking for help. Later on, he expressed his feelings about this in his prayer: "Let us discover the footprints of the Kami of the Shining Sun."

It was in this way that Kurozumi-kyō's desire to propagate the Way and save people began. It is based in Munetada's Direct Acceptance of Divine Mission. This experience had two characteristics: enlightenment in the Way and the mission to propagate the Way.

## Subsequent Development of Kurozumi-kyō

The history of Kurozumi-kyō after the acceptance of divine mission can be divided into two periods. The first period was from 1818-1829, and the second was from about 1836 until 1850. In the first period especially, many samurai from Bizen joined Kurozumi-kyō. Many of the intellectual class, and two of the four High Disciples, Ishio Kansuke and Kawakami Tadaaki, can be found among these followers. By contrast, the number of followers in the first period was small.

However, in the second period the number of the followers increased. Because his son succeeded him in his position at the Imamura Shrine, Munetada could concentrate on his propagating efforts. Not only members of the intellectual class but also middle and lower class people joined Kurozumi-kyō. Examples of famous disciples of the second period are Akagi Tadaharu and Tokio Munemichi, who also were among the first four High Disciples. There were many tales concerning Munetada's teaching. He saved people who were suffering from illness and from problems in their lives and in their families.

The official founding of Kurozumi-kyō came in 1846. The period was relatively stable socially, and believers rapidly increased in the early 1840's. In 1846 Kurozumi-kyō decided to proclaim its creed; but after four years, in 1850, the Founder Munetada passed away at the age of 70.

## The Spread of The Teaching

After Munetada's death, his Seven High Disciples devoted themselves to missionary work. They decided to focus on nine areas of western Japan. These disciples widened the scale of proselytizing in order to deliver the Founder's great teachings which they had received.

This missionary work was the first to go outside of the present Okayama prefecture. When Munetada was still alive, his missionary work only covered parts of Okayama. However, after his death, his teachings were delivered to people outside of these areas by his disciples.

These seven disciples did this proselytizing work for three years, from 1850 to 1852. People who joined Kurozumi-kyō had to present a document in which they declared themselves to be believers. This was in the form of a letter addressed not to Kami, but to the Teacher Munetada. The disciples' missionary work was evaluated by the number of these sacred letters and they brought back many of them.

After they finished this period of work, 1,000 followers went on pilgrimage to the Ise Grand Shrine to pray. They left Okayama in twenty groups, fifty followers in each group. On their way to Ise they healed many people who were sick. By the end of their pilgrimage many people had heard about them and asked them to come to their communities to save people.

Here is the most famous story about this event. Okamoto Kyōzaemon, one of the disciples, saw a crippled person and healed his legs. However, when this was reported to the government officer, Okamoto was arrested, He explained the teachings of Munetada to the officers, but they could not understand. Finally a Shinto priest at the Ise Shrine came to listen. He was very impressed by Munetada's teachings and said, "Shinto's main stream is in Ise; the teaching's mainstream is at Nakano [Munetada's birthplace]."

The first aristocrat who became a believer was Kujo Hisatada, a regent at that time. Nijō Nariyuki was another believer who was a high regent in the last years of the Tokugawa period. He joined Kurozumi-kyō because his son was saved from illness by Akagi Tadaharu. It is recorded that Nijō visited Munetada Shrine in Kyoto[3] to thank Munetada. This was his poem:

> If in our world
> there were no Kami to convey
> True Sincerity,
> How would we ever learn
> the Way of Makoto?

The following two poems, found at this same shrine, are said to be by Rokujō Ariyoshi:

> If there were no Kami
> to teach the divinity
> of Amaterasu,
> How could we éven enter
> the Way of Makoto?

> From the land of gold,
> from the country of Kibi
> dawn has arrived;
> Spring of the "Age of Gods"
> does indeed bring joy!

Another poem in the Shrine is:

> Here in this land
> that knows nothing by the path
> of sword and strife
> There appears like the sun and moon
> the Kami Munetada.

This was said to have been composed by Emperor Komei.

Many aristocrats became believers in Kurozumi-kyō because of the missionary work of Akagi Tadaharu. When a rebellion occurred in 1864, and the soldiers of Chōshū were coming close to the gate, Emperor Komei asked the Munetada Shrine what he should do. Akagi prayed to Munetada and came to the conclusion "stay there." At the palace, the officers were telling the emperor to hide himself or run away. However, because of Akagi's answer, the emperor did not move. Therefore, it is said that Kyoto was not burned because the emperor stayed in Kyoto.

Later, the regulation of religion by the Meiji government was very strict. Kurozumi-kyō needed recognition from the government as a religious association in order to continue its mission. In 1871 the grandson of Munetada was making great efforts in Tokyo to get this permission. In August 1873, Kurozumi-kyō received official recognition. After that it still had difficulty establishing its identity as a religious organization because of Buddhist affinities in its kami belief, but it was finally recognized officially as an independent sect of Shinto in 1876.

## The Basic Message of Munetada

The written canon is officially called *Kurozumi-kyō Kyōshō*. The main contents of the canon are the seven articles and the poems and letters. There are more than 200 poems and 200 letters.

However, Kurozumi-kyō is characterized by the fact that Munetada's personality (*jinkaku*) is its message, because it was born through his religious experience. Its doctrine was created in experience, not in imagination (*sōzō*). In Yoshida Shinto, for instance, Yoshida Kanetomo[4] built theory mainly through the classics of Confucianism, Taoism, and Buddhism on top of Shinto. Certainly he had some religious experiences. However, Yoshida Shinto was created using doctrines which were based on other teachings. Kurozumi-kyō does not have any texts in that sense because it was born through one person's religious experiences. The main and most important aspect of Kurozumi-kyō is that Munetada's personal qualities themselves are its doctrine.

Moreover, this characteristic is its strongest feature as compared to other sects. There is a special word which is used only by Kurozumi-kyō: *Misebumi.*[5] The original meaning of this term came from people who led travelers across big rivers. Long ago, when travelers crossed big rivers, they could only get to the other side safely if they followed the footsteps of those who led the way. The people who led the way were called *sebumi-sha*. *Misebumi* applies to Munetada because he leads people to the way of Amaterasu Ōmikami. Buddhism has a similar concept, but it uses the term *senshō*, meaning the sole of a foot. The term *Misebumi* is another way of saying that it is Munetada's personality which is the basis of Kurozumi-kyō doctrine.

The healing of diseases was a major reason for people to join Kurozumi-kyō. For instance, the Kujō family became believers because Akagi Tadaharu was asked to cure their daughter's serious illness, and he saved her. In many other cases this healing of disease helped people to become believers. Usually a religion based on miracles does not last very long. However, Kurozumi-kyō had a strong basis in the doctrine and experience of Munetada. Most important, it has Amaterasu Ōmikami as its leading kami. Therefore, even aristocrats became interested in it. If these healings had been based only on the saying of traditional prayers these aristocrats would not have become believers.

## The Unity of Kami and Humans

The doctrine of Kurozumi-kyō says that Kami and humans are never of two bodies (*funi*). There is a similar saying, but different from the view of Kurozumi-kyō, that kami and humans are of one body (*ittai*). In a sense they both say the same thing because both imply that kami and humans are in the same soul and body.

However, there is a slight but important difference between the two sayings. That kami and humans are never of two bodies implies that kami and humans are in the same soul and body from the beginning because the mind of a human is but a portion (*bunshin*) of Amaterasu Ōmikami. On the other hand, saying that kami and humans are of one body implies that humans and kami are not in the same soul and body at the beginning, but only reach that state by attaining fulfillment (*kyōchi*).

Both concepts have the same result, that kami and humans are in the same soul and body. However, there is a difference with respect to reaching that state. Kurozumi-kyō, in saying that kami and humans are in the same soul and body, means that humans do not need to become kami because they already are kami. All they have to do is follow the doctrine in order to maintain their divinity.[6]

Kurozumi-kyō practice, by which divinity may be maintained, is based in Shinto but was developed distinctively by the Teacher

Munetada. The main exercise in Shinto is purification (*harai*). This exercise traditionally concerns the body, but Munetada interpreted it as applying not only to the body but also to the mind (*kokoro*). He also emphasized that it should be continual. We have two large purifying ceremonies in the shrines every year, following the old calendar, every June and every December. Both these large ceremonies and the continual, everyday purification are very important.

Continual purifying cleanses the mind, allowing one to return to unselfishness (*muyoku*). In practice, people recite the words of The Great Purification Prayer (*Ōharai*) when they pray. Priests of Kurozumi-kyō pray for about an hour around 1:00 P.M. in the hottest part of the summer, and early in the morning in the coldest part of winter. This exercise (*shugyō*) is officially done in front of Kami, but it is all right to do it in other places because the important point is to return to selflessness by reciting the words of the prayer.

The Teacher Munetada emphasized that it was very important to leave everything up to Kami. Leaving everything up to the deity means that body and Kami are united. In doing this, it becomes possible to have inspired communication (*kannō*) with Kami.

This unity of Kami and humans concerns daily life. This may be seen by noticing a special expression used in Kurozumi-kyō, "utilization," or "making the most of it" (*ikasu*). There are three ways of using this expression: (1) making the most of your own mind; (2) making the most of another person's mind; and (3) making the most of materials. Making the most of your own mind implies what has already been said, that you should return to your own mind which is a portion of Kami.

Making the most of another person's mind implies that you should try to find the other person's good points. For instance, when you educate your children, you should emphasize their strong points, not only try to correct their weak points. The Teacher Munetada said that it was very important to make good use of yourself since your mind is but a portion of Kami. You can say the same thing about other people. We should look for other people's strong points, not their weak points. Munetada composed this poem:

> We need to strive
> to retain within ourselves
> all things that are good;
> It is the bad within us
> that needs to be abandoned.[47]

It is simple enough for everybody to understand. However, the more you try to get rid of the weak points, confusions, and distrusts in your mind, the more you become obsessed with them. It is much harder to do than you think. Since this is so, just leave the weak points, confusions, and distrusts in your mind alone, and look for your own good points. In doing this, your weak points will be weakened naturally. This is a good way to purify your mind.

It is hard to believe that Kami and humans are the same soul and body because you can see many bad points in humans. However, you have to believe in humanity's divinity; otherwise, you can never see this divinity. On the occasion when someone attempted to set fire to his house, Munetada never blamed this person, and did not even try to find out who had done it. Moreover, he prayed for him to return to his own mind, a portion of Kami. After a few weeks, this man came to Munetada to apologize for what he had done. Because Munetada believed that Kami and humans were not of two bodies he was able to lead this man back to his original state.

## The All-Encompassing Divine Virtue

Kurozumi-kyō has another important doctrine, that everything comes from divine virtue. Here is a poem:

> If we remember
>     that everything that exists
>         comes from Heaven,
> Then worries and daily life
>     are not matters of concern.[23]

If you find something to be right and correct, it is good. If you do not find it right and correct, it is bad. In this case, *good* and *bad* do not refer to moral behavior, but to the fact that people usually find things to be good or bad by their judgment that it is so.

However, everything comes from Kami. This is how all things are arranged by divine blessing.[7] Therefore, people should not interpret things in their own way, or judge things by their own preference. Since everything exists through divine order, everything is good. Even though you are facing hard times, they will turn to good times.

The Teacher Munetada explained this from his own experience. He faced his parents' death, and he himself became seriously ill. He could not think of Kami at all. He was sunk in great sorrow and could not understand Kami's mind at all. However, he looked back on his life after he had recovered from his illness, and realized that the important thing is how you react to any situation.

If you react well to a bad situation, it will become better. You have to accept the way situations are because they come from divine virtue. As long as you do this you will not have a bad result. Kami is our parent; therefore, Kami does not treat us badly. However, we sometimes do not understand and we complain about our situation. We should understand our parent Kami and learn well from what is happening. Here are two poems about this:

> When we are aware
> of the divine virtue
> of Amaterasu,
> Whether asleep or awake
> we will feel such gratitude.[25]

> If we remember
> that all things around us
> are divine reflections,
> Whether asleep or awake
> we will know such gratitude.[20]

The teaching of leaving oneself to Kami (*kami ni makasu*) is similar to the idea of Natsume Sōseki,[8] to "leave oneself to Heaven." The ideas are similar, despite the fact that one is religion and the other is literature, because this is the way humans should follow.

Our teachings include the following sayings: "Once you leave yourself to Kami, you are fulfilled and you know the way you should be." "There is no better way than leaving yourself to Kami." "Following the Way of Heaven is the safest way in this world." "Following the Way of Heaven is the same as following the way of your parents." Thus, when you leave yourself to Kami, you go into the stage of "Nothingness" (*mu*). You just follow the Way of Kami.

## Health and The Mind of Kami

Here are some poems about thankfulness, cheerfulness, and happiness:

> A sense of gratitude
> along with feelings
> of wonder and joy
> Will, if we maintain all three,
> bring us true Sincerity.[48]

> People who know
>> no more than the feeling
>>> of Gratitude
> Hold today as precious,
>> the Nowness in their hearts.[31]

> Ah, the gratitude
>> of being born in a world
>>> filled with such joy,
> And to live a happy life
>> free, indeed, from any strife.[28]

The word *thankfulness* is used often in the teachings of Kurozumi-kyō. For instance, Otake Tsurusaburō, one of the followers, read this poem:

> With gratitude,
>> and given that alone,
>>> it will come to pass
> That illnesses will be cured,
>> homes will be in harmony.

If you spend every day in thankfulness, cheerfulness, and happiness, you will see the way of Kami. These three should be the basis of everyday life. In contrast, you should not have frustration and anger in your life because they are against the teaching of Kami. If you lived in a way that is against this teaching you would become ill. Therefore, if you follow it you will not become ill. If you do become ill, you will recover as long as you believe in the teaching of Kami.

Ito Sahei had been ill for 26 years, and his condition was getting worse. However, the Teacher Munetada told him that if his mind and the mind of Kami could become one, he would get better. He recovered from his disease.

Ogata Chōjirō gave up the idea of recovering from illness. When he came to Munetada, he was told that he was not trying to overcome the illness. He recovered also.

Okumura Enzaemon was blind. He visited the shrine every day for three years to pray, but he could not get back his eyesight. When he came to Munetada, Munetada said to him "You should be thankful to Kami that for three years you have never had any accidents. The reason you cannot get back your eyesight is that your mind is not open to Kami." On the way home he regretted his behavior. He too recovered.

Because of Munetada's preaching, Akagi Tadaharu got back his eyesight after he had been ill for eight years. These stories can be found in the anecdotes about Munetada.

When Munetada himself was seriously ill at the age of 44, he told his followers: "I do not worry about my illness at all. I leave myself to Kami. If I do not need to exist in the world, I will die. But, if I do need to exist in this world, I will recover from my illness." Soon he did recover. "If you believe in the way of Kami, everything will be achieved."

## Religious Practice in Kurozumi-kyō

Finally, let us consider the actual practice of Kurozumi-kyō. When people join they receive a sacred book (*seiten*). The seven principles[9] are in it, and people declare that they will follow them. This is the first thing to do.

Next, they pray before the sun. The best time to do this is at the time time of sunrise. However, so long as you can feel as if you were praying at sunrise, it is all right to do it at any time, even on rainy or cloudy days. The purpose of this praying is to thank the sun which is the source of life. The Teacher Munetada composed a poem:

> Day after day
> we face the morning sun
> aware in our hearts
> That our lives are limitless,
> a feeling of such joy.[44]

After sun worship, people do breathing exercises (*go-yoki shugyo*). The purpose of this is to become calm in spirit (*chinkon*). It is good for our health, too. People should practice abdominal breathing. Recently, some studies in Germany about the brain explain that a big brain is in the skull and a small brain is in the stomach. The big brain functions through intelligence and the small brain functons to express emotional feeling. The terms *resolution* and *a plucky act* refer to the functions of the small brain; the Teacher Munetada emphasized the practice of abdominal breathing strengthening these qualities.

The last training [or practice] is purification. People should say the Great Purification Prayer while they are carrying out these practices.

A training session for *michizure* at a Kurozumi church in Kochi prefecture. Photo courtesy of Kurozumi-kyō.

Finally, five articles may be given in this modern way:

1. Worship the sunrise;
2. Love and admire your parents and ancestors;
3. Use nice and warm words;
4. Be kind to people, especially mentally and physically handicapped people;
5. Pray for people.

These are the teachings of the Teacher Munetada, and the doctrine of Kurozumi-kyō.

Behind Chief Patriarch Kurozumi Muneharu is the altar of the church. Photo courtesy of Kurozumi-kyō.

# 4

# Following the Way

## Study Sessions for Kurozumi-kyō Members (Michizure)[1]

**The Reverend Muneharu Kurozumi**

*These lectures were given during a period of three years beginning in 1981. The Chief Patriarch (Kyōshusama) visited 120 different meeting places, explaining clearly how to become able to win enlightenment. Each session lasted a whole day. He presented the precious teaching he had mastered for himself in the course of praying before the sun at sunrise at Shintōzan.*

*Listening to the teaching of the Chief Patriarch, the eyes of the members grew more and more lively as they gained pride in being devotees of Kurozumi-kyō and as they grasped the guiding principle of their lives from these teachings.*

*In presenting these lectures in response to the requests of many people, I remember the enthusiasm felt at these study sessions.*

—Nobuakira Kurozumi

### First Lecture

#### We should practice *Ōharai*

The root of our religion lies in the fact that our Divine Founder was enlightened through *nippai*. Praying before the sun at dawn, he received his divine mission through this practice. *Nippai* is the most important occasion of prayer for us. It is, in fact, the source of Kurozumi-kyō.

Ōmoto, our Holy Place,[2] has suffered from the growth of the city of Okayama. The pastoral appearance it once had has been lost, and it can no longer be considered an appropriate environment for Kurozumi-kyō as a sun-worshiping religion. We therefore moved to Shintōzan in quest of the graceful sunrise where we can share the sunrise prayer of our divine founder. Since then we have been practicing it in a different style from what was done in Ōmoto: we have been practicing *nippai* of *ohimachi*, beginning the *Ōharai* prayer before dawn.[3]

In our religion, our prayer starts with the Great Purification Prayer (*Ōharai Norito*). It may safely be said that Kurozumi-kyō depends a great deal on its practice.

Occasionally someone asks the meaning of this Prayer. Personally, I have not looked into the meaning of the words because from infancy I have studied it by ear. In fact, when I ask eminent Shinto scholars, such as those of Kokugakuin University in Tokyo or of Kogakukuan University in Ise, they seldom agree with each others' theories. Furthermore, the Divine Founder did not explain the meaning of the words though he prayed it up to five or six hundred times a day.

Through continuous *Ōharai* practice he was linked more and more closely to Great Kami [Ōmikamisama; Amaterasu Ōmikami], so that under her guidance he provides her virtue[4] for us. Thus, I often say, "If you have time to ask the meaning of the prayer, please use that time praying it as often as possible. Instead of asking the meanings of words, ask about the teaching of the Divine Founder." I mean that we put emphasis on practice: you can find the way to become one with Kami if you overcome your egoism in practicing it intently. Only when you make use of the prayer in this way are you actually purified. When you are able to enjoy this ultimate sense of purity you can feel something precious all through your body. I think that this is the charm of *Ōharai* practice.

The words of the Purification Prayer maintain the beauty of rhyme and rhythm of the ancient Yamato language, the root of modern Japanese. Its words are in themselves a song of praise of life. In ancient times it was said that every word has its own soul, called *kotodama*.[5] Since the distant past our ancestors have chanted the words of the *Ōharai* as they prayed. When we also chant them, the long history of "Japanese-mind" since the era of the kami ["age of the gods"] comes alive in our minds even today. To understand one should adhere to Ōharai practice, and not be misled by the literal meaning of the words.

Some people apologize saying, "I feel so sorry that I have various worldly thoughts even though I try hard to devote myself to the prayer. Perhaps it is because I don't have enough self-discipline." Don't worry about it. We don't need to feel sorry when we practice Ōharai. The human mind is a vessel of the virtue of Kami. In this practice you are washing the vessel. Suppose we were to try to remove dust from a large jar filled with water, so large that we cannot turn it over. But if we pour in clear water until it spills over, the dust will float on the surface and go out as the water spills. In just this way, when you have worldly thoughts during prayer, let them just be there in your mind. This gives promise that you are being purified. While practicing in earnest, I'm sure you will experience a moment of ecstasy when you can touch Kami's virtue, though you might not notice it at first and it might not last long. The important thing is to practice the prayer as much as you can, every day.

Your faith in Kami without Ōharai practice is something like a canary without its beautiful song. Please be sincere when you practice it. Two fundamentals of our religion, namely, daily occasions of prayer at home and attending the Kurozumi church,[6] may be compared to the two legs of men. Just as weak legs bring about the decline of health, so weak use of fundamentals leads to unhealthiness of our belief. So, at the beginning, I beg you to pursue the healthy religious life through practicing the fundamentals.

Meanwhile, I want to explain how to practice Ōharai. At nippai we say it facing the eastern sky, feeling as though we are throwing ourselves toward the sky on the rhythm of the prayer. In front of the altar, on the other hand, set your eyes on the mirror, or if you are home, set your eyes on the character "ten" or "dai" of Amaterasu Ōmikami [i.e., Tenshodaijin; Tenshōkōdaijin].[7] Throw youself into the bosom of Kami, or into the embrace of the Divine Founder, as a small child runs into the bosom of his mother saying, "Mom, I'm home!" Please practice Ōharai in this way.

Another thing you must be aware of in Ōharai practice is that you need to breathe using your stomach. Relax your shoulders and pull in your stomach. You may then feel it easy to breathe air out. Then, thrust your stomach out so that you can breathe fresh air in naturally. Keep this in mind as you pray the Prayer, saying it from the stomach. To breathe using the stomach guarantees that you

An American student before sunrise at the place of *nippai* at Shintōzan. Photo by Willis Stoesz.

breathe one hundred per cent, while in ordinary breathing we take in 70 to 80 percent of our capacity. By using the stomach we breathe in oxygen to the full, and receive the divine virtue which is surely good for health.

It is very important to lower your center of gravity (that is, with respect to the mind) by stomach-based breathing. Things fall over when their center of gravity is high. When the center of the human mind goes up, you get upset and worry about things. Young men who get angry may say of this that "something came up to the head": the center of the mind has gone upward. People tend to become restless when it happens. Therefore, the Founder teaches in the second of The Seven Principles not to be upset and not to worry about things.

Sometimes we hear of students who are so nervous that they cannot do their best in examinations, in spite of having real ability. You see, the center of the mind of such a student has gone up. To breathe using the stomach means keeping the mind's center of gravity down in the stomach. It is a practice by which the mind is put in repose.

Practicing Ōharai while breathing from the stomach lets you find various ways of gaining enlightenment.

**Receiving** *yōki*

At *nippai* we practice *yōki*, which means fully taking in the "*ki*," the essence of Kami.

Once when I was walking through downtown Okayama I met a friend from junior-high school days whom I had not seen for thirty years. He asked me about his neighbor who is an enthusiastic member of Kurozumi-kyō, saying "My neighbor claps facing the eastern sky every morning to pray to Kami, and then she moves her lips like a goldfish (*kingyo*) to swallow the air. I wonder what she is doing." I explained, "We call it *yōki* practice. She was not swallowing air, much less is she a goldfish. She swallows sunshine, the virtue of Kami, to unite with Amaterasu. While doing it, she

*Yōki* practice during *nippai* at Wright Brothers Memorial.
Photo by Willis Stoesz.

inevitably breathes in air also." It is not correct to understand the practice of *yōki* only in terms of swallowing air.

Through *yōki*, with the guidance of the Divine Founder who is identified with Amaterasu Omikami, we make efforts to unite with Kami. The point of *nippai* practice is to keep your breath at the same pace as the breath of the universe. The founder talks about this when he says that *inori* (prayer) is *hinori* (riding on the sun).

In *nippai* practice at Shintōzan we greet the sunrise during *yōki* practice. We swallow the morning *ki* with mouth wide open, deeply moved in the shower of sunshine as we receive the virtue of Kami.[8]

To do it, relax your shoulders and breathe out the air with your stomach pulled in. When you have released all the air, open your mouth widely and swallow the *yōki* in just the way that you drink water. If you cannot manage it well, try it lying on your back, doing the same as above, after you go home. This will somehow help you. Like *Ōharai* practice, this is a discipline to calm your soul, sinking the mind into the stomach. You will receive plenty of the virtue of Kami as well as health of both body and soul.

At a study session in the church at Asabara I met a gentleman in his sixties, who came to attend our session with the assistance of his wife since his body was badly diseased. He was hospitalized at the time but his doctor gave him permission to attend our session.

Later, at a session in the church in Kurashiki, he reappeared to thank me saying that he had been so much impressed by *yōki* practice that he had done it in bed every morning at the hospital, beginning with *nippai*. According to him, he was able to leave the hospital after three months of practice. As you can tell from this story alone, there is nothing better than *yōki* practice for the health of body and soul.

As I mentioned before, in Shintōzan we start *nippai* practice every morning before dawn, waiting for the rising sun.

It was in February of 1977. The day was really cold. It was reported on television or in the newspaper that it would be the coldest day of the year. It might have been less than ten degrees Fahrenheit at the *nippai* place. It got really cold, so cold that I felt it almost hurting me, or more than that, that I was almost so numb as to lose consciousness. My cheeks were frozen and my teeth chattered with cold, which prevented me from reciting *Ōharai* smoothly. Though I was afraid that only I chanted in a strange voice, I found that people behind me also could not chant well. In a condition like this we started *yōki* practice. The sun was rising among the mountains far away when it got the coldest. It was at the moment when the sun appeared that something very hot arose from deep inside my body and soon spread all over my body. My frozen ears and fingers got more and more warm and even the cold breeze felt smooth and comfortable. It was a really precious and joyful experience of *yōki*. This *nippai* experience verified the familiar knowledge given by the Divine Founder, that human beings are "children of Kami" who share the *bunshin* of Amaterasu Ōmikami. It showed me what this inner presence of Kami really is. At this *nippai* I learned that the point where the "something hot" arises is the portion of divine spirit (*bunshin*)[9] of Great Kami present within. This is why this occasion was precious and joyful for me.

### The presence of *bunshin*

Now I will focus on this *bunshin*. Among the teachings of the the Divine Founder you will find this statement: "Since the center of my mind is a portion of Amaterasu Ōmikami, my mind gets really rich only when I respect Kami living in my mind."

We can get water by turning a faucet. This is because the faucet is directly connected to the source of water supply. Now, consider the source as Amaterasu and the faucet as the inner spirit. Our life-activity goes on smoothly by receiving the virtue of Kami without ceasing. This is solely because we are directly connected with Kami through our inner spirit just as fresh water flows in torrents from a source to each faucet.

Many think that people live because they breathe, they eat, they sleep, or their hearts beat. On the contrary, they live, and that is why they can breathe. They do live, and therefore they can eat, they can sleep, and their hearts can beat.

To live means to be allowed to live by Kami in being directly connected with her through her inner presence and in receiving her virtue (*shintoku*) ceaselessly. This is Kurozumi-kyō's view of life. Breathing, eating, sleeping, and the beating of hearts are all subordinate conditions for life, just like tributary rivers. The main river of life flows directly through the inner spirit from Great Kami. However, people tend to think that the body is the human being, and that the self lives by itself. This idea alienates men from Kami. The farther away a faucet is from the source of the water supply,

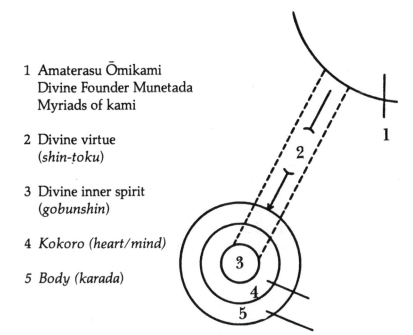

1 Amaterasu Ōmikami
  Divine Founder Munetada
  Myriads of kami

2 Divine virtue
  (*shin-ṭoku*)

3 Divine inner spirit
  (*gobunshin*)

4 *Kokoro (heart/mind)*

5 *Body (karada)*

the less water and the less water pressure you will get. Just so, the more distant human beings are from Kami, the less the divine virtue can be provided, in turn causing more problems. To keep trying to be close is what we call "religious belief."

There is a verse of a *michizure*:

> As a young child
>     gradually becomes aware
>         of worldly wisdom,
> He begins to move away
>     from Amaterasu.

The Founder warns:

> Up near its source
>     a flowing stream may indeed
>         be clean and pure,
> But when crossed by boats of life
>     its waters become cloudy.

So as not to be as the boat, he teaches:

> For those who go forth
>     together with the Kami
>         Amaterasu,
> There will come day after day
>     the feelings of gratitude.[49]

"I am always with Kami," "I am a child of Kami," or "Kami lives in my mind." If you live with these beliefs in your mind, you are living a *michizure* religion.

> Were we to join
>     these hearts of ours with the heart
>         of Amaterasu,
> We would live in unity
>     In that abiding life.[10]

Thus, we are to move toward the final goal of our religion, as sung in this verse.

People often say in conversation "He is lucky," or "I have no luck in my life." Let's think about this idea of luck.

This story happened during the world war. The man who is now the representative (*sōdai*) of the members of the church in Abashiri, Hokkaido was in continental China when his corps was assaulted. Though the men on either side of him were killed, he was spared as he was praying unconsciously. At the time he thought it was because he was lucky, but later he found that it was because of the religious faith of his deceased mother. After he returned from the battlefield he applied himself to *michizure* religion and now he is active as a church representative.

There are many similar stories of personal experiences. Those who live so-called lucky lives are the children of virtuous parents who enjoy benefit from their ancestors. It happens regardless of the social position of the family. If you keep in mind that you live under the grace of your ancestors, you will be sure to find fulfillment in a fortunate life.

On the other hand, those who overestimate their own ability and think they owe nothing to others will often cause disaster for their offspring even if they are able to live a good life themselves. A "lucky guy" is one who is close to Great Kami and who therefore has a large inner spirit. To live a fortunate life it is essential to cultivate as large an inner spirit as possible.

When the Founder was still alive a terrible incident happened. An extremely drunken samurai named Matsuo Chōzaburo injured some innocent passers-by with his sword at the western gate of the castle in Okayama. Matsuo met our Founder who was walking there just then and threatened him with his sword. However, our Founder thundered at him, "Think where you are now!" His immediate thought was that since Matsuo had drawn and brandished his sword in such a sacred place as the front of the castle, he would have to do ritual suicide and his family would be destroyed. Then Matsuo, beside himself, became weak and just sat down on the ground.

This samurai could calm down this way because of the virtue of Kami which the divine founder provided with his large inner spirit. In other words, he was enlightened [received *okage*] at that moment.

## To cultivate *bunshin*

We who are priests cannot communicate[11] the message of Kami if our inner spirit is smaller than yours as believers. It is just as impossible as throwing a bucket of water upstairs. We the priests should always try to develop a larger inner spirit. We need to keep on doing *Ōharai* practice in order to keep clean its location, namely our heart.

As the Patriarch (*Kyōshu*) I must put you in touch with (*toritsugi*) the virtue of Kami, more than pursuing my personal happiness. One of the important tasks of the Patriarch is to communicate the richest virtue of Kami that I have myself received. At *nippai* practice I always pray "Give me a larger inner spirit. Let me be as close as the Divine Founder is. Let me communicate a greater virtue of Kami." And, thanks to Kami, as my students become more enlightened, I become more "lucky" myself. I am so fortunate in this way that it sometimes scares me.

Remember the phrase "I am a *deku*, they use me to dance." The *deku*, a puppet in *Bunraku*, moves as though it is alive when it is controlled by a puppet showman. We who are way-companions should practice being a *deku* of the Divine Founder, who is the showman of human life. It is not you who communicate the virtue of Kami. You are just a *deku* who communicates this virtue at the wish of the Divine Founder. It is important to be consistent in the *deku* role. In order to do this, you need to develop your inner spirit as large as you can.[12]

Now I want to explain how to practice the prayer of inner spirit enlightenment which I myself pray during *nippai* while doing *yōki* practice. This is so you can continue to receive the virtue of Kami through stronger and closer relationship with her.

Relax your shoulders, close your eyes, and press your hands in prayer in front of your chest. Then pray:

> Oh Great Kami Amaterasu
>> One in body with Munetada,
>> Our Divine Founder,
> Allow my inner spirit,
>> Like the rising sun of morning,
>> Grow in size and vividness,
> Let it be pacified.
>
> Ooh, ooh, ooh,
>
> Let all our sins and impurities
>> Be purified away,
>> Be purified away.

Say this to yourself silently, and pray it within yourself believing the Divine Founder is there mediating with Kami. Staying in this condition, please open your eyes. Haven't you felt an electric shock at your fingertips?

Our ancestors in the distant past referred to the virtue — or, we may say, the divine work — of Kami, using the character *chi*. This character is found in the words *inochi* (life), *chichi* (mother's milk), *kochi* (eastern wind), *tachi* (kami of the rice field), and so on.

The blood (*chi*) is the first thing in which you may notice the virtue of Kami that you receive through the inner spirit. You feel something like an electric shock at your finger tips, which means that you are receiving this virtue. This is why, without thinking about it, we touch the teeth or stomach with our hands when we have pain there. Also, we use the phrase "touch with the hands" (*teate*) to refer to healing.

Pray every day until you feel the shock at your fingertips. Pray for the good fortune ("luck") coming from the inner spirit. And if you feel sick in some part of the body, touch that place and put yourself in touch with (*toritsugi*) Kami to receive virtue, saying silently "Munetada, Divine Founder, in the same body as Amaterasu Ōmikami, please give me your virtue." Practice this for about a month. You are sure to receive divine blessing. You will more and

more experience what is called "unexpected good future." I'm sure
your life will turn out to be larger and more glorious.

## Second Lecture

### Watch your mental condition

Our human mind (*kokoro*)[13] is of course in our body, though
we cannot see it. It is the mind that makes us angry and anxious.
We feel happy and grateful because of our mind. Its center, which
may be compared to the core of fruit, is the inner spirit. The human
mind is its vessel, set calmly within.

Even if you receive the divine virtue like water from a faucet
with the right attitude, if the vessel is dirty the precious water would
be polluted. Or, if the vessel is distorted, the virtue also would work
in an undesired way. Water takes the shape of the vessel it is in.

I have a story that may sound funny to you. Some ten years
ago I went to a church where I was in charge of a ceremony, and I
stayed in the church representative's home that night. He treated
me very well, offering sake and fresh fish from the Japan Sea. It was
served in a valuable inherited drinking set belonging to the family,
since he knew that I appreciate pottery. His wife served me sake in
a fine cup (*guinomi*). When I had thanked Kami and was about to
drink, I saw something on the surface. I knew what it was immediately because I had it seen it before at home. It was a piece of mold.
They must have kept the cup in a paulownia[14] box wrapped with
cotton. Of course they must have washed it, but a remaining piece
of mold rose to the surface as the hot sake melted it. Perhaps I should
have told them about it but I could not do it. I was quite at a loss
and tried to drink it without getting any of the mold, filtering it with
my lip and often wiping my lip gracefully with a handkerchief. I
took a second sip, and a third, but the mold remained until the last
sip. Finally I finished all the sake, but without really tasting it.

About a week later the minister (*shocho*) of the church came
to headquarters to greet me. He said, "The representative was so
impressed when he saw you drinking. He said he had not ever seen
such a polite person who drank sake wiping his lips at each sip. He
said the person who is to be the Patriarch in the future has something genteel about him." Though I tried to correct the situation
somehow, almost saying "To tell the truth ...," I could not. I was
really at a loss for words and could not tell the true story.

Even good liquor does not taste good if you drink it from a
dirty glass.

We have to try to avoid mold in our mind, since it is the place of the inner divine spirit. Even at our houses we have mold if we keep out fresh air and sunshine and keep in the moisture. It is taught in the Seven Articles "Do not become angry nor worry about things," and in another place, "not to worry about the future." Also, "To lose your way (*mayou*) means that a devil is approaching you (*mayoru*)." When you lose your way some bad idea is entering your mind, leading you to do things that injure you. Be careful. You need to keep your mind free from mold by making it sunny and dry.

Therefore, I urge you to practice the following three things in your daily life so that you will keep your mind healthy as well as keep your house free from mold.

**The importance of greetings**

First of all, I would like to ask you to be careful about greeting people. I want each of you to be able to greet your neighbors freely with a fresh smile, as well as those at home. In regard to such greetings, I've heard a story from a friend of mine who studies monkeys.

Tha Japanese monkey (*nihonzaru*) behaves in the interest of the group, and there is always an ostracized monkey on the outskirts of their territory. According to my friend, once a Japanese monkey is shunned it can never return to the group. On the other hand, when he went to Africa to do field research on gorillas and chimpanzees, he never found a monkey alone by itself.

He was somewhat perplexed by this. So, when he found a gorilla that had been shunned he followed it a whole day. He found that though it stayed by itself for a night, it was welcomed by another group the next day. He says that the gorillas bowed to each other when they met. In the case of the chimpanzees, they shake hands, hug, and pat each other on the back. In a sense, he says, the gorilla greets others in Japanese style while the chimpanzee does it in a western way. In contrast, Japanese monkeys do not give greetings to each other. He told me that he thinks children in Japan are becoming more like the Japanese monkey all the time.

Greetings are the first step in communicating with others. Please be an expert in doing it with the best kind of smile. Where there is a person who does this the air itself becomes brighter. In spring, wild cherry blossoms bloom all over our headquarters at Shintōzan. I found some in places where I had not noticed them before. And I noticed that where the wild cherry blooms, the whole atmosphere around it gets brighter. I often think that I want you to be a wild cherry blossom in your community. I want you to practice greetings in daily life to keep your mind with its inner spirit always bright.[15]

Two years ago at the big Ōharai festival, an old lady aged about sixty-five gave a refreshing speech about what she had learned when she had attended a members' study session. This is what she said:

> At that time I was listening thankfully to the Patriarch's teaching, but when he talked about greetings I began to feel gloomy. In fact, I was having a bad relationship with my daughter-in-law. Later at home I realized that I needed to choose to take some action to change the relationship, as Patriarch had taught us. The next morning I immediately prayed to Kami asking for inner blessing, and asked the Divine Founder to help me greet Keiko, my daughter-in-law. Then I soon went into the kitchen to approach her, but it was hard to say good morning. I prayed every day that I would be able to greet her. One morning, I finally was able to greet her, saying "Good morning, Keiko." I felt relieved, but then she turned away as though displeased. I was very angry with her at the time. After several days in misery, an idea occured to me: 'The Divine Founder must have understood my sincerity when I greeted Keiko, even though she did not!' Then I truly felt relieved.

> After I had kept on with one-sided greetings for several days, one day she returned my greeting from the next room. I was really glad to hear that, and I opened the screen (shōji) and said "Good morning, Keiko" quite naturally. Now we greet each other quite easily and keep up a good relationship. Though I had spent some really bitter days, now I think I have received the true virtue of Kami.

This lady did a really difficult but good thing. The point is that she believed the Divine Founder was sure to understand her sincerity in meeting all those obstacles. Our way to heaven is by no means beyond our reach. We can find it everywhere in our daily life as this old lady discovered. In this way we are able to be enlightened.

## Thanks and apologies

Second, it is important to express thanks (orei) and apologies (owabi). Greetings are still rather easy, but not apologies. This is true for all of us. This is because we stick to our "self." It is a great

thing when one can express an apology frankly. I think Kami will
save you only if you can do it.

I want to talk about an apology given by Godai.[16] As you
know, my father Godai died because of a heart attack. He was
rather plump and had been born a premature baby, so that from
birth his heart was weak. During his final year he had been in critical
condition five times because of heart attacks. At the wedding ceremony of an heir of a related family of ours, he suffered his sixth
attack.

At the ceremony, he gave a speech as Patriarch of Kurozumi-
kyō to the bride and bridegroom, saying:

> If your partner throws a pottery rice bowl to you, catch it
> with some genuine cotton, so as not to break the bowl and not
> make noise. As you know, cotton is soft and warm. When a
> husband feels under strain, a wife can warm him up like genu-
> ine cotton, and vice versa. When you help each other, you
> can make a really warm, good family. Once a woman came
> to tell me to preach to her husband to be soft cotton, since
> she was herself just like a rice bowl. I was at a loss for words
> at the time.

As he said this, he fell slowly into my arms like a balloon subsiding.
His life ended as I held him. It was a really calm and dignified occasion.

Anyway, my point is to tell you what he said on the morning of
July 19, 1972, a year before his death. That morning he recovered
from three days in coma after a heart attack. Godai then said:

> I have just received a very precious divine blessing. I clung to
> the Divine Founder who encouraged me saying, "Come with
> me, I will help anyone who longs for me." An idea suddenly
> occurred to me then. "I haven't said thanks to my own heart
> which has worked for me for seventy years to support my big
> body. I've owed you so much, thank you very much!" I apol-
> ogized and thanked my heart.

This is the point. His sincerity, which let him express thanks
and apologies frankly, is the key to receiving the blessings of Kami.

Sometimes ladies who weigh a lot will hit their knees because
they hurt, as though wanting to be rid of them. Even such people
would receive divine blessing if they would give apology and thanks,
saying "I am obligated to them for supporting my big body," and,
relying on divine inner blessing, put themselves in good relation

with Kami. In fact, many people have received divine blessing in the past.

It's not such an unusual thing to receive divine blessing. We miss out simply through carelessness, not using a little wisdom and learning from experience. We all have the divine inner spirit within us and live under the virtue of Great Kami. Only if we keep our mind clear and dry will we receive the maximum virtue of Kami. I want you as way-companions to be able to say thanks and apologies sincerely.

I want to tell another good story about this subject. There was a lady in the Hioki church in Hyōgo prefecture who was about to sign a divorce contract. This lady was told by Mrs. Fujiki, a priest and an arbitrator of the Family Court, who is also the daughter of the minister of the church, to wait to sign the paper until the next day when I would come to preach to them at a study session. It was the first time she had been to the church.

The lady, after hearing my sermon, went directly to her husband's house to say she was sorry. She said to them,

> While listening to the sermon of the Patriarch I became aware that I have many things to apologize to you for. I wrongly believed that you are to blame, while I had many things that I have to reconsider. I think it is not too late to sign the paper after I tell you I am sorry. Otherwise I cannot help but feel guilty the rest of my life.

Her mother-in-law who was there was so surprised that she burst out crying and apologized honestly and in tears. They both apologized for what they had done to each other. They all were reconciled and her husband understood that she was different now.

At night, soon afterward, they prayed in front of our Kami giving thanks for the blessing. Since she was very much pleased, Mrs. Fujiki waited for my return and told me by telephone what had happened. I was very glad to hear it. It is a pleasure typical of believers' religious life.[17] I want you to be frank in the belief that the Divine Founder is sure to watch over you and to understand your sincerity.

### To forgive people

And thirdly, I want you to forgive people open-heartedly when they apologize to you. You will attain a brighter and more healthy family atmosphere if you are always frank in practicing greetings, thanks, apologies, and forgiveness in your daily life. This will also result in a clean and bright environment for your inner spirit within your mind. This is the well-tried way of life for keeping your mind (*kokoro*) always clean.

## The basis of the human mind

I talked about fundamental problems in the first lecture, and now want to talk about how they apply to daily life. It would be dangerous for a large building to have an unstable basis. The main shrine building at Shintōzan, for instance, has sixty-nine ferro-concrete pillars one meter in diameter and ten meters long holding up the huge roof made of *gensho* stone and roof tiles of Bizen ceramic. The stable foundation of the human mind consists of the souls of parents and other ancestors. Religious belief in our country depends on the sincerity with which people respect kami and maintain ancestors' achievements. I am myself now thinking that even our own Kurozumi-kyō has somehow treated the achievements of our ancestors lightly, though we have been deeply concerned to respect Kami and have enlightened many people.

As an ancestor of our religion I can name the High Disciple Akagi[18] together with the other High Disciples. It was especially auspicious that we were able to build a new shrine to honor him, and that we received the visit of the two chief priests from Ise Shrine at the festival commemorating the 120th anniversary of Kaguraoka Munetada Shrine in Kyoto in 1982. Akagi Kotei contributed much when Kaguraoka Munetada Shrine was built, enabling us to worship Kami and to maintain the achievements of our ancestors. We make pilgrimage to the graves (*okutsuki*)[19] of the High Disciples with this in mind.

In considering the basis of the mind we ask, what does it really mean for a human being to be born and to stop breathing — that is, to die? We need to make this point clear to begin with.

I want to compare our lives to a runway used by airplanes. Let's say that the time of landing on a runway is when we are born, and the time of takeoff is when we die. A man is born to be given another occasion of learning to be enlightened, giving him a novitiate for gaining the status of the myriads of kami (*yao-yorōzu-no-kami*) on the basis of Great Kami.

We pray to three Kami as objects of worship (*gosanzin*), namely Amaterasu Ōmikami, the *yao-yorōzu-no-kami*, and Munetada,

the Divine Founder. I shall compare this to a tree. Amaterasu Ōmikami is the thick trunk of the tree. All the numerous branches are
the myriads of kami, and the thickest bough among them is Munetada, our Divine Founder. This is the trinity of our religion, and
this is how they relate to each other. None of them is the same, just
as any two human beings are different from each other and have
their own roles in society.

Life, in other words, is like a runway where as former kami we
enter in order to learn to be purified kami. After practicing on the
runway called life, we may take flight at death as real kami to the
place where Great Kami is. However, many people think that
human life starts at the time they are born from their mother's
womb and ends when they stop breathing. Therefore they pursue
only entertainments, amusements, and pleasure in life. But this is
not real life. I want to be able to explain the invisible part of life to
you, as a captain expert in navigation does who knows how to
direct his ship among the icebergs invisible underneath the surface
of the northern sea. As a way-companion of Kurozumi-kyō, I want
to explain this invisible part — that is, the life before we are born
and after we die — as well as the life that is visible.

I want you to be sure of the fact that your life is in the hand of
Great Kami throughout your life. The Divine Founder teaches that
"*hito*" (human being) means "*hidomaru*" (where the spirit of the
sun dwells); that is to say, a portion of Great Kami dwells in the
human mind. So, when a woman becomes pregnant it means that
this "separated" portion has come into the core of the cell at the
moment when the condition is met that two cells from the two
parents have become one. Then a life is born and a human being is
made. And so men begin their walk on the runway called life.

Now I will discuss death.

On September 24, 1940 my great-grandmother Masu-toji, the
wife of Muneatsu the third successor of the founder,[20] died. I was
three years old. I remember my father cried tears beside her, who
lay calmly in front of the shrine of the house. I, a child, stretched
out my hands calling her name, wondering why she kept on sleeping in our presence. Then my father took my hands and told me that
she had become a kami, which made me feel solemn. Through this
experience and through the later experience I have told you about,
of my father Godai dying calmly in my arms, I grew to grasp the
death of a human being and that being kami is an actual matter.

In sharp contrast to the death of these two was the death of five people, not Kurozumi-kyō members, who were victims of cancer. I was asked to come to take their hands to calm them down, as they were writhing in agony. In looking at the difference in these two kinds of deaths, I see the difference between the words "to die" and "to be a kami." The common characteristic of these five people was, to put it in a word, the egoistic nature of their lives. It's something like the crash of an airplane.

### About those who have died (mitama)

Why do we hold a funeral when people die?[21] In a sense, there was no need of it for Godai or Masu-toji, because they became kami immediately at their deaths. For others there is a definite purpose.

An airplane named "human being" can hardly take off if it is stained with filthy sin or if it lacks the fuel called virtue. A funeral is a prayer that these "airplanes" take off smoothly.

We accomplish our mourning period in a series of ceremonies (the funeral itself, the tenth, the twentieth, and the fiftieth day memorial services). Throughout this period we pray for the dead to be one of those myriads of kami in the bosom of Great Kami. Thus, the funeral is not simply an expression of sorrow and grief, nor is it merely a social convention.

A human being, originally a kami, should not stagnate at the mitama stage. Everyone should practice our religion seriously and at death rise to be a kami in the realm of Great Kami. Yet, most people at death still need assistance. We help a mitama to be a kami at a funeral; thus, we have to pay much attention to it.

Fortunately enough for us, we have landed safely on this earth for our learning period. However, a considerable number of miscarried or aborted children (mizuko) are abandoned with no care. How many of these nameless children are there who are left neglected without a funeral? Please deify these small nameless mitama as well. This should be considered an obvious human responsibility.

There are many questions about mitama that have not attained full status as kami, or buddhahood (jōbutsu) as they put it in Buddhist circles. For instance, people sometimes lament, saying "Because of all my struggles, I can never be happy." I've experienced many cases that lead me to consider that such things happen because the mitama of their ancestors have not attained to the calmness of kami.

Aged parents rely on their children, and the children take care of them. This is a stable truth of humanity, as well as a means of education. Three generations living together is the natural way of human existence, while *kaku-kazoku*, the two-generation family, is a family that lacks something important.

The two-generation family is not a natural way of human life. In this incomplete and makeshift situation *mitama* cannot help remaining on the minds of their children or relatives, and inevitably this brings trouble. Although this is sometimes referred to as an ancestors' curse, it is not something intentional like a curse at all, but something the *mitama* cannot help. It is a bitter thing for them as well as for us. Thus, we have to pray in earnest that, with the guidance of the Divine Founder, *mitama* become kami as ought to happen.

Offering thanks at the memorial mound for Munetada Kami at Shintōzan. Photo courtesy of Kurozumi-kyō.

Be sure to pray for *mitama*. Keep it in mind that our lives owe much to ancestors, and be sure to thank them. Pray together at the altar where ancestors' spirits are present in the Kurozumi church, practice the *mitama* mourning, pray "let me be a real kami" every day before the shrine of the Divine Founder set in each home, and pray to be held safely in his hands.

The Divine Founder preached:

Let me lead you on
    over this path of life
        that knows no end,
Throughout the countless ages,
    through the next ten thousand realms.[57]

He promised "I'll lead you to the place of Great Kami. All of you, follow me!"

To live each day in thankfulness is to be joined with the mind of Kami; it shows the eternal way to the place of Great Kami. Hence, "living through" (*ikidōshi*) means "temporality"; you "live through" each specific moment.

Thankfully to accept the fact that you are living under the guidance of Kami is to cultivate sincerity (*makoto*). If you continue to practice, this will lead you to Great Kami and you are sure to be one of the myriads of kami led by the Divine Founder. *Michizure* religion should lead us to this result.

Twelve or thirteen years ago an old lady about seventy-four or seventy-five years old came to tell me:

Since I came to this family I've been glad to accept its *michizure* belief, coming to know the Divine Founder and to gain enlightenment. Now I think I was born and got married and entered this family for the sole purpose of meeting the Divine Founder. However, my family has been the representative of all the families affiliated with our Buddhist temple for generations, as well as of the members of the Kurozumi-kyō. That is why my funeral will be performed in Buddhist style. I feel very sorry to lose my connection with the Divine Founder.

Although the Founder thankfully wrote,

Being the same age
    as Heaven and Earth themselves,
        Oh friend of the way,
Do not now turn away
    for the next ten-thousand years,

many people seem to share the concern of this old woman. She was lamenting fearfully that she would lose her relation to Kami at the last moment, when she would become kami.

I recommended to the lady that she ask her family to enshrine her soul in a divided way (*bunrei*), in the altar for prayer for the dead (*mitama-ya*) of the church and in the Shrine for Ancestors in the Daikyōden at Shintōzan. Anyone may in respectfulness be dedicated under the Divine Founder regardless of family religion. She was relieved to know this, and I suggested that she leave a will about her wishes before long.

Some people argue that if one whose family religion is Buddhism is committed to our religion, his *mitama* may be perplexed and lose the way to heaven. But I don't think *mitama* will lose their way. Think of the fact that if you believe in our Kami you will by no means lose your religious basis, even if you are a member of a Buddhist family. Moreover, three-fourths of the kami of war victims in Yasukuni Shine[22] had Buddhism as their family religion. So, please dedicate your relatives' *mitama* to our Kami. I'm sure this will lead to your own happiness.

While many people are dedicated in the *mitama-ya* of churches, few people are dedicated in the Shrine for Ancestors of the Daikyōden at our headquarters.

Frankly speaking, a main reason why I practice *nippai* is to pray to the Divine Founder and the other former Patriarchs in behalf of those *mitama* dedicated in the Daikyōden Shrine for Ancestors, to protect them and lead them to Great Kami. I pray also that Kami will provide blessing for people who pray all over the world.

You may know the term *mitama-shiro* (*ihai* in Buddhism).[23] *Mitama* don't stay in the *mitama-shiro* all the time. Instead, they usually stay with Great Kami to work as kami. However, when one prays in front of it they are immediately present there, beyond time and space. The *mitama-shiro* is a window where we keep in touch with *mitama*. To do the service of *Gōshi* is to set the window open. Please dedicate your ancestors at home even if your family is a minor branch, or a newly divided family, so as to anticipate main family status.

One *michizure* family of the Kurozumi church in Ogi in Saga Prefecture, who believe in Buddhism as a family religion, invites both a Buddhist priest and our minister to the ceremony for ancestors (*soreisai*) each spring and fall. Accordingly, the priest suggested that our minister perform the ritual first, saying, "This family ordinarily says "*shin-butsu*" (kami, Buddha), rather than "*busshin*" (Buddha, kami)." And, our minister did his part wearing a Buddhist robe. What a fine story that is!

I want to make the tenth anniversary of the move of the main shrine to Daikyōden at Shintōzan to be a festival of *mitama-na-gome,* for ancestors of all members.[24] Without any doubt we celebrate the prosperity of our new era at Shintōzan today because the Divine Founder and the *mitama* of our ancestors have given us the proper orientation. In that festival, I want those *mitama* who became kami before we built the Main Shrine at Shintōzan to come to join the Divine Founder there.

I hope all the priests, believers, and *mitama* of our ancestors will unite together around the Divine Founder. I want the first decade of our Kurozumi-kyō after our move from Ōmoto to Shintōzan to bring us closer and closer to the divine hope:

> It is our wish
> to have Amaterasu's
> Goodness be known
> to all the world's people
> soon and without exception.[61]

## Third Lecture

### Joy in giving and in offering

So far I have talked to you about the importance of *Ōharai* practice, the preciousness of *nippai*, and, sometimes by comparing it to our houses, the way to keep clean the human mind, the place of the inner divine spirit. I have also talked about the foundation or basis the inner divine spirit gives for eternal life, and have discussed *mitama* by comparing human life to the runway used by airplanes. Now I want to finish these lectures by explaining to you how to give shape to these ideas in your daily life, and how you may attain *ikidōshi*, which means living eternally.[25]

When airplanes go up with a heavy load and without enough fuel, they won't fly; or if they do, they will crash. In order to take flight gracefully like Godai or like the wife of the third patriarch, one needs to practice *Ōharai* in order to wash all stains from the wings, and to take on the fuel called virtue: the virtue of having joy in giving and in offering things. Moreover, we are asked to make these preparations for take-off at any moment in life.

Every time I go to Tokyo I go to worship at the Yasukuni Shrine. Suppose I was reaching for a 10,000 yen note to give as a gift for the kami but my hand fell on a 5,000 yen note. Then, my first thought might be that 5,000 yen is enough for today. My egoistic will would be about to rule my mind who usually am urging you not to let this happen. After a moment of struggle to abandon the idea, I give the 10,000 yen note to kami and pray to them. Now I feel really purified in overcoming the thought. Or, when I go abroad, I buy souvernirs for the staff at headquarters. When I choose things to buy, I have particular persons in mind for the good things I have chosen; however, when I get home, I might feel some item is too good to use as a souvenir. But, if I give it to that person after all, he will really be delighted, and I who present it feel more happy than the one to whom I give it. Although everybody knows this delight-fulness, egoism often invades people's minds.

The Reverend Fukumitsu, Main Priest of Daikyōden, often preached that accumulating virtue would work to one's disadvan-tage. To give something might appear at first glance to lose it. Yet, by doing this one grows in virtue. You get several times as much delightfulness by keeping away egoistic will and giving things. By doing this one can wipe off the stains on one's wings and get enough fuel. I believe the delight of the inner spirit comes from sincerity in offering, while physical pleasure comes from receiving things.

I practice karate at the Martial Arts Gym (the former Daikyō-den) in Ōmoto. One day when I had arrived early for a children's class and was walking around in the shrine, the mother of one of the children found me and asked me to go over and have some *yomogi-dango*[26] which the boy's grandmother had sent. While I was receiving this treat the boy came home saying, "Mother, I'm home!" The mother gave him some and said, "Grandma fondly made these for us to eat. Say thanks to her in your heart before you eat." The he ate it with satisfaction and asked, "May I bring some to Ken-chan?"[27] "That's fine. Do that," the mother replied.

I felt something warm when I listened to this conversation, because I sensed the warm atmosphere of the family through their conversation, allowing them to offer things they enjoy so naturally and frankly.

In contrast, some people would tend to say something like "Grandma sent us these *dango* so we could eat them ourselves. Bring some rice-crackers instead." Many grown-ups even trample down innocent sincerity, saying "You don't need to do that ..." I think such selfish ideas of grown-ups prevent children's innocence from growing rich in their mind. Such ideas make children lose human dignity, leading to adolescents committing crimes or causing domestic violence. In a sense, they are victims suffering from the selfishness of grown-ups.

Though it is hard to abandon one's ego, offering things is not so hard for us to do. To live up to this principle of offering things would be splendid education for children today. Please develop sincerity through offering things.

The roundness of the mirror in front of Kami stands for the sun. While for purpose of representing the sun it would be enough just to have it painted red, it also reflects things for our benefit. To pray to Kami doesn't simply mean to admire the symbolized Kami. It also requires that you pray for the kami within your mind through watching your own praying figure in the mirror. The mirror is letting you know that Kami, that is, a portion of Kami, dwells silently within you.

If you take away the syllable "ga" from "kagami" (mirror), it reads "kami." It is difficult to erase "ga," which means "self" or "ego." However, sincerity (makoto ) and self (ga) may come to mean the same thing when the spirit of "mirror" is lived up to. In the case of the boy with the dango, sincerity in giving was the true spirit of "kagami." The more you develop the "kami" part by showing the sincerity which is the spirit of Kami, the more the "ga" part shrinks. Furthermore, by controlling the fickle "ga" so that the "kami" part becomes more purified, you find a way to ikidōshi, wiping off the stains on the wings and loading enough of the fuel called virtue.

Whether you can attain ikidōshi depends on how you express thankful feelings, showing your sincerity to Kami and to society. It is this way of living that raises up the inner mind. To fast, to be beaten by water at the bottom of waterfalls, to practice Ōharai, these are not everything when it comes to life-long practice. To be always sincere in life, controlling the fickle ga and developing sincerity which leads you to Kami, this is the larger matter and the real practice of living.

Those who become involved with michizure beliefs should develop their religious morale, continuing to be interested in what they can do for the Divine Founder, for the church, and for the headquarters of Kurozumi-kyō. A church where there is a minister who devotes himself to the members, to the church, to the headquarters and to the Kurozumi-kyō as a whole, has a promise of prosperity.

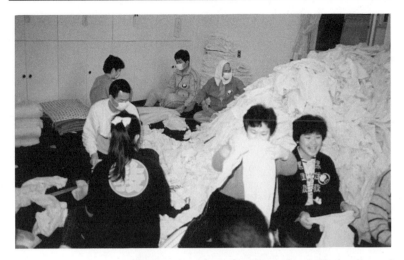

Doing service at the Asahigawa-so, a hospital for handicapped children from many courtries in Okayama. 10,000 diapers a day are folded. Photo courtesy of Kurozumi-kyō.

Kurozumi-kyō has always been concerned with contributing to society and to the nation. To continue this depends on your co-operation in the *Arigatō-gozaimasu* movement[28] and in contributing money. In this way Kurozumi-kyō can carry on the work for society, for the nation, and for the modern world that was taken up anew in coming up to Shintōzan. I think we have done some really valuable things, such as raising the next generation to support Kurozumi-kyō and carrying on social service and cultural diplomacy, on the basis of your unselfishly-given money. I give thanks to Kami for our rising social status and confidence and also that the name of the Divine Founder is increasingly well known on earth.

I seriously feel the responsibility of people's reliance on Kurozumi-kyō and the high expectation they have for us.

Please keep on believing in Kami and receiving virtue every day, continuing to be concerned with the church, with Kurozumi-kyō, with society, and with the world, through the *Arigatō-gozaimasu* movement.

By participating in this movement you may grasp how way-companions overcome egoism by showing sincerity, something that leads you to *ikidōshi*.

I want to finish my speech for this study session with your deep understanding and cooperation. Thank you very much.

# 5

# Kurozumi-kyō in Japanese Culture

## The Reverend Muneharu Kurozumi

*This chapter was The Reverend Muneharu Kurozumi's main address to an American audience. He proposes that Shinto is a universal religion. The late-Edo-period religious experience of Kurozumi Munetada and its current expression by Kurozumi-kyō today have their roots in primitive Japanese civilization. At each point in history the living presence of Amaterasu, Kami of the sun, animates the true life of all humans. It is a living tradition.*

*Enough of his original direct discourse to the audience has been kept to signal an essential part of the Kurozumi message: the immediate, here-and-now context in which the benefit of Amaterasu is experienced. In this way, in Kurozumi view, the universal religion of the founder finds its authentic expression.*

My subject is Japanese religion, and Kurozumi-kyō as an expression of it.

I want first to express my appreciation for having this study session on Kurozumi-kyō Shinto. I came to Dayton in the evening of the day before yesterday. Yesterday morning and this morning I practiced *nippai*, our sunrise worship, just as we practice it every morning at our main shrine at Shintōzan. This morning was a particularly splendid occasion, the kind I would like to take back with me to Shintōzan.

So far as I know this is the first time such a study session has been held in America.[1] This does not mean, however, that Shinto is in any sense an exclusive religion. We might speak of Shinto as essentially the religion of humanity (*ningen-kyō*). This is the message I have come to pass on to you. It might even be better not to use the word Shinto. When this word is used Buddhism and Christianity come to mind as equivalent entities. We should rather speak of Shinto simply as humanity's religion; or if a word must be found for it, as "Japanese religion" (*Nihon-kyō*).

## Origins in Japanese History

Though the comparison might not be entirely apt, I want to compare the situation of Japanese religion to the Galapagos Islands. I have heard that in this place many kinds of animals are found that have survived from centuries past and are still living there today. The evolution of these animals can be understood by observing them today. In some ways the situation of Shinto, or of Japan as a whole, may be likened to these islands in the way aspects of the spirit have been preserved from the past. Kinds of spirituality that existed in Europe, America, China, and Southeast Asia in ancient times are still alive and functioning in Japan at the present time.

The earliest period in the history of Japan is called the Jomon Period, beginning about ten or fifteen thousand years ago. In this period people lived by hunting. The people were physically strong, but life was very hard. They fought terribly and sometimes even killed each other over the prey they sought as food. If we look at the pottery of this era we find it reflects their way of life. The pots are very powerful and make a strong impression on us, but at the same time they leave us with a dark feeling as though the dreary spirit of the people is still alive in them.

This period continued for a long time until about 2,000 years ago when rice agriculture began.[2] Rice cannot be raised if people are wandering around or fighting one another. Only when they live in a settled place can they cultivate their land in a friendly and cooperative way, sowing seed in spring and harvesting in fall. Without harmony with one another during long periods of time, the crop cannot be tended and the way of life cannot succeed. It was out of the cultivation of rice that our civilization was born.

Our ancestors seem to have developed a simple and pious spirit in their pleasure at seeing the presence of life in a grain of rice.

Each grain would in growing be multiplied into many hundreds of grains by the time of harvest, and they were in awe at the power of its life. In searching for the source of this energy in the land, in the water, and in all the processes needed to grow rice, they began to realize that it was in the sun that the source of all this life and power was to be found. Later, people found the spirit of the universe in the sun, and they called it Amaterasu Ōmikami. Seeing her presence there is the beginning of Shinto.

This period in Japanese history is called the Yayoi. The pottery made in this period looks the exact opposite of what was made during the Jomon period. We find a very rounded, full, and bright sort of pottery that enriches our spirit like a large-hearted mother. As a result of rice agriculture, human life became secure and people for the first time obtained a peaceful life in which they could live in a friendly and cooperative way.

Pottery clearly reflects the characteristics of its times and of the people who make it and use it. In the Yayoi period people attained a human-like life for the first time and expressed their joy in living. It was then they learned to thank Kami for the first time. Shinto is truly a religion for expressing a feeling of appreciation and of the warmth of heart that is exchanged between Kami and humans.

In Kurozumi-kyō we don't make much of discussing the myths of the *Kojiki* and *Nihon-shoki.* I am particularly attracted, however, to the well-known story of the Kami Amaterasu emerging from the rock-cave.[3] When she emerged from the darkness the world was filled with brightness. I think this myth symbolizes how in the Yayoi period a bright and peaceful culture based on rice agriculture took the place of the long, dark, and brutal Jomon period.

Rice is a very important symbol. We think of it as having in it the power of heaven and earth. Rice is called *kome* because it contains (*komeru*) this power. It is also called *ine,* referring to the rice plant as a whole, because it is the root (*ne*) of life (*inochi*). At a time when people were still living on the bare ground a place was specially built to store rice. This place was called *miyake,* or in present times, *kura.* The term *miya* is also used to refer to the Shinto shrine.

The style of this early rice storehouse is preserved even now at the Ise Grand Shrine. In its buildings we can see the kind of structures used in the traditional Japanese farm house, originally designed for rice storage. Our own main shrine building at Shintōzan is actually a larger form of this early farm house.

From the symbol of a single grain of rice came the idea that kami reside in a grain of rice; and not only in rice but also in water and earth, fire and stone, and in everything associated with rice agriculture. The faith of Japan comes from this kind of animistic perception, just as most religious traditions begin in a period of animism similar to this. In general, *inochi* (life) is kami (divine).

Now we may turn to the main subject.

## Kurozumi Munetada, Founder of Kurozumi-kyō

Kurozumi-kyō was established when our Divine Founder Munetada was united with the sun in 1814. This is an experience full of meaning and mystery which we call the Direct Acceptance of Divine Mission (*tenmei jikiju*). The story of this event, in which the spirit of the sun — Amaterasu Ōmikami as we refer to it — and the spirit of the Founder were united, has already been discussed.

Before we come to this point, however, let us not forget the contribution of the Founder's parents and ancestors to his experience. The ancestors of the Founder had changed their status from samurai (*bushi*) to Shinto priest (*shinshoku*) at the beginning of the fourteenth century, so that behind the Founder's life there are five hundred years of service to the Shinto priesthood. The familiar "*geta* and *zori*" story about the Founder as a child wearing two kinds of sandals illustrates the depth of his trust in his parents. The other side of this story is that he developed this strong trust because they had raised him with overflowing affection. In this respect his attitude is just the same as our early ancestors' pious and simple appreciation of the life of nature, seen in the rising of the sun and in the ten- and hundred-fold multiplication of rice by its power.

Another factor in the background of his experience is the death of his parents, leading him to experience the depth in human life that is involved in accepting death.

All these factors indicate the great strength behind him leading to the event which united him with the spirit of the sun on the day of the winter solstice in 1814.

This strength can be seen by considering the pilgrimages he made to the Ise Grand Shrine. The first time he went to Ise he met an Amaterasu that is similar to the one we know from the myth compilations. Here Amaterasu Ōmikami is known as the deity of the Japanese people and the ancestress of the Imperial family. On the second occasion and thereafter, however, he did not visit Ise the way ordinary Japanese do. Having received the Divine Mission

The Chief Patriarch leading pilgrimage at the Ise Shrine.
Photo courtesy of Kurozumi-kyō.

Praying Ōharai (purificatory prayer) before Amaterasu
Ōmikami at the Ise Shrine. Photo courtesy of Kurozumi-kyō.

in 1814, the figure of Amaterasu had acquired for him a new and
universal meaning. Amaterasu Ōmikami had become the "spirit of
the universe."

We could put it this way: the Founder's acceptance of the Divine Mission, by which he was united with the sun on the winter
solstice day of 1814, meant he was returning to the original meaning of Amaterasu as we saw in the example of the discovery of the
life-giving power of rice. In a sense his experience liberated Amaterasu from mythical restriction, restoring her position as recognized by our ancestors at the beginning of rice agriculture. This is
not to deny her traditionally recognized role as Kami of the people
and Ancestress of the Imperial Family. That is to say, in the Divine
Founder's experience of her the Kami of the people was raised to a
higher level without losing that identity, and achieved a greater
and more essential existence as Kami.

The reception of the Divine Mission is at the same time a personal revelation, an event that may take place within anyone's
spirit. It means the discovery of the divine spirit within which comes
from Amaterasu Ōmikami (see chapter 4). The reception of mission

means coming to acknowledge what being a human being truly is. The one who experiences this feels a grateful appreciation which cannot be expressed in any words because of the great joy which results.

## Ethical Results of The Fundamental Experience

I want to tell you two or three stories through which the Founder taught us that all humans are the children of Kami and have received the inner spirit of Amaterasu Ōmikami.

Once when the Founder was going to visit the house of a follower, a river in that rural area was almost overflowing its banks after a heavy rain. While he was crossing over on a wooden bridge it abruptly moved and he took fright. If this had happened to one of us we would think, "Oh, I'm glad I didn't fall into the river." But the Founder, when he had arrived at the other side of the river, looked up to the sky and apologized to Kami, "Dear Amaterasu Ōmikami, I have injured my inner spirit by my fright and I have hurt your heart. Please forgive me." This shows he truly believed he was a child of Kami who had the divine inner spirit dwelling in his own spirit. I am deeply impressed by this story.

Here is another example. The Founder was often invited to followers' homes and he frequently went to visit them. Once when he returned from such a visit he was sitting in his house with a follower. His wife served them tea. As she did so, the Founder, before he drank the tea, clapped his hands to her as he would to Kami in his shrine. The follower was quite puzzled by this though he had often observed it, and asked, "Why do you worship your wife in the same way you worship Kami?" His reaction mirrors the Edo period in which the four-class system (samurai, farmer, artisan, merchant) was still strictly observed. This meant, within a family, male superiority and female inferiority (I hate these words!). In those times giving reverence to one's wife in the way in which one reverenced kami was considered very strange.

The Founder said to the follower, "This is not anything extraordinary. Though she is my wife, she is also a child of Kami just as I am. This child of Kami serves me tea with a generous and considerate heart. Her true heart is the spirit of Kami. I worship this spirit of Kami with the clapping of my hands."

Another story showing that humans are equally children of Kami concerns the seating arrangements when the Founder preached. As has already been related (see chapter 2), those who gathered before the Founder when he was speaking had to take their seats in order of their arrival. Even samurai had to sit far to the rear if they arrived late. Moreover, they could not bring their swords in with them. In the memorial house of the Founder, built late in his life, the sword-stand where the samurai left their swords remains today.

Another story concerns a rich follower who invited the Founder to his home to show with pride an Ōhinasama (an exhibit of dolls for the Dolls' Festival on March 3) which was a family treasure. The stand (*hinadana*) has the lord and his wife sitting at the top, and on the lower shelves each of the servants in their proper seats. A maid of the family was cleaning it on the morning of the visit and accidentally upset it. Fortunately, she was able quickly to set it up again, but because she was in a hurry she got the positions of the dolls entirely wrong. The lord was at the bottom and the servants were at the top. At that point her master proudly brought the Founder into the room and said, "This is my *Ōhinasama*, my family treasure." Then he noticed that the lord and servants were in reversed positions and was embarrassed about it. But the Founder, looking at it, laughed and said, "Oh yes, this is right. A time like this will come sometime in the future."

A time like that finally came about forty years ago as he had predicted. After World War II Japan was taught the importance of democracy, freedom, and equality by your country, America. But if our Kurozumi-kyō, which had such a great Founder, had been stronger we could have introduced these ideals in Japan much earlier and without the help of the United States [with a laugh].

The examples which I have given show the ethical aspect of Kurozumi-kyō, based on the idea that all humanity are children of Kami and have received the divine inner spirit.

### Inner Relation to Kami

Now I want to turn to another topic: that humanity is directly linked to Kami. We humans are directly connected with the origin of life, Amaterasu Ōmikami, because of the presence within us of the spirit of Kami. Figuratively speaking, the relationship is like that of a baby in its mother's womb, connected with the mother by the umbilical cord.

We have a tendency to think that we live on our own, by our own power and abilities. For instance, we think that we work and earn money by ourselves and that by ourselves we eat and live.[4] But, do we control the function of our heart? We hear with our ears, see with our eyes and we breathe; but all these functions are maintained by something beyond our control, and our lives are supported by such functions. It is not that we live because our hearts are beating, or because we eat and continue to breathe, but quite the other way around. Isn't it really that our hearts are beating because we live, that we eat because we are alive, and that we continue to breathe because we have the gift of life within us? These functions are like tributary rivers and the main river of our lives is alive because it is directly connected with Amaterasu Ōmikami by the inner spirit. In other words, we are alive because we are enabled to live. This is the philosophy of life in Kurozumi-kyō and in Shinto.

A feeling of appreciation will be naturally released when we get away from our belief that it is by ourselves that we live, and when we nourish our mind in realizing that we live by being enabled to live. This feeling of appreciation and gratitude gives the best nourishment to the divine spirit within our spirits. My own experience on a cold February morning in 1977 helped me to appreciate the rich presence of Amaterasu within (see chapter 4).

It is important for us to know how to keep this inner spirit big and round like the morning sun, and at the same time keep it vigorous. It should be vigorous without becoming a violent power which hurts other people. The teaching of Kurozumi-kyō is concerned to keep our spirit like the morning sun which enables others to live. There is a Japanese proverb: "Water obeys both square and round containers." Water does not have its own shape. In a round glass it is round, and in a square one it becomes square. Our spirit which is not visible but certainly exists can be thought of as a container for the divine spirit. If we pollute our spirits, then the life we receive from the divine virtue or power of Kami is distorted. It should have a round shape and perform a circular function.[5]

The most important means for caring for our spirits are the Seven Household Principles. Following them is the way to prepare our spirit to be a fit container for the divine inner spirit so that the divine virtue may remain clean and round like the morning sun. We nourish our spirit just as we eat meals for the sake of our physical body. Joy and appreciation are its nourishment; not poisons like being angry or depressed. These give pain to our spirit as poisons harm the physical body. Providing a time in which to experience appreciation and joy is the most important way to nourish the inner spirit. It is a time when the energy of life, the divine virtue, may burn perfectly like the morning sun.

Every religion tells us also that illness can be cured by developing one's religious belief. Particularly the new religions[6] proselytized on the basis of healing and in this way gained many members, but the same thing has happened in other times as well.

The same is true in Kurozumi-kyō. Even today there are many followers who have been healed of some disease or other through their religious belief. In our case there are two types of this healing, however. The first occurs when someone goes to a priest asking for healing. In this kind of experience one feels gratitude and thankfulness through putting complete trust in the priest. Through his mediation one gives one's self completely to Kami, and the power of Kami — the divine virtue — is transmitted through him. The result is a great sense of relief and a heightened sense of gratitude as one's life-force gains renewed vigor and the illness is cured. This is probably the most common type.

The second, the one that I hope will become more common in the future, is typified by *jiriki*, reliance on one's own power or ability. It may be illustrated by the following example. Once a follower came to ask for help because he was suffering from an illness. The Founder said, "Cure your illness by yourself." This was a respected person with a great deal of intelligence and will power. To such a person the Founder gave this command.

His meaning in saying this was that he should by his own effort cultivate the *bunshin* — the "portion" of the spirit of the universe within himself — to be larger and more like the morning sun. By doing this he would be strengthening his own spirit, and it would be only natural that his illness would be cured.

The Founder was fond of saying that his religion (*michi*, "Way") was not a way of healing illness, but a way of healing the heart. Healing illness is only a way of making a start in the Way. Our life, our "way of living" on this earth, should be given to cultivating our hearts to make them as perfect and pure as possible. When we do this we nourish and enlarge the presence of Kami within us.

It is joy and gratitude that are the best nourishment of this inner spirit. I feel this even now in the fact that all of you have come here, giving up your usual occupations to come and hear me speak. You are listening seriously to what I am saying about Kurozumi-kyō in which I believe. Even at this moment you are giving me a feeling of joy and gratitude that nourishes the spirit of Kami within me, and I am tasting great happiness. I feel that I must thank you for what you are giving me at this very moment.

Three years ago the Pope came to Japan for the first time. As one of the religious leaders of Japan I also had an opportunity to meet him. I wanted to give him a gift; through the advice of a Roman Catholic friend of mine, Professor Yoshinori Inagaki of Kyushu University, I presented him a quotation from a book he had written before he had become the Pope.

In that passage he had written:

It is precisely in becoming a gift to others that man becomes himself most fully. (Deep in the dynamic structure of the person there is inscribed what may be called 'the law of the gift.')[7]

This is exactly what we also want to have happen. We believe that the benefit of our action in sincere service to others comes back to us in a kind of circle. A kind of reciprocity is involved, so that our service to others is in fact the best nourishment we can find for our own soul. The happiness and appreciation gained in this way becomes the nourishment of our divine inner spirit; it is in fact *ikidōshi*, life eternal. I believe the sincere service the Pope spoke of is a fundamental doctrine in both Shinto and Christianity. We refer to this way of living as *toku o tsumu*, ("accumulating virtue").

## Conclusion

I have been speaking about the essential doctrine of Shinto. However, I am interested in doctrine as a method rather than as a goal in itself. Doctrine is a means to guide people to the goal and should not itself be the goal. When doctrine becomes that, it leads to dreadful fighting among religious people. The problem of religious people (including myself) arises when we make our doctrines absolute.

Whatever one's religion, the important thing is to practice the way of living taught by the Pope. I believe it is the way to live as a human being.

I thank you very much for your kind attention.

# 6

# Kurozumi Munetada's Poetry: The *Dōka*[1]

**Translated by Harold Wright**

## A

### 1

*Arigataya*
   *Ware hinomoto ni*
     *Umare kite*
*Sono hi no uchi ni*
   *Sumuto omoeba.*

Ah, how grateful
   to be born here in the land
     of the Rising Sun,
And to know that in the Sun
   I continue to abide.

### 2

*Amaterasu*
   *Kami no mitoku wa*
     *Ametsuchi ni*
*Michite kakenaki*
   *Megumi narukana.*

The divine virtue
   of Amaterasu
     fills Heaven and Earth;
Ah, in such abundance
   is this limitless grace.

### 3

*Ametsuchi no*
   *Uchini teriyuku*
     *Mitakara wo*
*Imazo torieshi*
   *Kokoro tanoshiki.*

That vast treasure
   here within Heaven and Earth
     continues to glow;
Having now accepted it,
   my heart indeed knows joy.

### 4

*Amaterasu*
   *Kami no mihara ni*
     *Sumu hito wa*
*Nete mo samete mo*
   *Omoshiroki kana.*

When one is living
   in the Deified realm
     of Amaterasu,
Whether asleep or awake
   one always knows delight.

### 5

Ara ureshi
 Kakaru ureshiki
  Ukiyo zo to
Shirade imamade
 Sugoshi oshisayo.

Ah, how joyful
 in learning of the joy
  of our daily lives;
Yet, I truly do regret
 not knowing this till now.

### 6

Ametsuchi ni
 Otoranu hodono
  Ikimono wa
Onoga kokoro to
 Omou ureshisa.

Being a living thing
 and equal in all ways
  to Heaven and Earth —
My heart has come to know this,
 and now is aware of joy.

### B

### 7

Ametsuchi no
 Kokoro wa onoga
  Kokoro nari
Hokani kokoro no
 Ari to omou na.

Heaven and Earth
 have the very same heart
  as these hearts of ours;
Do not think that it exists
 somewhere outside ourselves.

### 8

Kami Hotoke
 Onoga kokoro ni
  Mashimasu ni
Ta wo inoru koso
 Aware narikere.

It is in our hearts
 that the kami and Buddha
  are found to dwell;
Indeed to pray elsewhere
 would be truly a pity.

### 9

Ametsuchi no
 Kokoro no arika
  Tazunureba
Onoga kokoro no
 Uchinizo arikeru.

Whenever I seek
 the whereabouts of the Heart
  of Heaven and Earth,
I find, indeed, that it dwells
 here within this heart of mine.

### 10

Kami to ii
 Hotoke to yu mo
  Ametsuchi no
Makoto no uchi ni
 Sumeru ikimono.

Some call it kami
 some even call it Buddha
  this Living Thing
That dwells in the Sincerity
 of all of Heaven and Earth.

### 11

Umi areba
　　Yama mo aritsuru
　　　　Yononaka ni
Semaki kokoro wo
　　Motsuna hitobito.

Since there are oceans
　　as well as many mountains
　　　　in this world of ours,
Oh, people, don't keep clinging
　　to such narrowness of heart.

### 12

Ureshiki mo
　　Kanashiki mo mata
　　　　Kokoro nari
Mina ureshiki to
　　Omowazarukana.

Being delighted
　　and also being saddened
　　　　comes from the heart;
So why not, then, feel delight
　　in everything around you?

### 13

Amaterasu
　　Kami no mikokoro
　　　　Hitogokoro
Hitotsu ni nareba
　　Ikidoshi nari

Whenever the Heart
　　of Amaterasu
　　　　and a person's heart
Are joined together as one —
　　This is the Abiding Life.

### C

### 14

Asagao no
　　Hana no sugata ni
　　　　Mayounayo
Hikage matsumani
　　Shibomi nurukana.

Do not be deceived
　　by the morning glory's
　　　　flowering form;
Waiting for evening shadows,
　　it comes to a withered end.

### 15

Kagirinaki
　　Inochi to Shirade
　　　　Yoni utsuru
Hana morotomo ni
　　Chiruzo hakanaki

To leave the world
　　without knowing we possess
　　　　Everlasting Life
Is as sad as the scattering
　　of the flowers that fade away.

### 16

Tsuyu goto ni
　　Tsuki wa yadoredo
　　　　Ōzora no
Makoto no tsuki wa
　　Hitotsu naruran.

Although the moon
　　dwells in every drop of dew,
　　　　in the sky above
The moon of True Sincerity
　　certainly remains as one.

### 17

Ametsuchi no
　　Makoto no naka ni
　　　　Irinureba
Ukiyo no yume mo
　　Wasurarenikeri.

Upon entering
　　the True Sincerity
　　　　of Heaven and Earth
One can come to forget
　　dreams of the Floating World.

### 18

Ara ureshi
　　Kakaru tanoshiki
　　　　Yononaka wo
Tareka ukiyo wo
　　Ku no dō to yū.

Ah, such joyfulness
　　here in the delightfulness
　　　　of this world of ours;
Who can call the Floating World
　　merely a path of suffering?

### 19

Ukikoto wa
　　Mina yumenoyo to
　　　　Omoinaba
Samenan koto no
　　Tanomoshiki kana.

If we remember
　　that strife in our lives resides
　　　　in the world of dreams,
Then, indeed, awakening
　　would offer us much joy.

### 20

Mukau koto
　　Mina okagezo to
　　　　Omoinaba
Nete mo samete mo
　　Arigataki kana.

If we remember
　　that all things around us
　　　　are divine reflections,
Whether asleep or awake
　　we will know such gratitude.

### 21

Ikishini wa
　　Kokoro hitotsuni
　　　　Arumono to
Shiranu ukiyo no
　　Hito no awaresa.

Living and dying
　　are things that only exist
　　　　within our own hearts;
It is sad that that's unknown
　　by people of the Floating World.

### 22

Arigataya
　　Kokoro no kumo mo
　　　　Harewatari
Ukiyo no kumo wa
　　Tonimo kakunimo.

Ah, the gratitude
　　for having had the clouds
　　　　all swept from my heart,
Even though clouds still remain
　　throughout the Floating World.

**D**

### 23

Nanigoto mo
    Ten no nasu noto
        Omoinaba
Ku nimo sewa nimo
    Naranu mono nari.

If we remember
    that everything that exists
        comes from Heaven,
Then worries and daily life
    are not matters of concern.

### 24

Ametsuchi wo
    Wagaminoue to
        Omoinaba
Wakaki mo oi mo
    Kokoro naruran.

Were we to know
    that these very lives of ours
        are Heaven and Earth,
Then both youthfulness and age
    would be but in our hearts.

### 25

Amaterasu
    Kami no otoku wo
        Shiru toki wa
Nete mo samete mo
    Arigataki kana.

When we are aware
    of the divine virtue
        of Amaterasu,
Whether asleep or awake
    we feel such gratitude.

### 26

Sashiataru
    Koto nomi omoe
        Hito wa tada
Kinō wa sugiru
    Asu wa shirarezu.

People be aware
    of what is happening now ...
        there is nothing more;
Yesterday has departed
    and tomorrow is unknown.

### 27

Maruki naka ni
    Maruki kokoro wo
        Motsu hito wa
Kagiri shirarenu
    ⬭ Ki naka nari.

Inside of Roundness
    a person possessing
        a roundness of heart
Will never know of limits
    here within the ⬭ -ness.

### 28

Arigataya
    Kakaru medetaki
        Yoni idete
Tanoshimi kurasu
    Mi koso yasukere.

Ah, the gratitude
    of being born in a world
        filled with such joy,
And to live a happy life
    free, indeed, from any strife.

29

| | |
|---|---|
| *Ametsuchi no* | Dwelling within |
| *Makoto no nakani* | the True Sincerity |
| *Sumuhito wa* | of Heaven and Earth, |
| *Umu mo seishi mo* | One cares not about Being, |
| *Nanika itowan.* | Non-being, life or death. |

E

30

| | |
|---|---|
| *Umu no yama* | Crossing the mountains |
| *Seishi no umi wo* | of Being and Non-being, |
| *Koenureba* | the Sea of Life and Death, |
| *Kokozo anraku* | You come to the World of Here |
| *Sekai naruran.* | where, indeed, contentment dwells. |

31

| | |
|---|---|
| *Arigataki* | People who know |
| *Koto nomi omoe* | no more than the feeling |
| *Hito wa tada* | of Gratitude |
| *Kyō no tōtoki* | Hold today as precious, |
| *Ima no kokoro no.* | the Nowness in their hearts. |

32

| | |
|---|---|
| *Ari to mite* | When we see Being |
| *Naki koso moto no* | we do indeed have Nothingness |
| *Sugata nare* | in the original form; |
| *Naki o tanoshimu* | Rejoice in this Nothingness |
| *Kokoro yasusayo.* | and find comfort in your heart. |

33

| | |
|---|---|
| *Ari to mite* | When we see Being |
| *Haki koso onoga* | we do indeed have Nothingness |
| *Sumika nari* | as our dwelling place; |
| *Naki o tanoshimu* | Rejoice in this Nothingness |
| *Mi koso yasukere.* | and live your life in comfort. |

34

| | |
|---|---|
| *Ari to mite* | When we see Being |
| *Naki koso onoga* | we do indeed have Nothingness |
| *Sugata nite* | seen as some form; |
| *Naki sugata koso* | The form of Nothingness alone |
| *Ikidōshi nari.* | lives in the Abiding Life. |

### 35

*Ari to mite*
    *Aru koso onoga*
        *Sugata nari*
*Arite mayowanu*
    *Mi koso yasukere.*

When we see Being
    we do indeed have Being
        seen as some form;
Yet, not being deceived
    by Being frees us from strife.

### 36

*Naki to yū*
    *Naki niwa hitono*
        *Mayouran*
*Naki koso arino*
    *Moto no moto nari.*

People may become
    deluded by the Nothing
        in Nothingness,
Yet Nothing is indeed
    the basic basis of Being.

### 37

*Amaterasu*
    *Kami to hito tono*
        *Isshin no*
*Tazuna yurusazu*
    *Noritamae kimi.*

Amaterasu's
    heart and a person's heart
        are one and the same;
Do not let loose the reins
    whenever you're on horseback.

### F

### 38

*Kimiga yuku*
    *Higashi no hate mo*
        *Ima koko mo*
*Onashi makoto no*
    *Kokoro narikeri.*

As you now depart
    to the ends of the Eastlands,
        there still remains
Here in this place the Heart,
    the same True Sincerity.

### 39

*Namikaze wo*
    *Ikade shizumen*
        *Wadatsu kami*
*Amatsu hi wo shiru*
    *Hito no norishini.*

Be made tranquil
    in your blowing waves and winds,
        Oh, god of the sea —
One now aboard this boat
    knows of Amaterasu.

### 40

*Oni mo ja mo*
    *Mina kiriharai*
        *Ikimono wo*
*Yashinau hito ni*
    *Itatsuki wa nashi.*

Driving forth demons
    and the serpents from our lives,
        we can then nurture
This living thing within us
    and will keep from getting ill.

### 41

Mitabi made
　　Ikikaeritaru
　　　　Hito wa mata
Karatenjiku to
　　Waga chō ni nashi.

Now for the third time
　　a person has returned
　　　　to live once again …
Not in China, India nor here
　　had this ever happened.

### 42

Ōyamato
　　Kojima kojima to
　　　　Wakaredomo
Sono minakami wa
　　Awajishima yama.

This Land of Yamato
　　is made up of a number
　　　　of small islands,
Yet their single origin
　　is Awajishima Yama.[2]

### 43

Inishie mo
　　Ima mo mukashi mo
　　　　Konogoro mo
Kinō mo kyō mo
　　Onaji michi nari.

In ancient times
　　as of now and in the past,
　　　　as in recent times,
Even yesterday and today,
　　the Way remains the same.

## G

### 44

Nichinichi ni
　　Asahini mukai
　　　　Kokoro kara
Kagirinaki mi to
　　Omou ureshisa.

Day after day
　　we face the morning sun
　　　　aware in our hearts
That our lives are limitless,
　　a feeling of such joy.

### 45

Tsuki wa iri
　　Hino ima izuru
　　　　Akebono ni
Ware koso michi no
　　Hajime narikere.

The moon is setting
　　and the sun is appearing,
　　　　as dawn is breaking;
It is now, indeed, the time
　　to set out on the Way.

### 46

Tachimukau
　　Hito no kokorozo
　　　　Kagami nari
Onoga kokoro wo
　　Utsushite ya min.

Standing before you
　　others hold up mirrors
　　　　as their own hearts,
And there within you can see
　　your own heart being reflected.

### 47

Yokikoto wa
    Tsutomete mo mina
        Toritamae
Ashiki koto oba
    Harai tamae yo.

We need to strive
    to retain within ourselves
        all things that are good;
It is the bad within us
    that needs to be abandoned.

### 48

Arigataki
    Mata omoshiroki
        Ureshiki to
Miki wo sonou zo
    Makoto narikere.

A sense of Gratitude
    along with feelings
        of wonder and joy
Will, if we maintain all three,
    bring us True Sincerity.

### 49

Amaterasu
    Kami morotomo ni
        Yuku hito wa
Higoto higoto ni
    Arigataki kana.

For those who go forth
    together with the Kami
        Amaterasu,
There will come day after day
    the feelings of gratitude.

### 50

Ukifune ni
    Nagaku noritaku
        Omounara
Kokoro no kaji no
    Yudan surunayo.

Should you wish to sail
    on a lengthy journey
        in the boat of life,
You must never fail to heed
    the rudder of your heart.

### H

### 51

Yume no yo wo
    Yume to shiredomo
        Sameyarazu
Sametaru hito no
    Koishikaruran.

The world of dreams
    is, I know, a world of dreams,
        yet I cannot waken ...
For another yet to wake
    I know I shall be longing.

### 52

Kinō no hana
    Kyō no yume towa
        Kikitsuredo
Ima no arashi wa
    Urameshiki kana.

Although I have heard
    that the flowers of yesterday
        are dreams of today,
Towards this storm that rages
    I hold a deep resentment.

### 53

Nanigoto mo
    Arigatai nite
        Yoni sumeba
Mukau mono goto
    Arigatai nari.

If for all things
    we possess a gratitude
        as we live our lives,
Then the things we have to face
    will bring us more gratitude.

### 54

Ametsuchi ni
    Tada hitosuji no
        Sono michi wo
Suguni yuku koso
    Tanoshi karikeri.

There is but one path
    in all of Heaven and Earth
        and this is the Way
Over which I'll soon depart,
    and this indeed brings joy.

### 55

Izuru hi wo
    Onoga sugata to
        Omoinaba
Kasaneshi toshi mo
    Kurushi karumaji.

If we realize
    that we, as individuals,
        are the Rising Sun
Then this heaping up of years
    should not cause us any grief.

### 56

Waga sugata
    Tazunuru ni mata
        Oyobumaji
Tada Ametsuchi ni
    Teri wataru mono.

You will no longer
    have the need to visit me
        in my present form,
Yet, crossing Heaven and Earth,
    Something will be shining.

### 57

Kagirinaki
    Inochi no michi wo
        Michibikan
Kasane tamaeyo
    Yorozuyo mademo.

Let me lead you on
    over this path of life
        that knows no end,
Throughout the countless ages,
    through the next ten thousand
        realms.

### 58

Ametsuchi no
    Michi ni mayowanu
        Kokoro koso
Umarezu shinanu
    Kokoro narikere.

It is the heart
    that does not stray from the Way
        of Heaven and Earth
Which, indeed, is the heart
    that knows not birth nor death.

## J

### 59

Makoto hodo
    Yoni Arigataki
        Mono wa nashi
Makoto hitotsu de
    Shikai keitei.

True Sincerity
    is the one thing we must be
        most thankful for;
With Sincerity alone
    the Earth can be a Family.

### 60

Yononaka wa
    Mina marugoto no
        Uchi nareba
Tomo ni inoran
    Moto no kokoro wo.

In this world of ours
    we have all come together
        to form a Circle;
Let us pray to be joined
    by the Heart of all our hearts.

### 61

Amaterasu
    Kami no mitoku wo
        Yo no hito ni
Nokorazu hayaku
    Shirasetaki mono.

It is our wish
    to have Amaterasu's
        Goodness be known
To all the world's people
    soon and without exception.

### 62

Yono hana wa
    Chirabaya chireyo
        Ametsuchi ni
Tsukisenu michi no
    Hana wo sakasen.

Flowers of the world,
    scatter as you want to scatter
        over Heaven and Earth ...
Then along the endless Way
    burst forth in bloom again.

# Part III

# Perspectives on Kurozumi-kyō

# 7

# The Universal Attitude of Kurozumi Munetada

**Willis Stoesz**

When Kurozumi-kyō, centered in Okayama in western Honshu island, emerged in the first decades of the nineteenth century it was part of the cultural tide throughout Japan that would sweep aside the shogunate and prepare the way for that country's entrance into today's global interaction. A tendency toward universal attitudes was part of that tide; and although later in that century national Shinto and subsequent militaristic policies came as a countertide, the direction of development set within this Edo-period Shinto sect continues today.

The activities of the current Chief Patriarch in traveling to the United States, to New Zealand, and to Australia are an expression of the spiritual impetus given Kurozumi-kyō by its founder. It is useful to consider Kurozumi Munetada in the light of this nascent universalism. How did his own religious attitude gain its universal scope?

We will see that he set a personal example of openness to people without regard to traditional social differences, that his teachings emphasize the presence of a vivifying factor in every human being's life derived from the universal presence of Amaterasu Ōmikami, and that his way of explaining that presence relativized the moral basis of human interaction distinctive to Japanese society.

## Life of Kurozumi Munetada

In order to bring this out it is necessary again to review details of the life of Munetada already discussed in previous chapters.[1]

Our analysis reviews the stages of his development from his childhood piety to his mature, fully developed religious understanding as the founder of Kurozumi-kyō.

We note especially his developing intention. Though early in life his inner attitude was that of a conscientious Japanese boy heavily influenced by Confucian values, his vow to become a living kami (*ikigami*)[2] put into play in that inner life a set of concepts drawn from broader Japanese tradition which, melded in a new shape by his ecstatic experience of union with Amaterasu, established his originality. The distinctive quality of his experience is attested by the large numbers of people who venerated him as Kami and became his followers.

As living kami he expected to be of great benefit to other people and a great credit to his parents. He formulated a set of five rules to guide his efforts. He was convinced that if he devoted himself to introspection and constant attention to the quality of his every action as measured by these rules, and never did anything that he knew in his heart to be wrong, he would not fail to achieve this goal.

In the years 1812-14 he passed through the great crisis of his life. After a period of illness following the death of his parents he believed his own death to be near. However, after preparing himself to die, saying the appropriate prayers thanking the kami (including, of course, the Sun Kami, Amaterasu) and the spirits of his parents and ancestors for their favors to him in his life, he did not immediately die. It then occurred to him that his illness was due to his excessive grief at his parents' death and that his continued life would please them more than his death. He resolved to make a joyful, grateful spirit (*yōki*) rather than a negative spirit the basic motif of his life.

Two months later he was well enough to rise from his bed, bathe, and put on fresh clothes. Finally, at the time of the winter solstice of the same year, he had the pivotal experience of his life. As he worshiped the sun on this occasion,[3] he had an overwhelming sense of the obliteration of difference between himself and Amaterasu. The moment was characterized by inexpressible, ecstatic joy as he was filled utterly with the warmth and light of the sun; and not only the sun, but of the Sun Kami herself. His experience on that morning was paradigmatic for all that he said and did for the rest of his life; it was his charter (*tenmei jikiju*) from then on and it continues to have that significance for Kurozumi-kyō to this day.

No more than a few weeks later his career began as the founder of the religious movement known eventually as Kurozumi-kyō. He discovered in himself an ability to heal people from many kinds of illness and for the rest of his life devoted much time and energy to healing. He also devoted himself to teaching. His teaching activity probably expressed his fundamental concern better than did his healing, although interestingly enough the inspirational effect of it is by some accounts reckoned more highly than the precise content of what he said. He encouraged others to follow Seven Rules for daily living (his original five with small but important changes, plus two now added);[4] and in fact, a promise to keep them was made a condition of membership in the official roll of disciples. The roll of members increased, and during the remainder of his life his guidance of his followers was such that they came to venerate him as their Kami and as the authoritative guide for their lives.

We may now turn to a description of the stages through which Kurozumi Munetada went in developing the universal attitude that makes him of interest to us and that characterized his mature leadership of his association and his contribution to the Japanese religious and cultural scene.

## Stages of development

1. He first comes into view for us as a seven-year-old who wishes to be obedient to his parents in full detail. He wears a straw sandal (zōri) on one foot and a wooden clog (geta) on the other rather than disobey conflicting instructions from them. When he hears someone remark that his father is aging he engages in early morning cold water ablutions for some period of time, praying for his father's longevity. He is the kind of child who would take seriously the maxims used in the schools about respect and service to parents.[5] Confucian emphases on filial piety, respect for parents, and the five relations that structure harmonious and obedient life, inculcated in school maxims used for calligraphy practice, would have been presupposed in the family.

2. The second stage of his development visible to us comes with his making a vow to become a living kami. He intended for the rest of his life to be a source of benefit to others based in a high degree of personal purity. The vow was an outgrowth of childhood loyalty to parents, since it included the wish that they be honored by the intended achievement.

We may examine Munetada's Five Rules to discern the founder's frame of mind at this stage. They are as follows, in Wright's translation:

1. "Born into a home of faith you shall never be without faith;
2. You shall not be filled with self-conceit nor look down upon others;
3. You shall not increase the evil of your own heart by focusing on the evil of others;
4. When not ill you shall not be lazy in your work;
5. When following the Way of Sincerity you shall not lack sincerity of heart.

> Standing before you
> others hold up mirrors
> as their own hearts,
> And there within you can see
> your own heart being reflected.

The above articles are awesome. They shall be followed as principles of a religious discipline.[6]

We must be careful not to read into this statement meanings, arrived at only after the definitive experiences of 1814, including the centrality of Amaterasu.[7] Here he was intent on developing the inner purity of his mind/heart (*kokoro*). Two of the five (2 and 3) refer specifically to mind/heart-culture as he understood it. It is also important that they are (in the original) phrased as attitudes to be avoided. Thus, they function as diagnostic criteria rather than as prescriptions or commandments. One who on introspection could not find any impurity considered to be caused by what was to be avoided would have attained a highly developed culture of the inner spirit. Such a person would be characterized by a constantly benevolent and equalitarian attitude, an attitude not tied to the vicissitudes of circumstances or of the actions of others but sustained from within in its constancy. Sincerity is to be found in being sincere, and not only in something external to one's self called sincerity. The introspective mood the rules require is similar to the more subjective strains of contemporary Confucianism;[8] yet, without being out of keeping with that tradition, they read as a simple but original formulation.

Taken together, the rules have a coherent meaning. The first of them expresses his strong appreciation of and devotedness to the parental household (*ie*). Here lies the rootage of the purified life he at this time sought as living kami. Rules two and three reflect careful attention to the quality of relationship to others: such relationships should not detract from the essential task of personal character development. Indeed, attention to them promotes the purity of the inner heart. Rule four shows a practical concern: doing one's daily tasks is essential if the heart/mind is to be properly cultivated. Rule five gives the grounding of both family heritage and the several sorts of personal character efforts in sincerity (*makoto*) as an all-encompassing Way. The set of rules provides a structured connection of the highest values in life with its practical details.

By keeping these guidelines in mind, purifying the inner mind while remaining both attentive to other people and involved in the practical affairs of daily work, Munetada expected to become a living kami. He posted them in a prominent place so that he could always see them and be reminded to apply them constantly. We may assume they continued to shape his thinking during the next fourteen years until the next important turn in his life.

3. This happened in 1812 with the sudden loss of both his parents within a week. His excessive grief and his declining health thereafter indicate how fundamental a moral sanction for living his parents had been for him, even at his current age of 33. He did not give up his *ikigami* vow even when it appeared he would die, but restated it, now vowing that after death he would use his vantage point as disembodied kami to help people. Here an advance was made in that he now intended a broader framework in which his life would have effect than his mere physical existence could have given it. At the same time, no substitute for his parents as fundamental moral sanction had yet become effective. This stage in development continued until early in 1814 when it appeared that his death was imminent.

4. It was when his death did not after all follow that the next advance in his attitude occurred. He then decided to express gratitude to Amaterasu for his continued life. He would cultivate a positive principle of life (*yōki*), a *yang* attitude as opposed to the previous *yin* attitude of grief. Before this his attitude had been one of strenuous self-cultivation in the Confucian manner, with focus on the powers that he by his own effort would attain. Now he would

focus on the sun and on Amaterasu as source of benefit, a significant shift of sanction for his life. With this use of gratitude as a strategy for cultivation of mind that would turn on a receptive (*yin*)
rather than an assertive attitude, his health began improving.

5. Finally, the occasion of ecstatic identity of himself and
Amaterasu on the occasion of the "third sun worship" of 1814 cul-
minated his development. All sense of himself as other than Amaterasu was obliterated in that moment. He spoke of it as an experience beyond duality, using Buddhist terminology to express what
he meant (see chapter 6: *Dōka* 30-37); a constantly repeated note
of joy marks later recollections of it. The frame of mind it initiated
was the fundamental resource out of which he faced the varying
circumstances of life from then on. He drew forth its implications
in poetry and in letters and in personal conversation, in preaching
and teaching in his own unique manner, in the many occasions of
healing that marked his career, and in the guidance of personal
character formation to which the members of his group have devoted themselves from his times to the present.

We must characterize this mature attitude in order to lay a basis
for explaining its universality; but first it will be useful to look more
closely at the stages through which his mind went in its advance
toward this fifth point of view.

## Stages in universality

The first stage, childhood piety and moralism, can be called
universal only in a limited sense. His attitude was circumscribed by
the specific values he had been taught. These values are universal
in being shared in East Asian cultures and in being similar to values
present in other cultures. However, his intention cannot be said to
have reached beyond the particular circumstances of his life.

The second stage was much broader in the scope of what was
intended in not being limited to following specific rules. At least im-
plicitly, the five rules projected attitudes that could be expressed
by a broad range of specific actions. Childhood moralism was
being transcended, though the honor of his own parents and of his
specific family line of ancestors remained a sanction of action
necessary to him.

However, a state of mind had been affirmed that went beyond
the horizons in social relationships set by ordinary egoism. Rules 2
and 3 contain a fundamental equalitarianism (at least in principle);

indeed, the social class system of Tokugawa Japan might be considered set aside in principle by these rules. At this stage it would depend on how they are applied, since it might be possible to "look up to" someone faithful in fulfilling a role that one considers lower and more limited as expressed by Kipling: "You're a better man than I am, Gunga Din!"

A third stage of universality was reached when he accepted his imminent death. This was not so much a stage in itself, perhaps, as preparation for what was to come by diminished regard for his physical existence. The prospect of his death allowed an inner adjustment of attitude that prepared him for further broadening.

In the fourth stage his parents and family line no longer had a centering role for his attitude. The reformulated first of the Seven Rules shows the effects of this shift of attitude, referring now to his birth in a divine land [of Amaterasu] and not to birth in his own parents' household. He shifted focus from them to Amaterasu, referring thought and action thereafter to her as source of meaning. This was a significant step since a transcending frame of reference was thereby established. The sun as physical expression (*shintai*) of Amaterasu's presence shining everywhere in the physical world is a powerful symbol enormously broadening the attitude of a person keyed to it. Her light and warmth are felt both inwardly and outwardly; the focus she provides illuminates completely and universally. We should note, however, that Munetada had not yet given up commitment to self-cultivation though he had taken a significant step in that direction. Gratitude was here a strategy, a tactic to be followed in the effort at self-cultivation. That is, to attend to the positive life principle is to turn attention away from negative factors and simply to allow them to fade. In this way the self may be selectively developed through cultivating attention to Amaterasu as empowering presence.

In the culminating level of universality this concern with self-cultivation was placed in deeper perspective when Munetada came to see Amaterasu as the driving force even within the self. He came to regard the immediately experienced self as a separated portion (*bunshin*) which is not other than Amaterasu. He now saw the difference between self and Amaterasu as apparent only; it is an appearance resulting from the inner presence of Amaterasu being uncultivated and therefore weakly perceived. The sense of difference should be overcome by the practice of cultus and of proper social relationships.

Munetada for the rest of his career developed the implications of the non-dualistic awareness initiated at the third occasion of sun worship. His poetry and his letters show that he was alert to the way inner psychic horizons derived from physical existence, from social roles, and from egoistic self-concern had in principle been transcended and how others could also transcend them.[9] He prac-ticed the realization of Amaterasu's ontological priority to the "separated self" in its apparent separateness.

He called this practice the Way of Truth (or, Sincerity; *Makoto no Michi*). It constituted his understanding of the structure of reality, and was the basis of his worldview. He understood this Way both as objectively omnipresent and as the operative subjective daily attitude to be followed. As the Seven Rules show, it was the framework to be referred to in all circumstances of life for the practice of gratitude (rule 7).

## Assumptions Underlying The Universal Attitude

Three points may be made in describing this attitude. They concern the centrality of Amaterasu Ōmikami, the non-dualistic inner connection with Amaterasu, and the concept of time that is assumed.

### Centrality of Amaterasu

The three occasions of sun worship in 1814 culminating in the pivotal occasion of *nippai* focused Munetada's mind progressively more strongly on Amaterasu. Always important but up to that time only one of a number of kami being reverenced, she now came to be regarded as central.

Hepner, assessing Munetada's work from the viewpoint of western philosophy and theology, says his concept of Amaterasu has the possibility of being a "thorough-going monotheism." Hepner draws attention to the universal reference of the concept of heaven with which Amaterasu is identified and to the devotional focus on Amaterasu who is to be reverenced in every circumstance of life. He then argues that this belief falls short of that possibility and falls into the "vagaries of pantheism." Munetada's "syncretic ideas are not well-coordinated," he says.[10]

He furthermore thinks there is a discrepancy between what he calls Munetada's idealistic assumptions and his practical ways of implementing those assumptions in dealing with people, since those means do not seem to regard such practical details as the illusions they should in such idealistic theory be. Hepner, not noticing the pastoral concern motivating their use (see chapter 11) regards Munetada's use of popular charms (*omamori*) and of various healing practices as unworthy of his otherwise high spirituality; but this criticism extends to Munetada's concern for healing generally.

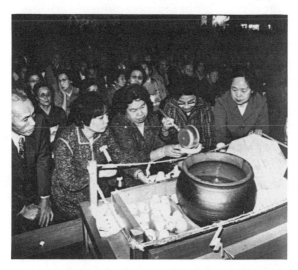

Receiving *goshinsui* (consecrated water) as a form of *majinai*. The practice was initiated by the Founder. Photo courtesy of Kurozumi-kyō.

Hepner's criticism of Munetada is two-fold: lack of logical rigor in his use of terms expressing who Amaterasu is, and lack of logical consistency in his basic view of reality (is the ordinary world an illusion, or is it not?). As a result, says Hepner, Amaterasu becomes an indefinite object of trust so that Munetada's religion cannot avoid being unacceptably vague.[11]

While it may be admitted that various terms Munetada uses about Amaterasu are not logically coordinated with each other,[12] this criticism misses the point. Another kind of expressional definiteness than logical consistency may be seen in Munetada's teaching. It has long been a commonplace in the comparative study of religion that the three elements of belief, practice, and social relationship may be found in all religions.[13] It is also clear that different religions place varying emphases on these three elements. Christian faith, for instance, places much emphasis on belief about God and about various aspects of the human condition, while Buddhism and Judaism in different ways place emphasis on praxis. Japanese religion also contains beliefs and praxis. But when we apply these comparative concepts, we see that its salient emphasis is on the quality of relationships among people, especially within groups, and between people and the various kami and spiritual presences. Herein, we may say, lies the religious genius of the *kami-no-michi* (*shin-tō*), the divine way of Japanese culture.[14]

The receptive and harmonious attitude which each person in this divine "way" should have to each other person is more fundamental than what each believes about the other. Hence, in looking for clarity of expressional reference we find it first in some aspect of relational attitude rather than in the contents of what is believed. The consistency Hepner asks us to look for is found in the quality of sincerity (*makoto*) rather than in logic. It is here that "truth" lies, in Munetada's view. *Makoto* implies the constancy of the well-cultivated mind which is always able to discern how to build a larger harmony (and, incidentally, how to elicit bodily well-being as a result) than had existed before. In Munetada's mature view this constancy derives from Amaterasu as its universally present source.

Harmony, or rather, *unity* with (that is, "in") Amaterasu, the transcendent source and reference point, provides the capacity to engender harmony among people; constant recourse to the presence of Amaterasu makes that social harmony possible. The way of Amaterasu and the ability to follow that way consist in being attentive in each moment both to Amaterasu and to what it takes to express that attention in practical circumstances of social relationship and daily work, thus replicating in this deepened way the structure given in the original five rules. Concepts are useful for Munetada in so far as they facilitate a harmonious attitude toward others, and he is not much concerned with their relation to each other as concepts.

Hence, Hepner's first criticism misses Munetada's meaning, and should not be taken as a negative judgement. In similar manner his second criticism also misses the point, since Munetada's concern for practical expression derives from his concern that others realize the way of Amaterasu in their own life. His approach parallels the Buddhist concept of skillful means (*upaya*) in that the practical means he employs are intended to assist literal-minded people with limited viewpoints to appreciate the inner presence of Amaterasu and to become transformed by that realization. What Hepner sees as logical inconsistency appears in Munetada's usage as compassionate assistance to those who in various ways have limited, literalistic, and egoistic (because dualistic) minds.[15]

Munetada regarded Amaterasu as central to the cosmos. He did not associate her much with the mythology of the *Kojiki*, even though he traveled to Ise six times and often lectured on the meaning of Ise pilgrimage. Without particularly rejecting her role as ancestress of the imperial line of Japan he emphasized her association with Heaven and with Heaven/Earth as understood in Confucian tradition. She is omnipresent as Heaven is omnipresent, and imparts to all people in every moment in every place a mandate for transformation of the inner mind. Munetada's empowering experience of Amaterasu (*tenmei jikiju*) is available to anyone in any place and time. She is that "living thing" (*ikimono*)[16] to be discerned as presenting to the inner heart the possibility of joyful, harmonious life in the circumstances of each moment. Her inner presence invites each person to "leave all [the details of life and even one's very self] to Heaven," and by practice of purification rituals to polish the inner mirror of the heart so that every action may reflect her primordial presence.

That this may happen at any place and in every time is underlined by his equating *makoto* and *marukoto* ("rounded thing").[17] Sincere expression of one's presence in Amaterasu takes place in the full round of life in every place and time. She is that "circular thing" shining in the sky and within one's heart, that living thing within (*ikimono*) enlightening the farthest circle, the widest horizon of existence. This idea is given formal expression in the conclusion appended to the rules for daily living. The *makoto* (relational) quality of one's life provides the constancy and stability needed to live effectively in this unbounded context.[18]

## Non-dualism

The second comment to be made concerns Munetada's use of the terminology of non-dualism. In this way he emphasized the completeness of Amaterasu's presence within him after the occasion of the third sun worship. The following *waka* is an example:

> Crossing the mountains
> of Being and Non-Being
> the Sea of Life and Death,
> You come to the world of Here
> Where, indeed, contentment dwells.[30]

No doubt this terminology lay ready to hand in Confucian and in Buddhist ideas current in his local circles, but he used it in a way that expressed his own perspective. He frequently referred to his teaching of the oneness of man with deity (shinjin ittai setsu).[19] As Kurozumi Muneharu has put it, the unity of human and Kami is a fundamental one that needs only to be maintained and to be cleansed of what impurely obscures it, rather than to be achieved by overcoming some prior dual condition (see chapter 3). This insight was arrived at, Hepner allows and Kurozumi Muneharu insists, not as a logical deduction from concepts but as an expression of the level of experience initiated on the third nippai occasion. The effect of the non-dualist view is to bring about the relativization of opposites. As Laube puts it, "Munetada understood that God and Man, Heaven and Earth, inner and outer were within himself as an undivided unity."[20]

Hepner cites the following passage:

> The Way is the Way of Heaven. It is not my Way. Since it is the Way of Heaven, if I trust all to Heaven, at once I have effaced myself and cease to exist. If I do not exist, then there exists only the Heart of Heaven. This Heart of Heaven is my Way. This way is a "Living-Thing" (ikimono). This "Living-Thing" is entirely "Not Is" (Mu). That "Not Is" (Mu) is the Supreme Thing.[21]

We may note two points in this passage, intended by Munetada to be so clear that anyone would be able to understand it. First, the emphasis on entrusting all to heaven places the dualisms of ordinary experience on a new footing. For instance, "trusting" indicates a receptive (yin) attitude; but since Amaterasu's energy is unobstructedly expressed when that trusting is complete, the yang attitude of yōki results. In principle, and, in ecstatic moments actually, the duality of yang and yin is transcended. Yang and yin are in principle simultaneous: it would, for instance, be possible to have a confidence in one's self that need not exceed limits required by harmony. Munetada's youthful assertiveness in self-cultivation thus is reestablished on a new footing, one which supports well-being in full receptiveness to universal harmony.

Second, a more radically universal way of comprehending the basis of human relationship is initiated here than had been possible under Munetada's earlier Confucian assumptions. Criteria of relationships making for equalitarianism were present already in the five rules of his original vow, and they persist into Munetada's mature view. Now however they are put on a deeper basis. To the extent that the non-dual assumption is taken seriously — and Munetada took it seriously indeed — it is not possible to regard differences in social rank as having any significance, in contrast to the way they might persist in the previous level even in a mutually appreciative relationship. Social rank differences are therefore even more radically relativized than in the earlier more strictly Confucian stage, and Munetada's universal attitude is broadened correspondingly. This relativization occurs through reference to the universal Amaterasu; it is given impetus as decisive factor in the motivational process by the perceived presence of Kami living within. Striving to achieve this universality is unnecessary. It exists as a prior condition that needs only to be recognized and is not to be achieved through effort.

The non-dualistic condition provides a basis for placing one's own framework of thinking aside and of taking into consideration others' frameworks of thinking and acting in full confidence that Amaterasu is present in and behind all that happens to one's self and to others, no matter how novel it may at first appear. The point is made neatly by a story retold by Nobuhara, one of a number of similar stories. Some person called on Munetada and lectured him in a very rude way. Munetada made no answer but sat silently with downcast eyes. When the man had gone Munetada's wife reproached him for being immature and vague and therefore giving poor leadership to others. His response, however, was that Amaterasu is glad when people are glad. The man who had rudely catechized him was benefited more by his feeling of triumph than he would have been if Munetada had answered his criticisms. Such an answer might have provoked him to speak ill of Kami and thereby to damage himself greatly. That man would come to have better ideas so long as the presence of Kami within him was not damaged, Munetada felt.[22] The story shows Munetada practicing *Mushin*, ("non-self"), and in a specific practical circumstance relying on *yōki* within another person (even though that *yōki* was not yet pure), understood as the active presence in that person of Amaterasu herself.

## Concept of time

A third point to be considered is Munetada's concept of time, or *ikidōshi*. While the term may literally mean "living through" one may also render it as "eternal life." However, something other than unending time is Munetada's concern. To "live through" each moment of time means being unconcerned in each moment with before-and-after but rather deriving complete satisfaction in the immediate presence of Amaterasu. It means not being preoccupied with distinctions between opposites, since a quality of experience that transcends opposites — namely, the joy-giving presence of Amaterasu — has been attained. It is the strength and constancy of this attitude or frame of mind that was the basis of Munetada's religious leadership.

Some *dōka* that express these views may be recalled:

> Day after day
>     we face the morning sun
>         aware in our hearts
> That our lives are limitless,
>     a feeling of such joy.[44]

> If we remember
>     that everything that exists
>         comes from Heaven,
> Then worries and daily life
>     are not matters of concern.[23]

> The divine virtue
>     of Amaterasu
>         fills Heaven and Earth;
> Ah, in such abundance
>     is this limitless grace.[2]

The frequent emphasis on joy will bear some comment. Munetada was joyful often to the point of nonchalance, appearing unconcerned about what others thought of him and about matters of ordinary importance such as personal finances.

What was the source of this joy? From within the circle of Kurozumi life and faith the answer is that joy comes from the presence of Amaterasu herself, as receptivity to that presence is cultivated by *nippai* and other religious practices.

In the study of religion we need to speak not (declaratively) out of intimate knowledge of such inner meaning but we must rather establish descriptive understanding of particular instances of religion by recourse to general theories of the function of religion in life. In this way we can generate interpretive hypotheses about particular people's religion, while remaining attentive to the way they prefer to express themselves religiously.

Here we may make an analysis based on defining religion as a transformative process.[23] In this definition religion is a process that moves from the perception a religious subject has that there is that which "ought-not-to-be" in life as it is, and that another condition of experience that "ought-to-be" should come about; and that some means exists or should be discovered in order to enable this transformation. The "ought-not-to-be" condition includes some factor which is undesirably limiting; in the corresponding "ought-to-be" condition that limit will have been somehow transcended. Religion is distinguished from mere problem-solving by reliance on power from beyond the active, willing consciousness in the process of transformation. The contrast between "ought-not-to-be" and "ought to-be" measures the structure of religious intention.

In this case, Munetada's great joy marks attainment of what ought-to-be; and we are led in our analysis to look for an ought-not-to-be condition of experience corresponding to it which had needed to be overcome.

At least two sorts of limit-conditions were removed as a result of Munetada's 1814 worshipings of the sun. The first was his illness which had brought him to the point of death. Indeed, throughout his career the overcoming of physical illness in others occupied his attention a great deal. The second, more important, limit that bounded his early life was that he found his basic sanction for his life so completely in his parents. Finding that sanction instead in Amaterasu, and finding it there so completely as to be describable only in non-dualistic terms, marked his move into a joyful, fully universal attitude.

At first, because of his form of parent-centeredness he descended toward death when they died; then, because of his shift toward gratitude to Amaterasu for the benefit of life he began to give thanks and to recover health; and finally because that benefit could be understood only non-dualistically he attained his joyful, infectious, non-self-concerned attitude toward life.

In order to underline the significance of this transformation we should notice what happens to the concepts of *on* (the giving of benefit) and of the obligation of the recipient to return the benefit (*hō-on; giri*) so fundamental to the moral basis of Japanese society, in these three stages of development.[24]

Up to the first sun worship in 1814 Munetada labored under an acute need to care about his parents, resolving to be an *ikigami* in order to honor them adequately, even after death if death were to come.

At the time of the first sun worship he experienced a degree of liberation from the burden of that limit upon his life in the realization that life ultimately comes from Amaterasu, far more than it comes from one's physical parents. Kurozumi Muneharu has emphasized the importance of this concept in contemporary Kurozumi-kyō teaching (see chapters 4 and 5). The founder shifted his mood from a negative to a positive one, to gratitude for whatever well-being he did in fact have, no matter how little at that time.

In the third of these three stages, no return benefit is possible since all is Amaterasu to begin with. She herself already possesses all that may be possessed and it is not meaningful to speak of return of benefit. The concept of *on/hō-on*, which, as Hori notes,[25] produces in Japanese culture the specific fields of social interaction distinctive to it, is in fact for Munetada transcended by the always-existing and universally-present Amaterasu. This transformation, we are led to suggest by our analysis, is the functional reason for Munetada's joy and the context for his entrance into his universal attitude. As the conclusion of the Seven Rules indicates, other persons are mirrors in whom one may see the face one has one's self projected toward them. The presence of Amaterasu perceived in social context is the ideal basis of human association, and the social horizon deriving from her inner presence is in principle completely unbounded and completely universal.

A moral and spiritual task remains to the adherent of Amaterasu. Overcoming the illusory sense of separateness from her requires the ritual and ethical cultus found in Kurozumi-kyō as a religious institution. The task ideally consists, however, not in expressing gratitude for favor received or in acting out of obligation to do something in return for favor. It consists in accustoming one's self to acting out of gratitude as an all-encompassing attitude toward all of life. The giving of favor and the return of favor cannot be distinguished from one another but are in principle a single act. They are the outflow of Amaterasu's prior presence. If in an earlier stage of development gratitude was considered a strategy for self-cultivation, it now appears as a constant attitude of looking for that in each situation which makes for harmonious interaction of all concerned. One's life need no longer be construed as an unending repayment to parents of illimitable debt for one's existence.[26] Even

Lebra's concept of a radically asymmetrical requirement of return favor owed to Amaterasu herself does not express Munetada's understanding.[27] Rather, life's primary motive is to be the expression of gratitude for all that exists within Heaven and Earth. The ritual and ethical cultus stemming from Munetada's teaching is intended merely to dissipate the inner clouds of self-limited awareness (*ga*) that obscure the reality of Amaterasu's presence. The heavy load of *on* and *giri* is part of that limitation. Ease of mind, joy of heart, and a universal social horizon are the fruits of Amaterasu's non-dualistic presence.[28]

Through the practice of *nippai* and of repetition of the *Ōharai* prayer, and through the ordered expression of open, harmonious relationships with others, one should purify the inner spirit and reduce one's sense of separateness from Amaterasu. In this way one may increase one's attentiveness to Amaterasu present as "circular-thing" (*marugoto*) both in the inner spirit and in the outer realm of Heaven-Earth. In that attentiveness one carries out one's daily work. This is the underlying purpose of the Kurozumi-kyō cultus and the point of its ethical expectations, as Kurozumi Muneharu has explained (see chapter 4).

*Ikidōshi* therefore means living through and transcending all limits imposed by what other people might do or by the exigencies of particular situations; exigencies which could tempt one to take a stance of opposition to rather than harmony with any of its details. Conceitedness, anger, anxiety, pride, and laziness (the conditions the Seven Rules are designed to remove) — and even death — might all have set such limits, but are now transcended. The *time* in which one lives is, therefore, defined not sequentially, by the tasks to which one might devote one's self, by ethical expectations per se, or by the objects of pleasure or distaste with which one's mind might be occupied. Rather, time means living in awareness of the whole of things as encompassed by Heaven and knowing one's self freely and harmoniously interactive with that wholeness. Time is continuing cosmic presence, focused relationally as Amaterasu but implying a frame of mind in no way horizon-attached. Though horizons remain present to awareness, they are meant to be seen beyond and do not constitute limits. *Ikidōshi* ("living-through") any and all of life's circumstances is the key to Munetada's universal attitude.

## Summary

Munetada's universality is not an abstract principle but a living attitude. It is a quality of mind at first gained by careful cultivation; even more, it is gained in the cultus of a receptive, participative quality of mind to what is perceived as the transcendent/immanent presence of Amaterasu. That she is non-dualistically understood as universal mind (or heart; *kokoro*) does not remove the force of Munetada's example. He provided the paradigm of what that non-dualism meant in practice.

That said, we may conclude this discussion with five points:

1. Munetada's religious viewpoint is universal first of all in that he intended to include all people as equally worthy of regard. From the first an impulse to share his experience with others was present; the relativizing of social difference was one result. Though faithful to the heritage of the divine land of Japan, this faithfulness did not cause him to set limits on that broad intention.

He also intended that anyone could become a sharer of his point of view. He understood that the same principle (Amaterasu) is present in every human being. All human beings have a common basis for their personal existence.[29]

2. He used concepts about reality as a whole which, though distinctive to East Asian culture, have a history of being used in a universally extensive sense. Central to his worldview are Amaterasu and the self in relation to her, comprehended with the use of concepts derived from Confucianism with Buddhist and Shinto contributions. Although these concepts are not universal in the sense of being accepted everwhere, the creation of categories by which they may compared with other sets of cultural presuppositions from elsewhere in the world is a task we are learning how to undertake. In such a task much depends on the attitude — exclusionary or inclusionary — of those who explore universality in this sense.

3. Munetada showed the flexible attitude that would be needed in such dialogue. That this flexibility is not an unprincipled eclecticism is shown by his constant emphasis on *makoto* as a basis for harmonious relationships among people. He himself was adaptable to the many sorts of people whom he met, and the social field in which that flexibility was to be exercised was, according to his worldview, present wherever the sun is present.

4. Munetada showed aptitude for discerning the inner limits within people by which they might otherwise hold themselves back from harmonious life. His was a universality that grew out of rich psychic/metaphoric soil in his own self, so that he was attentive to the causes of partiality in others' actions and able to guide them in overcoming those causes.

5. Finally, Munetada had a strategy by which to broaden people's attitude toward a more universal frame of mind. This was the expression of gratitude. He trained himself how to focus on factors in specific situations making for harmony and to minimize other factors making for disharmony. We may see in this strategy and in the worldview in which it is grounded the seeds of a truly universal contemporary attitude of mind. He showed the way to be receptive to ever-broader circles of experience reaching outward toward an ultimate wholeness of things.

Those who take Munetada's attitude as their paradigm, rooted in the immediate here-and-now as it is, can find themselves assisted in adopting a universalizing thrust in their actions in particular situations, enabling movement toward the harmony of the whole of things. For him this larger harmony was already an accomplished fact, needing only the practice of appropriate cultus to allow its power to be felt. One then needed only to act on it and thus allow it to be recognized. In this confidence and in this skill lies the specific genius of Munetada's universal attitude.

Morning prayer before Amaterasu Ōmikami at Shintōzan,
headquarters of Kurozumi-kyō. Photo courtesy of Kurozumi-
kyō.

# 8

# Internalization of Kami: Buddhist Affinities in Kurozumi-kyō

Alan L. Miller

## Introduction

### Goals and method

In undertaking the task of demonstrating Buddhist affinities in Kurozumi-kyō I have sought to extend our understanding of this tradition by deepening our grasp of the religious experiences and practices of its founder. These experiences and practices are both primordial and contemporary, available to present-day followers of the way of Kurozumi Munetada by means of rituals and personal devotions, and thus I have also made use of contemporary writing about religious praxis. I have sought to extend understanding of a living tradition with its own unique formulation of a way of life, its own internal coherence, its own integrity, and its own proper claim to an honored place among the world's religious bodies.

The use of the analytic tools of scholarship should not be allowed to obscure these facts. I find that there is considerable Buddhist influence, though this does not convince me that Kurozumi-kyō is a crypto-Buddhist group as was suspected by the Meiji governmental bureaucracy in the latter part of the nineteenth century. Showing Buddhist affinities of Kurozumi-kyō should not lead us into that genetic fallacy, any more than Christian affinities to the mystery cults of the ancient occidental world should lead us to suppose Christianity to be no more than a sum of such parallel elements.

The procedure I have adopted is typological. It is neither a comparison of sophisticated philosophical texts nor a tracing out of historical causality. Derived in a general way from the work of such scholars as Joachim Wach and Mircea Eliade, this approach seeks to discover a pattern of similarities in behavior, attitude, and expectation, which it claims reveals a deeper structure than either linguistic parallels[1] or conventional history can provide.[2] The patterns or types I shall suggest are classical configurations abstracted from Neo-Confucian, Buddhist, and Shinto traditions. Several will be defined and tested for fit; the degree of fit will tell much about both the similarities of Kurozumi-kyō to other religious traditions and its uniqueness.

Secondarily I wish somewhat to balance the excellent recent work done on Neo-Confucian affinities in Kurozumi-kyō with similar material that demonstrates Buddhist influences, ideas, and parallels. Munetada was a man of his times, and those times must be recognized as permeated as much by a Buddhist as by a Neo-Confucian spirit. Insofar as Munetada also was a unique individual, he must be recognized not as a philosopher or as an intellectual, but as a man of feeling, of experience, and of action. He was a folk or popular figure in the best sense of those words and must be approached in a manner appropriate to this fact.

### The problem of shared terminology

The problem of interpretation of popular religious language is compounded when several religious traditions have existed in long historical association, as have Confucianism, Buddhism, and Shinto in Japan. In such interpretation one must be constantly aware of context or internal signification. For example, religious vocabulary throughout East Asia strongly tends to be Chinese, a fact that gives us many shared terms. Among them are such basic items as *tao* ("way, nature"), *t'ien* ("heaven"), *t'ien-ming* ("mandate of heaven, fate"), *sheng-jen* ("sage, saint"), and *hsing* ("mind, heart"). Surely, we feel, this commonality must be an important fact; yet, concentration upon it can be very misleading. Words acquire their meaning according to their context, and they are greatly affected by their linguistic environment. Thus, *Tao* in Taoism and in Confucianism, despite a shared linguistic horizon, have very different practical referents; and, *T'ien-ming* as used in Confucianism has such a different tone that its usual translation as "mandate of heaven" may have quite different implications than when rendering the same ideographs in Munetada's usage.

Further, what does it mean that Taoism, Buddhism, Neo-Confucianism, and Kurozumi Shinto all share such a fundamental term as *mushin*? In a Buddho-Taoist context this term usually is rendered as "no-mind" or "no-thought," and is an attempt to point to that enigmatic state of mind characteristic of sages and saints. In the Buddhist context it is a state of mind characterized by extra-ordinary calm (Sanskrit: *samatha*) and concentration (Sanskrit: *samadhi*), often interpreted as a permanent state of trance. Perhaps because of this specific Buddhist referent it has become popular in academic circles to render the second part of this compound, *shin* (also Japanese *kokoro*, Chinese *hsing*), as "heart" rather than "mind" when it occurs in Neo-Confucian or Shinto contexts.

This usage is dubious in both contexts in my view.[3] *Mushin* in Neo-Confucian usage refers to the original nature of human beings, "before the feelings are aroused," in the phrase of Chu Hsi (d. 1200). In his view *shin* ("mind") contains both the originally pure and tranquil nature or essence of humanity and also the active emotional life, a characterization not permitted in Buddhism. Thus in the classical Yogacara texts so influential in Zen thought the mind of the bodhisattva ("Mahayana Buddhist saint") is tranquil and empty (and hence *mushin*), and yet the body continues to perform numerous acts of altruism. In neither Neo-Confucianism nor in Zen is there room for the context into which Munetada placed *mushin*, namely, a personal, shared spiritual and mental identity with a personal deity. *Mushin* for Munetada was more nearly self-lessness, or loss of personal identity within the realization of a higher identity with an ultimate and sacred person.

## Historical situation of Tokugawa Buddhism

The preceding Ashikaga period had been one of great vitality and creativity in Zen Buddhism, especially in the arts. Among its many influences one can cite the No drama, particularly in the person of the great theorist Zeami; the tea ceremony, especially as brought to an apogee by Sen no Rikyu; and the popularization of Zen, begun in early Ashikaga with the foundation of the *ankoku-ji* ("provincial Zen temples") and carried on by such illustrious fig-ures as Musō and Ikkyū just before the beginning of Tokugawa. And the creativity and influence, indeed the revitalization, of Zen was continued in Tokugawa times by such giants as Basho and Hakuin, both of whom had great popular appeal. The former's ascetic life and literary activity combined native elements, such as *mono-no-aware* ("the pity of things") and pilgrimage, with a Zen vocabulary and a clearly Buddhist quest for self-transformative experience. The latter's charisma and popular evangelical style did much to rescue Zen from a tendency toward routinization and complacency.

True, the Pure Land schools were largely quiescent. They had felt the brunt of the military power of the unifiers of Japan who helped inaugurate the Tokugawa era, as had the Enryaku-ji, headquarters of the Tendai school. Yet, concern for rebirth in Amida's Pure Land, however routinized, had not subsided. The people had not ceased to call upon the name of Kannon Bosatsu (bodhisattva) in adversity, nor to call upon the healing arts of Shugendō and Nichiren-shu practitioners. Their knowledge of Buddhist words of power, together with their largely Buddhist ascetic exercises, continued to be respected, particularly by the common people. People had not ceased to believe that Buddhas, bodhisattvas, and kami were intimately related in a vital if obscure economy of the sacred. Indeed, as to this last, we know that in the early Meiji period, when the decree came down that henceforth Shinto and Buddhism should be separate, many priests had taken both Shinto and Buddhist orders and were thus able to choose more or less freely which newly defined tradition they would follow.

For such reasons as these I am not persuaded that the hold of Buddhism upon the hearts and minds of the Japanese people was so much weakened in the second half of the Tokugawa period that it becomes improbable that Kurozumi Munetada should have been influenced by Buddhist ideas and Buddhist practice. Unfortunately, the prevailing view of Tokugawa Japan held by contemporary scholars is of a Buddhism sunk in unrelieved decadence from which it could muster neither internal creativity and depth of piety nor the allegiance of the masses. Many scholars hold the view that Neo-Confucian thought had swept all else before it, except perhaps for a few *kokugaku* ("Shinto renaissance") scholars who were too isolated from the mainstream of national life to matter. Established scholars in the field have never put the case so baldly of course, yet it seems to me that only such a radical state of Buddhist decline could justify such thinking about Tokugawa religion. The situation was manifestly different.

If we move from the level of historical context to that of the individual, there are a number of facts which more specifically associate Munetada with Buddhism. First, Munetada's home district of Okayama was an exception to the government rule that all households register as parishioners with Buddhist temples; here, registration with Shinto shrines was the pattern. Thus, the anti-Buddhist sentiment grounded in this enforced Buddhism would presumably have been much weaker. Second, Okayama, as the home district of such past Buddhist notables as Hōnen, Eisai, and Sesshū, might have continued to be a hospitable arena of Buddhist ideas and practice. Third, Munetada is known to have visited Buddhist temples on his frequent pilgrimages, namely those of Jodo, Jodo Shin-shu, and Zen. Fourth, and even more to the point perhaps, he is reported to have practiced Zen meditation "from his early years."[4] Fifth, his own copy of the Zen master Ikkyū's "Popular Sermons" (*Ikkyū Zenji Hogo*) has appended to it his own poetry thus: "Though Heaven and Earth are thought to be vast,/ They are contained within my human mind."[5] Certainly this is a rather clear reference to the Yogacara-Zen doctrine of mind-only.

Finally, we must take into account the argument recently made by Kuroda[6] that not until the Tokugawa period, and only slowly and incompletely even then, was it thinkable in Japan that Shinto and Buddhism were not of one essence. In his bold words, "before modern times Shinto did not exist as an independent religion."[7] Shinto meant primarily having to do with kami, and it was universally understood that kami and buddhas were aspects of the same thing. Although there is much in Kuroda's short article with which one might take exception, I accept his fundamental position. I believe the many statements of Munetada equating Buddha and kami, as well as his usage of Buddhist terminology, provide ample evidence of just this worldview. For example: "Call it kami or call it Buddha, it is the one living-thing (*iki-mono*) which dwells within the sacred reality (*makoto*) of Heaven and Earth."[8] "It is in our hearts/ that the kami and Buddha/are found to dwell;/ Indeed to pray elsewhere / Would be truly a pity"[9] (see chapter 6, *Dokā* No. 9).

## Internalization

This study will depend in part upon the general thesis that Munetada and Kurozumi-kyō exhibit a more or less clear Buddhist affinity not because Munetada had conscious Buddhist leanings or formal Buddhist training but because of a religious tendency or drift which affected Shinto at all levels of culture. This historical drift I believe to be primarily the result of the permeation of the kami cult by Buddhist ideals and attitudes. It is multidimensional of course,[10] but I want to concentrate upon one aspect of it which seems to have affected Munetada in a decisive way. This aspect I will call the internalization of kami. By this I mean a process of moving from a largely external and transactional relationship to kami to a more direct, emotional, and even mystical relationship.[11]

### Emergence of a new sense of unity

Internalization in Shinto led to a new sense of psychic unity between human and kami, comparable to what had been long known in Buddhism between the various types of sentient beings. All these beings, whether Buddhas, bodhisattvas, or humans, whether ghosts or *goryō* ("angry spirits of the dead"), animals and sometimes even plants and inanimate objects — all were thought of as one substance, so to speak. All could be led to nirvana because all shared in the Buddha-nature. But this was never merely a metaphysical principle of intelligibility as *li* ("principle") tended to be in Neo-Confucianism. It was rather a living, experiential, and to some extent personal reality because it was composed of mind, of consciousness itself.

As this was accepted into Shinto it meant that the communication between human and kami became at once more intimate and conceptually more subtle. As in Buddhism, "virtue," "purity," and "grace" became in Shinto primarily a matter of right thinking, right attitudes, and habits of mind; only secondarily overt acts or external circumstances. Intention became more important than action. This was not so much the discovery of a new moral sense as it was the discovery of a new basis for morality. It moved the center of consideration from external and often ritual matters to the inward state of the mind which directs the action. The rituals that were retained were infused with a new meditative spirit, a spirit of communion and even mystical participation.[12] For the kami cult it constituted a new understanding of the relation between human and deity. It required a new sense of participation in deity and in unity of purpose and of mind.

Genchi Kato had something like this in mind when he wrote of the developments in the medieval period: "Inner purity [is] emphasized, and sincerity or uprightness as the fundamental ethical principle becomes pre-eminent in Shinto."[13] In my view this way of stating the case is too narrow in that it fails to concern itself with what is fundamentally beyond the realm of ethics. In any case perhaps the earliest documented example of the attitude I have labeled internalization comes, significantly, from the approving brush of a Buddhist priest at the end of the Kamakura period. The monk Saka kept a pilgrim diary of a visit he made to the outer shrine at Ise (as a Buddhist priest he was not allowed to enter the precincts of the inner shrine), wherein he recorded the views of the Shinto priests:

> When anyone comes here to worship there is both an outer and an inner purity. The former consists in eating clean food and observing the ritual purification and keeping oneself from defilement, but the latter means ridding the mind of all ambitious desire.[14]

The *Shinto gobusho*, written by Ise priests at about this same time, corroborates Saka's testimony; "Virtue (*toku*) and sincerity (*makoto*) please kami, not all kinds of material offerings."[15]

Prior to this time the overwhelming tendency of Shinto was to emphasize purity rather than sincerity or a virtuous character (the meaning I give to *toku* here).[16] Now, although the dichotomies "sincerity/insincerity" and "purity/pollution" can and indeed have existed side by side in Shinto thought and practice since the medieval period, they are by no means identical. At the very least, taken together they offer a high level of redundancy in the explanation of evil (or misfortune, or suffering — I know no neutral word). If one examines the earliest recorded Shinto documents — *Kojiki* and *Nihon Shoki* — one will find but one example of something that looks like a concern for sincerity. I am referring to the contest sequence in the *Takama-ga-hara* myth. Here Amaterasu confronts her obstreperous brother Susano-o concerning his behavior, which consists primarily of violations of ritual purity.[17] A kami-producing contest ensues, described in many textual variations in *Nihon Shoki*, none of which agrees very closely with the version in *Kojiki*. For other reasons which cannot be gone into with any thoroughness here[18] it is clear that this text has been much tampered with — for one thing, the sexual aspects are uncharacteristically veiled.

In this context of ritual purity and pollution we find the following sentence spoken by Susano-o in triumph, since he believes his creativity in the production of new kami has proven his equality with or even superiority to Amaterasu:

"It was because my intentions were pure and bright that in the children I begot I obtained graceful maidens. By this it is obvious that I won."[19]

The Japanese gloss on this passage is *waga kokoro kiyoku akashi*, which can be rendered as either "My heart/mind is pure and bright" or "My heart/mind is proven to be pure." It may or may not have meant "My intentions are innocent," as is usually assumed.

Otherwise the attitude of Shinto myth is quite consistent with the ritual of purification (*Ōharai*) found in the Heian period *Engishiki*. Here "sin" (*tsumi*) is clearly pollution. It is contagious as moral turpitude never is, and thus can be got rid of by ritual transference to pieces of wood which are then thrown away. This is not to deny even at the earliest time a psychological benefit, even something like *suga-suga-shii*, that feeling of relief when all is again as it should be when the rite of purification is completed. In this regard perhaps the clearest example of this old Shinto attitude is to be found in the ritual *Ōharai* practiced by individuals when entering a shrine. One must be purified, that is, ritually made sacred, before one can approach the presence of the sacred, the kami.

### The Kurozumi approach to unity

The medieval attitude as exhibited by the priests of Ise occupies but a medial position when compared to more recent views. Kurozumi Muneharu, the present patriarch of Kurozumi-kyō, takes the medieval attitude considerably further when he refers to the "inner presence" of kami: "Since the center of my mind is a separated portion of Amaterasu-Ōmikami, my mind gets really rich only when I respect kami living in my mind."[20] Another very suggestive example from the same source is the practice of praying while watching one's own image in a mirror: "The mirror is letting you know that kami ... dwells silently in your inner mind." Of course the mirror is the primary *shintai* or divine manifestation of the Kami Amaterasu: in the Rock Cave myth she is drawn out of the cave by a mirror. Mirrors thus attract her as they seem to attract light. She saw her own image in the mirror in the myth. Thus to see one's own image in a sacred mirror in such a ritual context is symbolically equivalent to an act of identification with the deity.

More than this, the mirror has a long and hallowed history as a Buddhist metaphor for the mind in its absolute aspect. In such texts as the *Lankāvatara Sūtra*, *The Awakening of Faith*, and the *Platform Sutra* to mention only a few, the mirror is a prominent symbol. The process of enlightenment is described as polishing the dust from the mirror of mind. Mind as ultimate reality (the *alaya vijñana* of Yogacara Buddhism) is described as a perfect mirror in its ability to reflect defiled thoughts without itself being defiled by them. Of course this ultimate Mind is identical with the Buddha-nature, with the essence of buddhahood.

Munetada himself also provides numerous examples of this internalization of deity: "If only mind (*kokoro*) is alive, this is kami, this is Buddha, this is humanity."[21] Indeed, Munetada frequently reveals this tendency to identify kami and Buddha and to see them as united with human beings in the psychic unity of mind. "Call it kami or call it Buddha, it is the one living-thing (*iki-mono*) which dwells within the sacred reality (*makoto*) of Heaven and Earth."[22]

### Original mind and separated self

In Kurozumi-kyō as formulated by Munetada the basic problem to which the religion addresses itself is separation from kami. All difficulties, all suffering, all evil are derived from this one basic fact of human existence. It is, therefore, from this fundamental estrangement that people yearn to be saved. But because of the psychic unity of human and kami, all human beings are by nature kami. This original nature (*honshin*), of which we will hear more later, remains within us in a defiled state. As defiled and therefore human in the negative sense it is called *bunshin* ("separated self"). The task of the religious person is to purify the *bunshin* through rituals and good deeds. The primary rituals for this purpose are frequent repetitions of the *Ōharai* ("purification") prayer of ancient Shinto and *nippai* or sun-worship. Secondarily might be mentioned also *majinai,* or healing "magic" as performed by the founder, a practice that has largely ceased in recent times. The ultimate destiny of those who have achieved the proper level of purity is the experience of union with the mind (*kokoro*) of Amaterasu both in this life and after death.

It is impossible, given this formulation and the language employed, to miss the close parallel with the Buddhist view of salvation and evil. East Asian Buddhism also uses the term *honshin* ("original nature") to emphasize the unity of all sentient beings with Buddha-nature, the Absolute. All sentient beings — and among them humans have an especially privileged position — are in essence

Buddhas, are in essence enlightened. What is needed is to realize this in fact. Those who do realize this state of enlightenment are either bodhisattvas or "living" Buddhas, whose powerful presence in our midst is the means by which salvation is made available to the great majority of humans. [23]

In view of the previous discussion of purification it should be pointed out that the choice of the *Ōharai* text as the prime ritual means of bringing about the reunification of phenomenal self and true self, of human and kami, is not merely a historical accident. If my theory of internalization is correct it must be that the association of purification and sincerity had already been powerfully made in the minds of the Japanese people. It must be that the structural identity of purification and sincerity had been intuitively grasped and was thus natural if not inevitable. What has happened in the equation is a substitution: "Pollution requires the medicine of purification" becomes "Insincerity requires the medicine of purification." To be sure, purification by *Ōharai* practice itself undergoes some modification in that it is assimilated to some extent to Pure Land *nembutsu*, which in its own proper context is chanted as an antidote to the disease of ignorance, unenlightenment, and the burden of bad karma. Indeed Munetada is said to have repeated the *Ōharai* as many as 600 times in one day, a clear borrowing of the structure of Pure Land practice.

## Typology of Experience and Intention

### Munetada's fundamental experience

We have placed Munetada within the phenomenon of internalization largely through presentation of his thought and religious practices. To deepen our understanding we must now examine Munetada's own decisive religious experiences. Fortunately, his own descriptions have been preserved, although here as always description and interpretation are closely intertwined. The oft-quoted account in Hepner goes as follows:

On the morning of December 22, 1814, at the Winter Solstice ... He went out on the verandah and worshiped with his face toward the rising sun ... He felt the rays of light and life-giving warmth fill his breast and believed that the sun-spirit (*yō-ki*) had completely possessed him. His long illness seemed to vanish like the morning dew before the rising sun, and his whole nature thrilled with inexpressible joy and gratitude. He believed firmly that he had attained one-ness with Amaterasu-Ō-Mi-Kami , the source of universal life ...[24]

In order to interpret this personal religious experience of the Founder it is necessary to place it within the personal context of Munetada's own religious yearnings and ambitions and to place it within its cultural context, that is, to distinguish the several possibilities which the Japanese culture of the Tokugawa period could reasonably be supposed to offer as interpretive models. The first task involves us also in the second, inasmuch as Munetada himself seems to have had some kind of model in mind. Before the decisive mystical experience related above he had set himself the goal of becoming a "living kami": "*Ware iki-nagara ni shite kami.*"[25] This living kami ideal represents Munetada's own label for the goal for which he strove. We must ask ourselves what he meant by the term and how it relates to other ideal types.

Hepner's interpretation has several things to tell us about Munetada's view of the *ikigami* model:

1. It was first "embraced" at the early age of nineteen.
2. It claimed his lifelong effort.
3. It was motivated primarily by filial piety, "to make a name for himself to the honor of his beloved parents."[26]
4. It was to be accomplished by means of conscience-driven ethical behavior.
5. It was in method very similar to that used in the school of thought founded by Ishida Baigan.
6. It had its roots as a goal (as distinct from the method of attainment) in the "hereditary influences of ancestor worship" at the Imamura shrine, which Munetada served as a priest.
7. The goal was achieved, in the opinion of his followers.

Such is Hepner's interpretation which puts the experience, or at least the interpretation of it, strongly in the category of popular Confucianism, or at least acknowledges the Confucian role as an overarching theoretical construct to which was grafted a traditional Shinto field of practice. One need only substitute the term *sage* for *living kami* in the above account to see the point. Who can miss the emphasis upon filial piety? This view is rapidly becoming the standard interpretation of Munetada's intention, and it has been powerfully reinforced in Helen Hardacre's recent work.[27] In what follows I will subject this view to a more thorough analysis utilizing the typological approach.

### Three models of interpretation

I distinguish three ideal types or models which Japanese culture in late Tokugawa times can reasonably be supposed to offer as shapers of experience and self-interpretation: (1) the shamanic model, more or less closely associated with folk Shinto; (2) the sage, rather solidly the product of Neo-Confucianism, although it must be kept in mind that Neo-Confucianism is itself partly the product of a Confucian-Buddhist alloy; and (3) the bodhisattva, the central ideal of Mahayana Buddhism and one which I will argue is needed to complete our understanding of Munetada.

Each of these describes a specific life goal. That is, all presuppose that in this or a higher life one hopes to achieve a certain sacred personality and status. The last two particularly assume a more or less dramatic moment or series of moments during which this goal is realized. During such moments, self-transformation, appropriately termed enlightenment, is attained, resulting in a new set of attitudes and impulses in conjunction with the possession of a new and higher wisdom. The first, shamanism, is rather ambiguous on this score[28] because of its routinization in ritual forms; yet, particularly in its reemergence in the new religions, it retains its more ancient affinities to mysticism and thus to association with the more dramatic and decisive forms of personality change. All three models are alike in that they constitute programs — one might say "rituals" in the broadest sense of the term — by which the new status can be realized.

### The shamanic model

Taking them in chronological order, let us look first at Munetada as part of a new upwelling of ancient Shinto; specifically, of shamanism. Many have pointed out the special affinity of the new religions to shamanic structures in the decisive experiences of many of the founders, perhaps most notably Hori Ichirō.[29] More recently the work of Shimazono has again placed the role of shamanism in the new religious movements to the fore, this time in a manner which is quite suggestive of my theory of internalization.[30]

The classical definition of shamanism as a type is found in the work of Mircea Eliade[31] where the term is used to refer to an archaic religious technique of "ecstasy." This simply means that the shaman must have the ability to achieve a state of trance, an altered state of consciousness in which the personality is split. There are two basic types, the soul-travel type and the possession type. In the first the soul or conscious aspect of the personality is felt to leave the physical body and travel as a spirit to a spirit world. There it interviews the powers that control the world in order to return with knowledge, an "oracle" which can be of great importance to the inhabitants of the ordinary human world. In possession-type shamanism the spirit comes to the shaman, displaces the ordinary personality, and delivers the oracle directly to the human world. In both cases the shaman performs the essential function of mediation between the sacred and profane worlds and thus communicates sacred knowledge. The possession type is the only type of shamanism known in Japan. What Blacker calls the ascetic type of shamanism I call simply asceticism.

If we examine Munetada's experience in the light of this model we are immediately struck by an anomaly. Munetada is never possessed by Amaterasu, despite Hepner's use of the term. What he experiences is described as union and not possession. This distinction is not trivial. It is crucial to a full understanding of Munetada's exemplification of internalization. Shamanism is mentioned in the Chinese *Wei Chronicles* and thus is the most ancient documentable Japanese religious practice. Throughout its long history it has remained true to its primitive roots. Psychologically speaking it represents not a transformation of personality but a displacement of personality. When a kami possesses the shaman, the shaman's ordinary personality and consciousness are suppressed. The shaman is not even conscious of what she or he is saying in the trance-like state of possession. The kami takes over the mouth and body of the human, uses it long enough to deliver its oracle, and then departs. This is the reason there must be a second person, the questioner or the one to whom the oracle is delivered, at a shamanic seance. But Munetada delivers no oracular utterances while kami-possessed. His poems and other writings are regarded as scripture, and some of this material is certainly the result of reflection upon his own mystical experience. Yet they are not regarded as Amaterasu speaking directly through his mouth in the shamanic sense.

Thus we return to the description of Munetada's early vows. He seeks to be no mere vehicle for divine information, but a divine presence himself. He seeks not merely temporary contact with the divine, but to be a "living kami." He seeks to be transformed by the sacred, to be unified with Amaterasu. Out of the confirming mystical experience he articulates a rudimentary theology of the human as divine — that is, the *honshin* and *bunshin* doctrine already discussed.

In fact, Munetada's experience is quite similar to that of many founders of new religions. One could cite the founders of Konkokyō and Tenrikyō. While I do not deny the generally shamanic character of these experiences, I doubt whether in Munetada's case this is an adequate explanation. It seems to me a crucial point that something has been added, a something that transmutes the old structure of shamanic possession into something new.

To seek this something new, let us return to consideration of Munetada's mystical experience. What Hepner in his interpretation does not say is that Munetada's first-stated goal was altered in a later moment of personal crisis, with the result that we have not one but two "vows." Each involved becoming a kami, but each had its own unique roots. This is clear from evidence which Hepner presents.

The crisis involved a series of misfortunes. First, in 1812, he lost both his parents in one week to dysentery. Second, in the autumn of 1813 he developed tuberculosis of the lungs due, it is thought, to his excessive grief over the loss of his parents. In giving himself up to die he is reported to have said: "When I die and become a god (kami), I shall devote myself to the work of healing the diseases of mankind."[32] Thus, faced with his own imminent death and the consequent failure of his quest to become a *living* kami, he reverted to a more basic and indeed older goal. This goal was to be transmuted by passage into death. It is a concept bound up with popular views of the destiny of humans at death and of the after-life, which in Japan are the peculiar province of Buddhism and (to a much lesser extent) of Chinese folk religion (usually referred to in Japan as Taoism).

Before examining the Buddhist implications, however, let us look more closely at the Neo-Confucian side of things.

### The model of the sage

The old Confucian *chün-tzu* is the prototype of what came to be called the sage in Neo-Confucianism. The former was a "superior man" whose accomplishments, while much above those of the ordinary man, were still far below the mythic sages of the golden age of high antiquity. The *chün-tzu* was a person of high ethical standards, fearless and unconcerned for consequences so long as he conformed to the overarching way of life prescribed in *li* ("ritual"). Because of his *te* ("virtue"), he was charismatic in his effects upon the social world. His mere presence tended to bring about order and harmony.

In the hands of the Neo-Confucianists the earlier concept of *li*, as the ritual way governing social life, is replaced by a new concept. This new concept is also pronounced *li*, but its meaning is rather different. The new *li*, usually translated "principle," refers to a metaphysical absolute, which, like Buddha-nature, inheres in all things. Since the new *li* is the principle of intelligibility it is also the essence of mind, one's "original nature." Correspondingly, the old *chün tzu* ideal is no longer central for the Neo-Confucians, but is functionally replaced by a new ideal of the sage. For the sage as now understood, the realization of this inner principle constitutes a kind of enlightenment experience in which one's knowledge is transformed into a more esoteric wisdom. It becomes an insight into the underlying meaning and unity of all manifestations.

This sage is one who must practice meditation (quiet-sitting) throughout his life, for he is not perfect in any static sense. Rather, his original nature is always there but only while directly engaged in meditation is he fully aware of it. Otherwise he is fully engaged emotionally and intellectually in the everydayness of life. He must periodically reinvigorate his phenomenal mind by reopening communication with ultimate mind whose essence is *li*. In everyday life the old Confucian ethic is in full force as is its overarching ritual structure. Here as in ancient Confucianism filial piety remains a very important element.

It is quite impossible to force Munetada's "kami at death" ideal into the Neo-Confucian sage model. The death of a sage, like the death of any ordinary person in Neo-Confucian thought, ends the direct influence of that person. After-life is not a part of the sage model, although of course the popular belief in ancestral survival is not contradicted by the philosophers. Thus a sage would function after death in the way any other ancestor would.

Although Munetada's "living kami" ideal at first seems to fit rather well with the Neo-Confucian sage, emphasizing as it does filial piety and the virtue of sincerity, it lacks an emphasis upon *li* ("ritual")[33] But a more serious problem confronts us if we compare the second *li* ("principle") with the object and subject of Munetada's mystical experience. Clearly Amaterasu is no abstract metaphysical principle, no rational principle of intelligibility overlaid with emotional or mystical fervor. No, the psychic unity which Munetada discovered and experienced was a union of personality. It was the experience of a continuity, a communion of minds. What Munetada was, and all humans are, Amaterasu is also. We are living persons united in mind with the living creator of all. Thus can Munetada say of his Absolute what no Neo-Confucian can say, *"Ten-chi wa ikimono ni soraeba,"* "Heaven and Earth are living things;"[34] and, *"Amaterasu-kami no mikokoro hitogokoro / Hitotsu ni nareba, ikidoshi nari."*[35] "When the mind of the kami Amaterasu and the human mind / Are one indeed, this is truly life" (see chapter 6, *Dōka 13).*

The term *ikidōshi* means literally "living through," usually rendered as "eternal life," a translation which misses the point. For a student of Lao-tzu, Chuang-tzu, and Ikkyū Zenji such an understanding is impossibly pedestrian. Unlike the first two named, Munetada had an implicit belief in eternal life, nurtured in part by native belief in ancestor reverence and in part by the Buddhist doctrine of karma. In both these sources eternal life is not something to be grasped or to be achieved. It is a given, an inevitability. The issue is not whether or not one has eternal life but the quality of that life. This is what Munetada seeks to communicate in *ikidōshi:* the quality of the life one leads. *Ikidōshi* refers in very Buddhist ways to the life of immediate experience, of giving up ego considerations to live a spontaneous life of gratitude and wonder. In this respect it is a view fundamentally compatible with that of the great Taoist thinkers as well.

### The Buddhist interpretation

The notion of becoming kami has complex and obscure origins. Shinto mythology as we have it has no separate creation of humans. Far from being radically separate from kami, humans seem rather to be simply attenuated kami. With respect to the first "human" emperor, Jimmu, the legendary material is rather clear that he seeks for and is dependent upon divine aid in his deeds as a warrior. In power and status he is clearly a being subordinate to the great kami who assist him. Even so the implicit concern of the mythology is not with becoming a kami but with becoming a human — at least as concerns members of the imperial clan.

Deification or becoming kami seems to have two sources, both distinct from the mythic tradition. First, it is strongly correlated to what Nakamura calls a tendency to ascribe "absolutely divine attributes to the individual at the top of the hierarchy of Japanese society."[36] However, even in connection with the Japanese emperors it has been applied until the advent of State Shinto in the nineteenth and early twentieth centuries almost exclusively to the cult of dead emperors. Examples are the Meiji shrine in modern Tokyo and the Kofun tombs in the Nara plain of late prehistoric times. Thus, becoming kami seems more connected to the native ancestral cult which pervades Japanese society at all levels, with its expression of an almost universal human tendency to attribute special powers and status to the dead.

The second source seems to be primarily Buddhist. From classical times it has been customary in Japanese to say *Hotoke ni naru* ("He or she has become Buddha"), instead of the blunt *shimu* ("He or she is dead"). This of course can be dismissed as little more than a euphemistic cliche.[37] But as Kuroda has recently reminded us,[38] only in the Tokugawa period did the Japanese even begin to question the ultimate unity of Shinto and Buddhism. Further, Hori has well documented the importance of a more specific belief which he attributes especially to Buddhist influence: that is, belief in *goryō*.[39] *Goryō* were from the Heian period thought to be the often malevolent spirits of the dead, a belief much attested in the diaries of the time. The most famous *goryō* of course was the spirit of Sugawara Michizane (d. 903), the aristocratic government official who was exiled unjustly and died in great want and loneliness. His angry and vengeful spirit caused plagues and other disasters in the capital, and that spirit was finally pacified by being enshrined in the Kitano shrine in Kyoto.

To be sure, the influence of this belief was by Munetada's time largely indirect. That is, the Buddhist *goryō* had in part joined with the native ancestral cult to become the Shinto *hitogami*, the kami who comes from afar, and is, if properly ritually handled, a benevolent force.[40] In popular Buddhist lore this transformation was brought about by a number of ritual means, most notably by wandering ascetics, the *hijiri*. Among the most popular were the *Nembutsu-hijiri*, who could cause the angry spirit of the dead to be reborn in the Pure Land, thus benefitting both the living (by its absence) and the dead.

If, however, we move from consideration of "kami at death" to that of "living kami," the influence of Buddhism becomes much more obvious. Perhaps the most famous example is the tradition that Ieyasu, the founder of the Tokugawa shogunate, expressed a wish to become such a kami. He was from a Pure Land family and consistently favored that sect. In his old age

> Ieyasu was visited by the abbot of the Zojoji temple at Yedo and confided to him his ambition to become a god and pro- tect his country. The abbot replied that the way to attain his desire was to recite the Nembutsu and by the power of Amida become reborn as a Buddha in the Pure Land. Then he would be able to assume any form he might wish and bestow bless- ings on his descendants and the Japanese race. Ieyasu is said to have gladly accepted this advice and to have repeated the Nembutsu regularly till he died. Officially he was assumed to have attained his ambition, for the year after his decease the Emperor Go-Mizuno-O granted him the posthumous title of Tosho Dai Gongen, or the Great Manifestation of Divine Light from the East, Gongen being the name for a contem- porary manifestation of the Buddha, such as the abbot had described.[41]

In fact *gongen* strictly speaking is a manifestation or embodi- ment especially of the bodhisattva, a religious ideal to be described below. Although often called Buddhas in Pure Land tradition, such beings follow the classical Mahayana Buddhist path of the bodhi- sattva. Perfected in the Pure Land, such bodhisattvas have the power to manifest themselves at any time and in any form and are dedicated to leading all creatures to nirvana. They are clearly be- yond birth and death because they are lords of karma, which is the cause of birth and death.

### The model of the bodhisattva

The Mahayana religious ideal of the bodhisattva, like the *chün tzu*/sage, is a goal toward which ordinary humans can strive. This ideal includes a program for its attainment, through the cul- tivation of certain virtues and through meditative disciplines. Strictly speaking the bodhisattva is a "future Buddha" in that after many lives of striving he or she has attained to full enlighten- ment and is "deserving" of nirvana, the final state of release from embodiment and from involvement in the phenomenal world. But practically speaking, the perfected bodhisattva is nothing more nor less than an active form of Buddhahood. This is attested in the common confusion in Japan between the terms bodhisattva and Buddha, a confusion perpetuated in the above-cited quotation. The ultimate practical result of the bodhisattva vow is that one remains active in the world after enlightenment. That is, one becomes a "living Buddha" who somehow participates in the suffering of the world in order to benefit the worldlings.

The bodhisattva ideal takes meditation far more seriously than does the Neo-Confucian sage. Meditation, a practice leading to a specific experience, is the heart of the ideal, especially as it was pursued in the Zen schools. Not only is meditation more greatly stressed, but Zen also takes to its extreme limit a tendency which Mahayana Buddhism had exhibited from its early period. Along with the Pure Land schools, the other dominant form of Tokugawa Buddhism, Zen simplified the dharma as an intellectual thing and emphasized its saving realization. This was in contrast to the way traditional Buddhism often emphasized dharma as saving knowledge or gnosis in a way that excluded serious attempts to attain actual realization of this knowledge.

In the Pure Land schools, the task of understanding was to be postponed until one was reborn in Amida's paradise, where the presence of a living Buddha and his supportive Buddha-field could be directly felt. In Zen, knowledge and thus understanding became supra-rational: it was only through direct, mystical experience of the truth of dharma that one truly achieved enlightenment or self-transformation and overcame the estrangement between phenomenal self and true self. It is perhaps no accident that the Zen sects, the most creative and influential type of Buddhism throughout the Tokugawa period, at least at the elite levels of society, consciously sought to differentiate themselves from traditional schools on just this issue. They stressed the direct transmission of dharma or gnosis from mind to mind, thus removing it from the public domain. This truth beyond words was contained within the words of the Sutras, but not in a form graspable by the unenlightened mind.

This deemphasis of intellectual content of gnosis had two important consequences for the bodhisattva model and its availability to the creative religious virtuoso in Japan. First, it made meditation and its culminating mystical experience the *sine qua non*. All else flows, rather mysteriously it must be said, from this. Second, it in effect identified gnosis with the psychological state of mind metaphysically understood as the state of enlightenment, so that gnosis collapsed to the experience of *satori* or *kenshō* itself. The mind of the bodhisattva has no describable content. It has only a tone or feel and a set of identifiable practical results. That is, it is perfectly tranquil and "empty" and at the same time is the engine that drives compassionate actions. These actions "spontaneously" issue from the mind's mysterious core (in such a context, interestingly, often called Tao). The mind of the Zen master is the mind of the bodhisattva: it is empty, no mind (*mushin*), that is, the supra-rational essence of mind. And mind in its essence is the one ultimate reality.[42]

The anti-intellectualism of Zen was thus a historical factor which made it easier for Munetada to identify the ultimate goals of Buddhism and Shinto. Munetada could remain loyal to much of the content of traditional Shinto — most notably the person of Amaterasu — while at the same time making use of the structure of Buddhist enlightenment experience.

A third point must also be emphasized, namely, the vow to bodhisattvahood which Zen shares with the other great tradition of the period, Pure Land. In Zen and the mainstream of Mahayana, the rise of *bodhicitta* ("thought of enlightenment") was ritually sealed in the ordination to the monastic life. Mahayana monks were not merely seekers of enlightenment. They were bodhisattva-monks. That is, they sought the type of enlightenment which the bodhisattva embodies. As understood in *The Awakening of Faith*, for example, this vow was itself a powerful conditioning factor, an objective power operating in the life of the fully enlightened bodhisattva.[43]

The early Munetada's personal goals and the vows he made in order to promote them are comprehensible only in light of the bodhisattva tradition, however much of the popular Buddhist-inspired *goryō*, of Shinto-Confucian ancestor veneration, and of the Neo-Confucian sage there might also be in them. Munetada vowed to become a "living kami," that is a perfected and active sacred being comparable to the bodhisattva. As a result of his crisis, his first vow was transformed into a vow to become a "kami after death." In the Shinto-Buddhist system of thought which prevailed this meant *both* a *goryō*-type kami with its own shrine and cult, thought of by Munetada typically as a kami specializing in the healing of disease, and at the same time a bodhisattva/buddha who seeks the well-being of all living things and whose wonder-working power of *upaya* allows him to work actively in the world of humans. Because such a perfected bodhisattva is functionally a god, the bodhisattva-kami identity was not merely natural but inevitable in this context.[44]

## Conclusions

This study demonstrates the usefulness of a typological approach to Kurozumi-kyō and to the life and experience of Kurozumi Munetada. In doing so it has seemed necessary to sow a few seeds of doubt in the minds of its readers that the prevailing Shinto-Confucian view of Munetada is the only possible one. Partly as a means to this end the Kuroda thesis of the historical unity of Shinto and Buddhism has been affirmed, and an aspect of this, the phenomenon which I have labelled internalization, has been delineated.

The typological task when applied to popular religion in Japan has proven to be a complex one. I have argued not for an exclusively Buddhist interpretation but for the need to include the Buddhist dimension in any adequate view of Munetada. Within that Buddhist dimension I have abstracted the bodhisattva as the most appropriate structure serving as an organizer and shaper of Munetada's religious ideal. Whether it be regarded as a shaper of the Japanese "living kami" ideal or as an inheritor of it, the bodhisattva as a *de facto* "living Buddha" is a necessary ingredient in such an ideal in Tokugawa Japan.

It is in part by appropriation of this bodhisattva structure, therefore, that Munetada is able both to articulate his goal(s) in the form of a vow to become a kami (either living or at death) and also to interpret his decisive experience as unity with Amaterasu. This I have argued was understood by Munetada to be the sort of unity experienced by the bodhisattva himself. It is the unity experienced by the bodhisattva when he achieves the final breakthrough to Buddha-nature, in which he knows with absolute certainty that his mind in its depths is identical with the mind of Buddha. This mind is both personal in the sense of intimately and ultimately at the center of oneself, and impersonal in that the individuality of the ordinary phenomenal self is refined away.

# 9

# The *Dōka* in Historical Perspective:
## The Religio-Aesthetic Tradition in Japan

### Gary L. Ebersole

My intention in this chapter is to locate the *dōka* of the founder, Kurozumi Munetada, in terms of the larger religio-aesthetic tradition in Japanese history. I will relate the major religious concepts informing Munetada's worldview which find expression in the *dōka* to this larger tradition.

My goal in the first part of the essay will be to suggest something of the prestige that poetry has enjoyed in Japan both as a vehicle for communicating religious teachings and, in its recitation and composition, as a form of religious praxis. By reading the founder's *dōka* in light of the larger religio-aesthetic tradition he participated in and drew upon we then can go on to appreciate more fully the content of these verses. Let me begin with a look at the place of poetry in the history of Japanese religion.

### The Prestige of Poetry

The poems of Kurozumi Munetada are called *dōka* ("poems of the way"). From this one learns that they are held to contain useful information for spiritual salvation. As such they may be located within the venerable tradition of *kadō*, poetry as a salvific way or discipline. Although it is difficult if not impossible to precisely locate the origins of poetry as a religious way (*michi* or *dō*) in Japan, we can say that the earliest extant texts in Japan — the *Kojiki* (720), the *Nihon Shoki* (702), the *Man'yōshū* (late eighth century), and the *fudoki* (early eighth century) — all contain examples of ritual poetry. Poetry has long been a privileged form of communication in Japan.

The first poem (*uta*) found in both the *Kojiki* and the *Nihon Shoki* is attributed to the deity Susano-o and has traditionally been pointed to as the origin of Japanese poetry. While this claim cannot stand up to modern historical scrutiny, it nevertheless indicates the high value placed on poetry throughout Japanese history. That poem reads:

| | |
|---|---|
| *yakumo tatsu* | The many-fenced palace of Izumo |
| *Izumo yaegaki* | Of the many clouds rising — |
| *tsuma-goimi ni* | To dwell there with my spouse |
| *yaegaki tsukuru* | Do I build a many-fenced palace: |
| *sono yaegaki o* | Ah, that many-fenced palace![1] |

A song of praise, this *uta* was probably used in rituals performed at the Suga Shrine, where Susano-o was enshrined,[2] as well as more widely for blessing the homes of newlyweds in early Japan.[3]

The preface to the *Kojiki* suggests that this text was written down from the recitation of one Hieda no Are, who had both the ability to commit to memory whatever passed before her/his eyes and to retain everything heard. The Emperor Temmu (r. 673-686) ordered Hieda no Are to learn the *Teiki* and the *Honji* (or *Kuji*), earlier written histories. It is a source of some dispute among Japanese scholars as to whether this reciter memorized written texts which were then recited or whether he/she was the oral repository of certain clan histories.[4] For our immediate purposes, it does not really matter which of these was the case. It is enough to note that in the late seventh century the prestige of oral recitation was such that it was considered more reliable than available written documents.

It was not long, however, before orally generated and circulated songs and histories were displaced by the written word and relegated to the status of provincial art forms. An inevitable element of repression was inherent in this process, overseen as it was by the imperial clan. Various clan histories and myths were "corrected" to better accommodate the imperial clan's versions; in some cases such works were simply not recorded and were thus denied formal recognition.

All of the earliest extant texts from Japan date from the eighth century. Although they undoubtedly contain songs from earlier periods, relatively little can be said with certainty concerning the religious uses of poetry in these earlier centuries. A few points are clear, however. The prestige accorded poetry in these texts can be understood in light of the fact that they come from a period in which Japan had already undergone significant urbanization, with the concomitant emergence of a hierarchical social system. Virtually all of the poetry preserved in our texts comes from the ruling elite and thus provides relatively little insight into the lives of the masses. A number of folklorists, including most notably Tsuchihashi Yukata among contemporary Japanese scholars, have done much to restore imaginatively the popular religious ritual contexts of some of the poetry from the *Kojiki*, the *Nihon Shoki*, and the *Man'yōshū* by studying contemporary rural ritual practices and extrapolating those findings back into early Japan.[5]

We may note, though, that the *Kojiki*, the *Nihon Shoki* and the *Man'yōshū* were all part of a concerted historiographic project of the eighth century imperial Court; they witness to the development of a national consciousness and pride in Japan. At the same time, the evergrowing cultural contact with the Asian mainland and its great civilizations engendered a certain sense of inferiority among the Japanese. It is in this situation of having adopted the Chinese script and other cultural forms and adapting them to their own special needs, mixed with a sense of national and ethnic pride, that the Japanese came to assert, perhaps as a form of compensation, that their native language, especially that used in religious rituals, was something special and even divinely inspired.

## The Power of The Word

By the late seventh and early eighth century the Japanese had begun to speak of native Japanese *uta* ("songs/poetry") as the repository of *kotodama* ("the spirit power of words").[6] A number of scholars have suggested that this belief in the magical power of words (*kotodama shinkō*) represents a certain nostalgia for the pure, seemingly simpler and less harried past which was found among the intelligentsia in the Court. While not denying this, I would go on to argue that in cultural terms this was more than a romantic pastoralism. In some respects it was a response to one of the major developments in Japanese history: the introduction of writing in the form of the Chinese script. The references to *kotodama* represent a cultural memory of a recent past and a way of life quickly disappearing in which the spoken word, and especially ritual language and poetry, was effective (and affective) in ways the written word was not. Moreover, with the centralization of political power such that even religious institutions and rituals came under imperial sway, performance of the major rituals became the prerogative of imperial representatives or hereditary clans of specialists of the sacred. This, too, contributed to the loss of a sense of the presence of the work, for the local clan headsman (*uji-gami*) no longer was the sacred intermediary with the deities to the extent that once had been the case. This position and power had been usurped by the sovereign in the imperial capital. As in every instance of "modernization" and urbanization in history, these processes engendered a series of ambivalent responses.

The late seventh and early eighth centuries especially marked an important transition, at least within the Court circles, from a primary oral culture to a graphic or literary culture. The *Kojiki,* the *Nihon Shoki,* and to a lesser extent the *Man'yōshū* all come from period of secondary orality where previously orally generated and circulated songs (*uta*), clan histories, myths, legends, and so on were committed to writing.[7] In this period of secondary orality the early Japanese retrospectively posited a kind of Golden Age when the meanings of words had been crystal-clear, when words had power not only to say things but to do things. That is, there was a memory, albeit somewhat romanticized, of a time when poetry was truly a performative act. The poems that survived from this posited Golden Age were described by the early Japanese as filled with *Yamato-damashii,* the spirit of Japan — "Yamato" being the ancient name for the unified nation.[8] It was believed that in the Golden Age of Japan even everyday speech was filled with poetry, as witness the following famous passage from the *Kojiki,* which in the medieval period came to be valorized as recounting the origin of *renga* or linked verse. It concerns the Prince Yamato-takeru and an elderly and, let it be duly noted, unlettered servant:

| | |
|---|---|
| *sunawachi sono kuni yori koete, Kai ni idemashite, Sakaori no miya ni imashishi toki, utaitamaishiku,* | Then he [Yamato-takeru] proceeded from that land to Kai. While he was there at the palace of Sakaori, he sang this song: |
| *'Niibari Tsukuba o sugite iku yo ka netsuru* | "How many nights have we slept Since passing Niibari and Tsukuba?" |
| *to utaitamaiki. shika ni sono mi-hitaki no okina, mi-uta ni tsugite utaishiku,* | Then the old man tending the fire sang this song to continue his song: |

'kaga nabete                          "The number of days, altogether,
yo ni wa kokono yo                    Of nights, nine,
hi ni wa toka o                       And of days, ten."

to utaiki.  kore o mochite            Then [Yamato-takeru] rewarded the
sono okina o homete,                  old man and made him the Miyatsuko
Azuma no kuni no miyatsuko            of the land of Azuma.[9]
o tamaiki.

The resultant verse is, of course, hardly distinguished in and of itself. Moreover, it is of irregular syllabic count: 4-7-7-5-7-7. But to stop at saying this is to miss several more important points: (a) the Japanese claimed that conversational speech was potentially poetic;[10] (b) poetry conveyed useful and historical information; and (c) poetry could be a vehicle of social advancement. In early Japan poetry was not simply literature-for-literature's sake.

The Man'yōshū is one of the best sources of information we have concerning the ritual uses of poetry in early Japan. Its 4516 poems, plus variants, in ten books (maki) contain a number of different types of ritual poetry, including land-viewing poems (kuni mi uta), used in seasonal agricultural and fertility rites; poetry for the pacification of the spirits of the dead (tamashizume or chinkon uta); land-praising songs; funeral laments; and so on.[11] Ritual poetry was believed to have the power to magically coerce the kami to attract back the wandering spirit (tama) of an ill or a recently deceased individual, to ensure the safety of a person while on a journey, to attract the hoped-for romantic attentions of another person, to draw an unfaithful lover back again, to predict the future, and so on.

This conception and use of poetry as a privileged and powerful form of language continued well into the Heian period and beyond.[12] The belief in the magico-religious power of poetry was found at the popular or folk level, as well as among the most educated and cosmopolitan members of the aristocracy. For instance, Kukai (or Kobo Daishi; 774-835), the famous Buddhist philosopher and founder of the Shingon school, was himself a well-known poet and was instrumental in propagating a Buddhist understanding of the magical power of words.[13] In the Tendai school, mahashikan meditation was employed in the composition of verse, while others meditated on mandalas, pictures of the moon and even the moon itself, resulting in the genesis of poems.[14]

## Poetry and Nature:  A Seamless World

Probably the most famous statement of Japanese literary aesthetics is that found in Ki no Tsurayuki's preface to the *Kokinshū* (ca. 905), the first of twenty-one imperial anthologies of poetry complied under imperial commission over the centuries. The opening lines of this preface indicate that poetry retained its prestige in the 10th century, even though some modern scholars unfortunately have taken Tsurayuki's words as so much hyperbole. He wrote:

> The seeds of Japanese poetry [ *Yamato uta*] lie in the human heart and grow into leaves of ten thousand words. Many things happen to the people of this world, and all that they think and feel is given expression in description of things they see and hear. When we hear the warbling of the mountain thrush in the blossoms or the voice of the frog in the water, we know that every living being has its song [*uta*].

> It is poetry which, without effort, moves heaven and earth, stirs the feelings of the invisible gods and spirits, smooths the relations of men and women, and calms the hearts of the fierce warriors.

> Such songs came into being when heaven and earth first appeared. However, legend has it that in the broad heavens they began with Princess Shitateru,[15] and on earth with the song of Susano-o no mikoto.[16]

For our purposes it is enough to note that the exceptional status of poetry is clearly affirmed here. Moreover, it is asserted that all life is filled with poetry. Other Heian texts suggest that not only animate beings have their own *uta*, but nature has them as well: there is poetry in the gurgling stream, in the patter of rain, in the wind in the pines, and so on, if only one has ears to hear it. The Japanese religious worldview was and is such that the world is permeated with kami-nature. Mountains and streams, plains and waterfalls, and so on are all places where the myriad kami dwell. In this worldview there is no sharp bifurcation of the sacred and the profane or of the phenomenal world and a distinct divine world. Joseph M. Kitagawa, the dean of American historians of Japanese religion, has called this form of religious cosmology a "monistic" and a "seamless world."[17] Kurozumi Munetada participated in this same world view, which finds clear expression in the following *dōka*:

| *kami to ii* | What are called 'kami' |
| *hotoke to iu mo* | and what are called 'buddhas' |
| *ametsuchi no* | are the animate beings |
| *makoto no naka ni* | living in the ultimate reality |
| *sumeru ikimono* | of Heaven and Earth.[18] |

Western and even some Japanese observers have often spoken of the Japanese sense of nature as being uniquely colored by either Shinto or by Zen. I believe that it is a mistake to characterize the situation in these ways. The number of Japanese who were truly sectarian or exclusive in their religious beliefs and practices has always been relatively small. The Japanese traditionally have experienced no cognitive dissonance in worshiping both kami and Buddhist divinities. Similarly, it would be wrong to assume that the concept of a seamless world was an exclusively Shinto one. The identity of Heaven and Earth (*ametsuchi*) as a unified whole is found already in the *Kojiki* and the [*Nihon*] *Shoki*. While this may be regarded as a Confucian teaching, it also finds expression in Buddhist, Taoist, and Shinto terms. In the history of Japanese religion it is extremely difficult, if not impossible, to distill a "pure" Shinto out of the extant texts and other sources of data about early and early Medieval Japan.[19] Indeed, even Hitomaro, that paradigmatic poet of *Yamato-damashii*, may well have offered ritual poetic laments in a Buddhist or syncretistic locus.[20]

To return to Tsurayuki's claim that poetry is ubiquitous in nature, it should be noted that Japanese Buddhism also tended to valorize nature, first as a place for quiet meditation away from the distractions of urban life but finally as a locus permeated with Buddha nature.[21] It is here that one finds one of the most striking convergences between what has traditionally been thought of as the Shinto worldview and that of Buddhism. The phenomenal world is filled with the divine nature, whether one refers to it as kami-nature or as Buddha-nature. I would argue that this should be considered one of the central components of the mainstream worldview of the Japanese religious tradition in general.

Along these lines Helen Hardacre, picking up on Robert Bellah's earlier insight, has noted that Kurozumi-kyō arose in a cultural milieu where many "new religions" shared a similar set of core values and a basic worldview:

Humanity is the recipient of countless blessings (*on*) from superiors and beneficence from superordinate entities such as

Heaven, the Buddhas, and the kami .... In addition to (but not in competition with) superordinate entities was the idea of an underlying principle of the universe (Neo-Confucian *li*, the Buddha-nature, kami-nature), and of humanity's need to seek union with this principle. This idea is found in Confucian, Shinto, and Buddhist idioms, expressed as the quest to become a sage, to become a kami, or to attain Buddhahood. Toward this end, humanity must practice spiritual cultivation. ... Virtually all popular religions of the nineteenth and twentieth centuries originate in this matrix of ideas.[22]

## Buddhist Comparisons

Hardacre suggests that Munetada's knowledge of Buddhism was probably not of a specialist nature, but one wonders whether it is finally accurate and useful to distinguish Buddhism and Shinto as discrete religions in this way. Munetada shared the belief Hardacre points to in the passage above to the effect that the phenomenal world could both serve a soteriological function and be itself the spatial locus of spiritual salvation. This aspect of the religious worldview, though, predates the nineteenth century (as Hardacre would have it) for one finds it expressed in a number of different ways over the centuries. Moreover, even Shinto priests such as Munetada were generally aware of basic Buddhist concepts and tenets: one could readily absorb them from the study of classical literature and poetry.

One might counter that the Pure Land sects of Buddhism, which looked to a Western Paradise off somewhere in a different cosmic realm, constitute a major exception to this characterization of the Japanese world of meaning as being monistic. Yet even within the Pure Land groups there were medieval Japanese who located the Western Paradise in this world and more specifically in the Japanese archipelago (here one thinks especially of the views of those like Kamo no Chōmei in his *Hōjōki*). For Munetada too, though he was not an ardent nationalist, Japan was a sacred blessed land.

| | |
|---|---|
| *arigata ya* | When I realize |
| *ware hi no moto ni* | I live in the Sun, |
| *umare kite* | how grateful I am |
| *sono hi no uchi ni* | to have been born in |
| *sumu to omoeba* | the Land of the Rising Sun![1] |

Munetada rejected certain Buddhist concepts, including *mappō*, the belief that the present age was the age of the degenerate dharma. Similarly he eschewed all eschatological views, arguing that truth was unchanging. Once again his *dōka* encapsulate his views on time and change. The following are representative:

| | |
|---|---|
| *inishie mo* | In ancient times, |
| *ima mo mukashi mo* | the present and the past, |
| *konogoro mo* | in these days, |
| *kino mo kyo mo* | yesterday and today, |
| *onaji michi nari* | the Way is the same.[43] |
| | |
| *chihayaburu* | The Age of |
| *kamiyo mo ima mo* | the Myriad Kami and today |
| *onaji yo o* | are the same age! |
| *mina sue no yo to* | How sad everyone thinks |
| *omou awaresa* | it the end of the world. |
| | |
| *mukashi yori* | From ancient times |
| *ima ni kawaranu* | until the present, the world |
| *yo no naka o* | has not changed, |
| *kokoro kara shite* | so why believe in your heart |
| *sue to omou zo* | it is coming to an end? |

It is perhaps in the popular esoteric forms of Buddhist practice that one finds the closest parallels to Munetada's religious ideas, especially in terms of his *unio mystica* with the sun (*tenmei jikiju*). The final goal of the various forms of esoteric meditation such as those in the Shingon school founded by Kukai and other related practices was *sokushin-jōbutsu*, the attainment of (or perhaps better, the realization of) one's Buddhahood in this phenomenal body. This involved the realization of oneness with the Dharmakaya Mahavairocana, the Great Sun Buddha, who was at once the principle of the material universe and the universe itself. In general terms at least, this is very close to Munetada's own understanding of and worship of the sun. Munetada believed that the power of the sun had saved his life. This experience found ritual expression in the practices of *nippai* and *majinai* whereby the divine vital essence, *yōki*, was incorporated into oneself.

## Munetada and The History of Japanese Poetry

Before pursuing the topics of Munetada's anthropology and his concept of mind further let me suggest a few points of continuity and discontinuity between the *dōka* of Kurozumi Munetada and the poetry of others in Japanese history. Even in the Man'yō period

Japanese poetry was colored by Buddhist concepts and ways of experiencing the world introduced with Sino-Korean culture, although the resultant hues were usually recognizably Japanese. MYS V: 805 is an envoy to a long poem (*chōka*) by Yamanoue Okura (ca. 660-733) entitled "Poem sorrowing on the impermanence of life in this world." Quite Sinified in theme, tone, and expression, the envoy reads:

| | |
|---|---|
| *tokiwa nasu* | Like the rock cliffs |
| *kaku shi mo ga mo to* | eternally unchanging |
| *omoedo mo* | I'd like to be, |
| *yo no koto nareba* | yet being of this world, |
| *todomikanetsu mo* | there's no stopping time.[23] |

Here one finds a common theme in Japanese poetry: everything in the world is subject to the ravages of time. The poet laments this even as he recognizes the inevitability of the situation. The following verse by Ki no Tsurayuki on the death of his cousin, a noted poet, is similar to Yamanoue Okura's in its stance towards death:

| | |
|---|---|
| *asu shiranu* | Although I realize |
| *wa ga mi to omoedo* | my body will not know the morrow, |
| *kurenu ma no* | in the darkening |
| *kyo wa hito koso* | space-time of today |
| *kanashikarikere* | I grieve for him.[24] |

## Death and The Acceptance of Nature

At first glance human grief may seem an inevitable response in the face of death, but Munetada's *dōka* dispute this. In his verse Munetada presents a different understanding of aging and death based on his religious worldview. Hardacre has suggested that Munetada taught a doctrine of immortality, yet this must not be understood as implying that he denied that the material world, including the human body, was subject to decline. Rather, he taught that one must not be deluded by the phenomenal world into supposing one was immune from the ravages of time. This is the burden of the following *tanka*, for instance:

| | |
|---|---|
| *asagao no* | Be not led astray |
| *hana no sugata ni* | by the form and appearance |
| *mayouna yo* | of the morning glory. |
| *hikage matsu ma ni* | In the space-time of waiting |
| *shibomi nuru kana* | for the shade it withers.[14] |

The phenomenal existence of the world is not to be denied as a material "fact," but is to be affirmed and even rejoiced in. Yet, as matter, it is subject to change. Rather than lamenting this, however, Munetada taught that the "fact" of its existence should be calmly and dispassionately accepted. This could be achieved through realizing one's oneness with Heaven and Earth. Here we must understand Munetada's anthropology and his concept of mind to appreciate the full existential meaning of this. Again I will rely on his *dōka* as guides:

| | |
|---|---|
| *ametsuchi o* | When I realize |
| *waga mi no ue to* | that Heaven and Earth |
| *omoinaba* | are my very body, |
| *wakaki mo oi mo* | youth and old age |
| *kokoro naruran* | are but states of mind.[24] |

Another verse speaks to the same theme:

| | |
|---|---|
| *ari to mite* | Precisely because we see |
| *aru koso ono go* | existence as existing |
| *sugata nari* | we have form. |
| *arite mayowanu* | Relief comes from not |
| *mi koso yasukere* | being deluded by 'existence.'[35] |

And again:

| | |
|---|---|
| *izuruhi o* | When one realizes |
| *onoga sugata to* | the rising sun is |
| *omoinaba* | one's own form, |
| *kasaneshi toshi mo* | one does not mind |
| *kurushi karumaji* | the accumulating years.[55] |

At least one *dōka* seems to suggest that at one point Munetada temporarily slipped into believing he was immune from aging, although it also suggests that he had soon abandoned that view:

| | |
|---|---|
| *kokoro kara* | Believing in |
| *ikidoshi zo to* | my heart that I would live |
| *omoinaba* | eternally, |
| *toshi no yoru no mo* | the coming of old age |
| *wasurekeru kana* | slipped my mind. |

Hardacre cites two verses in support of the assertion that Munetada taught a doctrine of immortality. They are:

| | |
|---|---|
| *Amaterasu* | Those who dwell |
| *kami no miya ni* | within the precincts of the shrine |
| *sumu hito wa* | of Amaterasu |
| *kagiri shirarenu* | shall have eternal |
| *inochi naruran* | life. |

| | |
|---|---|
| *Amaterasu* | The heart |
| *kami no mi-gokoro* | of Amaterasu |
| *waga kokoro* | is our heart; |
| *futatsu nakereba* | when they are undivided, |
| *shi suru mono nashi* | there is no death.[25] |

The question which must be addressed is whether Munetada indeed held a belief in immortality and if so precisely what form it took. I would point out a few things regarding the translation of these two verses. Hardacre's rendering of *kagiri shirarenu/inochi naruran* as "shall have eternal life" may be misleading. A more literal translation would be "will come to have life (or lives) that knows no end." The difference may seem negligible, but if the former suggests unending life in unchanging form (i.e., something akin to the popular Christian belief in a corporeal life in heaven), it is misleading.

Turning to the second verse may help clarify matters a bit more. There Hardacre translates *shi suru mono nashi* as "there is no death." Again a more literal rendering would be "there is no-thing to die," or "no-thing exists to die." This, I think, is the essence of Munetada's view of life and death. The realization of oneness with the divine nature overcomes the distinctions of life and death; they are states of mind only, not ontological states. Only when ego is invested in them do they become sources of pain, suffering, and anxiety.

| | |
|---|---|
| *iki shini mo* | Those who leave |
| *ten no makasehi* | life and death to the will |
| *hito nareba* | of Heaven |
| *umarezu shinanu* | will travel on the Way |
| *michi ni ikanan* | of no birth and no death. |

Munetada seems to have taught that the body passed away, but that mind was eternal if it was united with the universal mind of Heaven and Earth. The realization of this identity brought, we are told, great joy.

| | |
|---|---|
| *ametsuchi ni* | To think |
| *otoranu hodo no* | my mind is a living thing |
| *ikimono wa* | no less than |
| *ono ga kokoro to* | Heaven and Earth — |
| *omou ureshisa* | what joy![6] |

Munetada's teaching is one which was voiced by others earlier in Japanese history, though it was never the only stance towards

the world and the human condition adopted by the Japanese. Ari-
wara Narihira (825-80), a famous courtier and poet, for example,
who enjoyed all of the amenities of life in the Court, could perhaps
afford to adopt the following poetic pose:

> yo no naka ni          If there had
> taete sakura no         never been cherry blossoms
> nakariseba              in this world,
> haru no kokoro wa       our hearts in spring
> nodokekaramashi         would still be tranquil.[26]

## Parallels in Saigyō's Poetry

A major stream of the religio-aesthetic tradition in medieval
Japan, however, adopted precisely the opposite stance toward the
ephemeral nature of the world. In important ways the medieval
Japanese came to affirm the ephemeral world (*mujō*) and human
emotional responses to that ephemerality as essential for one's
salvation. Perhaps the Buddhist poet-monk Saigyō best epitomizes
this valorization of nature and the identification of the human condition with that of the world, for he took the cherry blossoms, one
of the most famous symbols of ephemerality, and turned them into
a living symbol of the world in general and an object of enlightening
meditation. Compare the following poems by Saigyō with that by
Narihira above:

> hana ni somu           Does a blossom-dyed
> kokoro wa ikade        mind-heart still
> nokoriken              remain
> sutehateteki to        in my body I thought
> omou waga mi ni        had cast off the world?[27]
> (*Sankashu* No. 87)

> hana chirade           If the world came to be
> tsuki wa kumoran       such that blossoms did not scatter
> yo nariseba            and the moon did not cloud over,
> mono o omowan          my mind-body would not be
> waga mi naramashi      concentrated on such things.[28]
> (*Sankashu* No. 83)

> haru goto no           Each and every spring
> hana ni kokoro o       the cherry blossoms have
> nagusamete             soothed my heart and mind
> musoji amari no        while more than sixty years
> toshi o henikeri       have come and gone.[29]
> (*Sankashu* No. 1775)

| omoikaesu | Today's satori; |
|---|---|
| satori ya kyo wa | such a change of mind would |
| nakaramashi | Not have occurred |
| hana ni someoku | if I had not immersed myself |
| iro nakariseba | in the color/passion of the blossoms.[30] |

(Sankashu No. 1956)

I suggest that Saigyō's worldview shares much with that expressed in Munetada's dōka almost seven centuries later. This is not to say that Munetada drew directly on Saigyō or even on the immediate religio-aesthetic tradition Saigyō participated in. I only want to suggest that a similar view of the world and the human condition was widely shared over time and space and among "Buddhist" and "Shinto" poets. One does not find the sense in Munetada's dōka that he wished to change the world or wished it were somehow different. The world is accepted as it is. Rather than imagining what human existence might be like if the world were different, Munetada uses his verse to suggest that it is the individual's understanding and perception (even reception) of the world which must change, not the world itself. This theme is repeatedly stressed in the dōka, as the following examples will demonstrate:

| tanoshimu mo | Experiencing pleasure |
|---|---|
| mata kurushimu mo | and experiencing pain as well |
| kokoro kara | come from the mind-heart |
| katteshidai no | creating the conditions |
| ukiyo naruran | of this floating world. |

This verse represents a basic Buddhist teaching first delineated in the doctrine of codependent origination. The world-as-experienced is a function of the operations of the human senses and of the false assumption that through them one is in touch with reality. In a number of verses Munetada makes the point that all that exists does so only in mind and has no separate reality. The following is representative:

| nanigoto mo | Not realizing |
|---|---|
| kokoro hitotsu ni | everything that is |
| arumono o | exists in one's mind |
| shirade ukiyo ni | people wander lost |
| mayou hitobito | in this floating world. |

Munetada's dōka present his understanding of the relationship of the human mind to the cosmic mind and the phenomenal world to ultimate reality. Like certain Buddhist poet-monks of the late medieval period, Munetada wholeheartedly affirms emptiness or nothingness.

| ari to mite | That viewed as existence |
| naki koso moto no | is the original form |
| sugata nare | of non-existence. |
| naki o tanoshimu | Enjoy non-existence |
| kokoro yasukere | and soothe your mind-heart.[31] |

Material form is subject to change, but true mind is unchanging.

| sugata kiso | Although forms |
| mina sorezore ni | are all transformed |
| kawaredomo | into this and that, |
| kokoro no moto wa | the original heart-mind |
| hitotsu naruran | is one. |

There is some question in my mind whether Munetada's religious world view is better described as a "henotheism" (Hardacre) rather than as a form of cosmotheism, since ultimately all is one Mind. Time and space, life and death are but the play of Mind for Munetada. In reading the *dōka* I could not but recall the medieval poet-monks' invitation to "play and cavort in the ephemeral world" (*mujō ni asobu*). Munetada never tired of preaching that:

| ametsuchi no | The Mind |
| kokoro wa onoga | of Heaven and Earth |
| kokoro nari | is your mind. |
| hoka ni kokoro no | Don't think there |
| ari to omouna | is another mind![7] |

And:

| mayoi hado | There is nothing |
| yo ni omoshiroki | in this world as delightful |
| koto zo nashi | as delusion. |
| mayoi nakereba | Without delusion |
| tanoshimi mo nashi | there would be no pleasure. |

For Munetada,

| yo no naka wa | All things |
| mina marugoto no | in this world are within |
| uchinareba | the cosmic circle.[32] |
| tomo ni inoranu | Together let us pray |
| moto no kokoro o | for the original heart-mind.[60] |

## Conclusion

I have tried to locate Munetada's *dōka* within the larger religio-aesthetic tradition in Japan and to explore a few of the central elements of his religious anthropology and cosmology as found in these verses. My intention has not been to deny originality and value to the *dōka*. To make such a denial would apply an essentially modern and western emphasis on originality to the religio-aesthetic products of a culture in which continuity with tradition is more in the foreground than originality per se. Munetada's religious worldview, expressed in encapsulated form in the *dōka* and more fully in his other writings, has an integrity of its own. I suggest that the *dōka* are important texts for historians of religions to consider in their study of Kurozumi-kyō and of the Japanese religio-aesthetic tradition in general.

As to the ways followers of Kurozumi-kyō today use the *dōka*, we can say briefly that these poems have never served the type of magico-religious functions poetry did in the Man'yō, Heian, and later periods. They are not considered the repositories of magical powers, nor do they seem to be used for purposes of meditative practice. Instead, they seem to be used largely as didactic devices. To that end their short and regular 31-syllable form makes them useful mnemonic "handles" for conveying sometimes complex and subtle concepts. Moreover, as a part of the sacred scriptures of Kurozumi-kyō, the *dōka* continue to serve as the basis of sermons and of aid to reflection by members in their own immediate situations.[33]

Let me end by citing my favorite verse by Munetada. It captures his mythic vision and playfulness, while still conveying important elements of his religious worldview in typically everyday (yet extraordinary) terms:

| | |
|---|---|
| *waga sono no* | While I watched |
| *ari ga ametsuchi* | an ant in my garden |
| *hitokuchi ni* | swallow Heaven and Earth |
| *nomu o miredomo* | in a single gulp, |
| *hara mo fukurezu* | its belly did not swell. |

# 10

# Kurozumi Munetada's Use of the *Tanka* Form

### Harold Wright

Japanese poetry, to some readers in the West at any rate, is synonymous with *haiku*, the popular 17-syllable poem which was traditionally related to one of the four seasons. But in reality, poetry written by the Japanese, both in the past and at present, encompasses a diversity of verse forms and styles. Today most of the poetic energies of the country are going into *shi*, or free verse poetry, although *haiku* and other traditional fixed forms are written and published widely.

## The *Tanka* Form

One important form of poetry in Japan, older than the *haiku* by nearly a thousand years, is perhaps less familiar in the West than its well-known 17-syllable offspring because it is known by so many names. This 31-syllable poem, subdivided into five phrases of 5, 7, 5, 7, 7 syllables, is commonly referred to as the *tanka* ("short poem," to distinguish it from the *chōka* or "long poem") or *waka* ("Japanese poem" to distinguish it from poetry written in Chinese). But this same 31-syllable poem goes by other names as well: *uta* ("song") *gyosei* (when composed by an emperor), *miuta* (when composed by other people of high rank like other members of the royal family and some Shinto deities), *kyōka* ("mad poem" when they are meant to be humorous), and even *Shikishima no michi*. *Shikishima* is an old poetic name for Japan, so "the path of *Shikishima*" can be used to mean the same 31-syllable verse form when you are really trying to impress or be archaic.

Kurozumi Munetada, founder of Kurozumi-kyō, preferred to call them *dōka* ("Poems of the Way"). He expressed much of his teaching in this little 31-syllable form.

In form, this 31-syllable *tanka* (to use the most generic term) is probably as old as the Japanese language. Early records are incomplete, of course, but it has been suggested that this verse form, on themes of love at any rate, sprang out of songfests as associated with ancient Shinto fertility rites. The earliest recorded *tanka*, however, appears in Japan's oldest extant book, the *Kojiki* (A.D. 712)[1], the major source of Japan's creation myth and early history. The first *tanka* is said to have been written by Susanō no Mikoto, brother of Amaterasu Ōmikami, the Sun Goddess herself. Due to misbehavior, Susanō was banished from his sister's kingdom and eventually ended up at Izumo on the Japan Sea side of the islands. There he slew a drunken dragon and married a local woman. In building his new home he recited, perhaps sang, the following 31-syllable verse:

> Yagumo tatsu
>   Izumo yaegaki
>     Tsuma-gomi ni
> Yaegaki tsukuru
>   Sono yaegaki wo.

Each time I approach this poem I see new things. My current attempt at translation goes:

> *Many clouds are rising,*
>   *Izumo's many fences*
>     *surround this couple;*
> *I am building many fences,*
>   *a home of many fences.*

It is certainly doubtful that this is the very first *tanka*, but the verse does indicate to us that the form has been in existence for a very long time. Later this fixed form of 31-syllables became the mainstay of Japanese poetry almost until modern times. Most of the poems in the *Man'yōshū (Collection of Ten Thousand Leaves)*,[2] Japan's first major anthology of poetry, were of the *tanka* type. The later imperial anthologies also focused on *tanka*. Even today the poetry of the Emperor's annual New Year's poetry contest is in this form. Hundreds of magazines and even newspapers still publish them. *Tanka* writing is taught everywhere both in private homes of established poets and in adult education centers, like the schools established by newspapers, YMCAs, Shinto Shrines, and even department stores. The parks and temples of Kyoto continue to be full of *tanka* poets seeking inspiration. Some of the writers, however, in order to widen their vision, no longer write merely of the cherry blossoms and autumn leaves. As is also the case in some schools of *tanka*, commuter trains and public telephones are now fit topics for the *tanka* poem.

Faced with the many years in which *tanka* have been written as well as the vast number that have been collected over the centuries,[3] I have felt the need to create several groupings or categories of *tanka* poetry into which I can sort the poems encountered for research and translation. The categories I use are based primarily on the reasons they were composed, although in some cases a poem may have been written for one reason and then ended up being used years later for another purpose entirely. Let me suggest these four categories: lyric, social, ritual, and didactic.

## Lyric *Tanka*

The lyric nature of traditional Japanese poetry is no secret. Any work that deals with the *tanka* at all will without doubt discuss the poetic form in terms of its lyric history. Earl Miner and his colleagues in their insightful *The Princeton Companion to Classical Japanese Literature* write, in describing early Japanese poetry,

> If what transpires in the human heart is the cause of poetic words, then one central feature of classical Japanese poetics must be termed expressivism ... Surely this kind of poetic expressivism is particularly appropriate to a theory of literature based on lyricism as the norm.[4]

And indeed this lyricism did become one of the main elements of Japanese poetry, if it had not already been the norm from prehistoric times. Let us look at two examples of *tanka* in the lyric category.

The first lyric poem presented here is an anonymous one found in the eighth century *Man'yōshū:*

> I look back at her
> and wave my sleeves in parting
> from between the trees
> Praying the clouds won't cover
> the moon that has just appeared.[5]

A much more recent example was composed by the Emperor Meiji:

> In the palace tower
> Each and every window
> Was opened widely,
> And then in four directions
> We viewed cherry in full bloom![6]

In both these cases it appears that the poets were moved to pick up a writing brush when their hearts were overflowing with emotion. And it is this expressivism that remained the norm for most poets for over a thousand years. Yet, the lyric is not the only type of Japanese poetry. Some poems had other functions even though in some cases they may well resemble lyrics.

## Social *Tanka*

One of the major social uses of *tanka* poetry has been communication, often between lovers who were not always permitted to meet openly. Traditional fiction and drama are filled with the social uses of poetry. Many were written by a man attempting to initiate an affair by presenting a flattering poem, or a woman saying "yes" or "no" (often "maybe") in verse. There was the morning-after "thank you" poem for a lovely night; often these were worded in the hope that there would be another meeting as soon as it got dark. Sometimes it was the women who were more outspoken. In the tenth century Izumi Shikibu, known for her "passionate" poetry, wrote:

> Caring not at all
> of tangling my long black hair
> I fling myself down:
> Only to begin to yearn
> for the man who stroked it smooth.[7]

Other uses of communication through poetry are not limited to lovers. Emperor Meiji, for example, communicated to the people of his country in mini "state of the nation" communiques in the form of the *tanka*. To encourage modernization of Japan he wrote:

> Nation
> By gaining the good
> And rejecting what is wrong
> It is our desire
> That we'll compare favorably
> With other lands abroad.[8]

On an everyday level, we find in contemporary Japan another social use of the *tanka* in those placed in guest logs of temples, shrines, some homes, art openings, and even weddings. Of course, not all the entries can be scanned in terms of their 31-syllables; many of them are written in prose.

To appreciate a principal social use of *tanka* more fully, let us go back nearly a thousand years and look at one poetic exchange between lovers. This is described by Lady Murasaki in her masterpiece, the *Tale of Genji*.[9] Toward the end of the novel the woman Ukifune is unhappily being half-heartedly wooed by two high-ranking aristocrats, Kaoru and Niou. Kaoru has set her up with a place to live in the then-awful town of Uji (now known for tea) south of Kyoto. Throughout history people have made puns on the town's name: *Uji = ushi* (sorrowful). Niou visits her at times, so Ukifune is not that lonely, but she is upset because she is neglected by Kaoru. Kaoru writes an insincere sounding *tanka*, saying he is sorry he can't visit her but he does wonder how she is getting along. It is the rainy season and he assumes she is alone. In my own translations he writes:

> I am wondering
>     how you distant villagers
>         are faring in the flood,
> As I stare into the gloom
>     of these times of darkness.

In her reply she makes a pun of the name of the village of Uji which, like Kyoto the capital, was situated in the Province of Yamashiro:

> I have come to know
>     the meaning of the name of
>         this Yamashiro Hamlet,
> Near an Uji River crossing
>     my life is filled with grief.

Niou, the second lover, busy with other matters back at home, also uses the rain as an excuse not to visit her. His messenger does get through, however, with the poem-message:

> Gazing as I am
>     I cannot even see
>         those distant clouds,
> For all the sky has darkened
>     and my days are spent in grief.

Let us look at one more attempt at communication through
*tanka*. In the eighth century a person by the name of Tajihi Mahito
had a poem in the *Man'yōshū*.[10] Little is known about him and even
less is known about the women involved. Because they wouldn't
even tell him their names their poem is anonymous. Tajihi apparently was walking along the sea near present-day Osaka:

> As I walk along
> the seashore at Naniwa
> young fishing girls
> Gather in seaweed for food
> and I call and ask their names.

The reply:

> Please consider us
> merely as fishing girls
> and continue on ...
> You're a traveler far from home
> and we can't reveal our names.

Although anti-social in content, the reply poem is certainly social
in type because a message was communicated. Now let us look at
other types of *tanka*.

## Ritual *Tanka*

Poetry is much used in ritual in Japan. Perhaps the Noh theatre
itself could be described as ritualized poetry. Historic events are
still portrayed in ritual dance to a chant of *kanshi* or Chinese poems.
For ritual use, Shinto prefers the 31-syllable *tanka*, and these little
poems are often embedded in prayers, chants, songs, or in the
music of sacred dances. In the Meiji Shrine in Tokyo the poetry of
the Emperor Meiji is often used in shrine ritual. In this way too, the
poetry of Kurozumi Munetada is used in Kurozumi-kyō ritual.
The Founder's poetry is not only studied, memorized, taught in
texts, quoted in sermons, and sung as hymns; it is also incorporated
into actual prayers and danced in sacred dances.

This is conveniently illustrated by a ritual held in the Spring of
1987 when the Chief Patriarch of Kurozumi-kyō welcomed to
Shintozan a visiting couple from the United States. They were not
mere tourists. The man was a member of the city council of his
home town and had been presented with official letters of introduction from a businessman member of the Kurozumi congregation
who lives and works in the United States. So, befitting an official

visit of this nature, a ritual was created in the main hall for the purpose of bringing the visitors closer to the blessings of Amaterasu Ōmikami. The visiting couple was requested to offer a sacred branch of the *sakaki* tree to the enshrined deity. The *norito* written for the occasion contained a 31-syllable poem that was composed by the Founder. This *norito* and the poem used in it can serve as an example of the Founder's poetry being used in ritual, though numerous other examples could be provided.[11]

### John Smith
### Prayer on the Occasion of His Visit to Shintozan

Oh mighty and most revered Amaterasu Ōmikami, we stand before thee as we stand before the host of eight hundred thousand deities of the earth as well as the deified soul of our Founder Munetada no Mikoto. It is with awe and reverence that I, Muneharu, Chief Patriarch of Kurozumi-kyō, speak in humility.

In these multitudes of days it is today, a most auspicious day, on which we have from the United States of America, Mr. and Mrs. John Smith, who have been living in the city of Midland in the state of Ohio, and who, in coming closer in their hearts to the teachings of the Way have deep appreciation of the words of our Founder Munetada no Mikoto who composed as a sacred hope:

> It is our wish
> to have Amaterasu's
> Goodness be known
> To all the world's people
> soon and without exception.[61]

Now offer, here in the great teaching hall of the Deity of the Sun, the treasured sacred branch in the humble hope that, being plainly and easily heard, our prayers be granted. It is our hope that from this day our guests, by the grace of divine blessings, be daily granted more and more gratitude, wonder, courage, and freedom from all afflictions; and that they will in health and renewed spirit be able to enjoy prolonged good fortune in a safe home. Furthermore we pray that our guests, having had these divine blessings bestowed upon them, will then in turn relate to other thoughtful people of America their knowledge of the Way in order, as a blessing and in happiness, to bring about and maintain the opening of a path of eternal peace.

It is with awe and reverence that we offer up these prayers.

Ceremonial prayer before the central altar at the Main Shrine
(*Daikyōden*). Photo courtesy of Kurozumi-kyō.

### Didactic *tanka*

Poetry in Japan has been used throughout the centuries as a
vehicle for conveying religious, spiritual, or moral concepts or
attitudes. Zen priests wrote Zen poetry, often in the Chinese language. A great many Buddhist attitudes towards the universe have
been captured in *haiku* and in *tanka*. Perhaps "didactic" is too narrow a word to describe a poetry which combines a lyric beauty and
a statement on the human condition. The priest Saigyō in the twelfth
century, for example, wrote:

> Denying my heart
>      even I am quite aware
>           of beauty's sadness:
> A woodcock flying from a marsh
>      on an autumn evening.

> Every single thing
>> has no choice but to change
>> in this world of ours,
> Yet, with the same brilliance
>> the moon is still shining.[12]

The Emperor Meiji, more in a Shinto vein, akin to the Kurozumi spirit, wrote lyrics that could also be called "didactic" in intent.

### Sun

> The morning sun
>> Rises so splendidly
>> Into the sky:
> Oh, that we could attain
>> Such a clear reviving soul![13]

Perhaps it it difficult to ascertain whether Kurozumi Munetada composed his poetry for the purposes of ritual, but it is quite obvious that he used his poetry as a vehicle for teaching the Way. His letters, for example, are filled with 31-syllable poems that make a didactic point. This is not to say that he didn't write poetry in other modes, even the lyric. Take for example the powerful emotions he expresses in poetry at the time of his wife's death:

> The world of dreams
>> is, I know, a world of dreams,
>> yet I cannot waken . . .
> For another yet to wake
>> I know I shall be longing.[51]

Or:

> Although I have heard
>> that the flowers of yesterday
>> are dreams of today . . .
> Towards this storm that rages
>> I hold a deep resentment.[52][14]

But then we are told that "after thinking things over" he wrote again on his wife's death, still lyrically, but more positively:[15]

> Flowers of the world
>> scatter as you want to scatter
>> over heaven and earth.
> Then along the endless Way
>> burst forth in bloom again.[62]

It was one of the major principles of his teaching to turn the painful experiences of life into "religious practice" to enable his followers to grow along the Way. So we can see in this last poem his ability to turn even something as painful as his wife's death into a didactic message for himself and others.

Later he was able to use even his own approaching death as an opportunity to provide a message of faith to his followers.

> There is but one path
>      in all of Heaven and Earth
>         and this is the Way
> Over which I'll soon depart,
>      and this indeed brings joy.[54]

## Conclusion

*Dōka* (Songs of the Way) is the name Kurozumi Munetada gave to his 31-syllable poems. They cover a variety of themes and subject matters as broad as his teaching: blessings of Amaterasu Ōmikami, gratitude, existence and non-existence, kami and Buddhas, death, and life of True Sincerity. They are quoted everywhere in Kurozumi-kyō circles. I even have a beautiful set of seven bookmarks that have been printed with Munetada's poetry. Every sermon given in Kurozumi-kyō worship contains quoted poetry of the Founder.

Although the poems serve to express the founder's personal feeling and are used on ritual occasions, they were primarily intended to serve as didactic expressions. In Kurozumi-kyō usage, they continue to serve that function, communicating the Way taught by Munetada to a broad range of people.

# 11

# *Omamori* in
# Kurozumi-kyō

Eugene Swanger

The distribution of amulets and talismans was an important activity
of Kurozumi Munetada. He gave away tens of thousands of them
during his lifetime. Called *omamori,* amulets and talismans have
two general functions. If the object is said to have apotropaic power,
that is, the ability to dispel unfortunate or malign forces, it is an
amulet. On the other hand, if it is believed to effectively attract
what is beneficial, it is a talisman. Each power is a complement of
the other and often a single *omamori* will have both functions.

## Religious meaning of *Omamori*

Seen essentially as conduits through which the sacred power
of life flows to human beings, *omamori* and their use are one of the
persistent characteristics of the Japanese religious traditions. Most,
although certainly not all, of the traditions make use of them,
especially Shinto and the Buddhist movements which sought to
meet the needs of the common people: Tendai, Shingon, Nichiren,
and Soto Zen. Exceptions are the Pure Land movements. Jōdu Shu
and especially Jōdu Shinshu rejected their use because of their theological insistence that one is saved, not through one's own effort,
but solely by the grace of Amida. They looked on carrying an *omamori* as an attempt to save oneself (*jiriki*) versus trusting completely
in the grace of Amida (*tariki*). But this Pure Land interpretation is
not shared by most priests whether Shinto or Buddhist.

The fundamental belief that everyday needs can be influenced
by sacred powers present in the *omamori* is not in itself magical.
That is, *omamori* are perceived by most priests, including those of

Kurozumi-kyō, to be neither automatically effective nor to represent a mechanical means of manipulation. *Omamori* are not coercive.

Amulets and talismans are better understood if they are thought of as tokens of the divine presence, requiring the complete and sincere effort of the persons possessing them. They do not automatically guarantee success in examinations or safety in driving or prosperity in business. Without spiritual cultivation, intelligent energy, and care, the individual cannot avoid failure or achieve success. There is no virtue in the mere possession of an *omamori*, as several traditions clearly indicate. Although Kurozumi-kyō does not follow the practice, it does share the attitude of several other Shinto and Buddhist traditions which issue cards with their *omamori* stating that their effectiveness partially depends on the spiritual and moral condition of the recipient. Often specific counsel will be given: do not be greedy, do not dwell upon your anger, be patient, and persevere in the face of difficulty.

Kurozumi-kyō participates in the *omamori* culture. That is, it too believes that *omamori* can function as effective transmitters of the presence of the sacred, enabling its people not only to meet the problems and vicissitudes of life with resolution, but to triumph over them. It sees their distribution as an act of concern, even compassion, toward people confronting ordinary but often daunting problems. Kurozumi-kyō values it as a humanitarian practice first established by its founder who knew that most people find an expression of concern to be more real if it is accompanied by something tangible. Amulets and talismans can shift the sense of divine support from peripheral to focal awareness. In its use of *omamori*, Kurozumi-kyō shares a sacramental view and a pastoral concern with many other Shinto and Buddhist institutions in Japan. Certainly too, the forms of its *omamori* in their shape, color, and material are common to other Shinto and Buddhist communities.

## Symbolism in *Omamori*

One of the largest of Kurozumi-kyō's *omamori* is pictured in figure 1. Consisting of a hollow box covered with white paper and measuring 27 cm. long by 7 cm. wide by 5 cm. deep, it has printed in black down the front *Munetada Jinja Futotamagushi* ("Munetada Shrine Respectful Offering"). A red seal of the shrine appears at the bottom, and one third of the way from the top are gold and red bands tied in a bow. Inserted behind the bow is a triangular folded paper with a grain of rice inside. On the front it states *osen-mai*, the honorific for rice conveying a sense of its holiness. Here are found a cluster of symbols common to *omamori* throughout the range of Japanese religious traditions.

Figure 1. Photo courtesy of Eugene Swanger.

The sealed empty wood box is an important symbol and it shares meaning with a host of vessel symbols found worldwide. According to Erich Neumann, who has examined this symbolism more extensively than anyone else, a basic equation in all cultures since prehistoric times has been "woman equals vessel" because of the experience of woman bearing the child within her. Thus, "the body-vessel and mother-child situation — the positive elementary character of the feminine — spring from the most intimate personal experience, from an experience that is eternally human." Inside the dark and powerful interior of woman new life is mysteriously generated, contained, nurtured, and protected.

Extending this elemental symbol of woman as the generating, transforming, and protecting vessel, cultures universally expand the equation to read "woman equals vessel equals world." That is, the experience of the mother as the container which generates, transforms, and protects is projected onto objects within the world. Natural objects such as gourds, cows, pigs, owls, pomegranates, and rice are seen as primordial wombs of life. Among cultural objects of this sort we might observe pots, jars, ships, barrels, enclosed bells, hollow mallets, bags, and boxes. All of these objects, both natural and cultural, can be viewed as the very reservoirs of life, as ontic centers of generation and regeneration, and as inexhaustible springs of vitality, strength, and power. In the darkness of the vessel, whether a woman or a cave, a gourd, or a box, life gestates and grows until it breaks its covering and emerges into the world.[1]

Yanagida Kunio was the first person in Japan to recognize the fundamental importance of vessel symbolism. Without any knowledge of western scholarship on the subject, his investigation and explanation proceeded along somewhat similar lines of reasoning. Yanagida used the word *utsobo* for the "mother equals vessel equals world" equation. The word *utsobo* means "empty" or "hollow." But, as Yanagida employs the term, it does not mean a space which is merely empty. Rather, it is a space which is full as well as empty. That is, the empty space is animated by the mysterious and numinous power that produces and reproduces, nurtures and transforms life. He cites as examples Japanese fairy tales and folk stories in which strange but powerful children are born out of trees, gourds, fruits, and so forth. One is born from the bamboo tree, another comes forth from a melon, and a third appears from a gourd.[2]

Boxes are also presented in popular lore as containers of power from the suprasensible world which must be kept sealed. In the story of Urashima, a fisherman is taken to the undersea palace of a beautiful princess where he lives for a time. When he expresses his intention to visit his home, the princess gives him a closed box to protect him on his journey and to assist him in making a safe return to the palace beneath the ocean. He is instructed never to open the vessel. When he arrives at the site of his home, he discovers that over three hundred years have elapsed since he left. Compelled by curiosity he opens the box and instantly a purple cloud is released. In the same moment he becomes an aged man and dies.[3] Inadvertently he had destroyed the protective mother-vessel.

In the same way the *omamori* is never simply the material from which it is made. Whether an enclosed box, a bag drawn tight, or paper folded to make an enclosure, it is a repository for a numinal presence alive and highly charged with energy. If opened, its power is lost.

Colors too are important characteristics of *omamori* because color also gives power to an object, charging it with *mana*. The object takes on the qualities of its color, and the acquisition enhances the ability of the object to attract and repel because the color itself is seen as an extension of a higher reality. That is, colors embody the various qualities of the life force, and through the use of color different aspects of the mysterious sources of being can be made present.

Red and gold are the dominant colors of the fourteen kinds of *omamori* Kurozumi-kyō makes available to its people. Of the fourteen, thirteen employ gold and fourteen make use of red. None of the fourteen are without one or the other color. Six are exclusively red and gold. The third dominant color is white, while green is employed on two.

In all cultures universal meanings are ascribed to gold, red, and green. Gold is associated with the sun, with the transcendent, the eternal. Gold is the only metal known to be immune to time. It does not rust, corrode, or tarnish. It does not after a period of time turn green, brown, or grey as do other metals. So it is perceived as immortal, transcending time and all of the corrosive events occurring in time.[4] Thus gold is believed to contain an unusual amount of vitality. It is a reservoir of being and as such it can overcome the effects of time.

Red is the vital color of animal life. Since it is the color of blood, it radiates the energy and vitality of blood. Consequently red became the color considered most offensive and distasteful to evil and most inviting of good fortune and success. Because it is considered the luckiest of all colors next to gold, instances of the apotropaic use of red abound in Japanese folk culture. For example, pieces of red cloth were used to protect against smallpox. Patients were given red caps and red *tabi* to wear. Sometimes red candles were also placed in the room. Red papier-mache figures of dolls were placed near the sickbed, and red paper was used to decorate the bottle of *sake* from which the patient drank.[5]

White is a propitious color. The appearance of a white fox, horse, or dog is a good omen. White symbolizes purity, simplicity, sacredness, the presence of the ultimate or absolute.

Green is the color of plant life, springtime, youth, the wind, and long life.

A grain of sacred rice is contained in a folded paper enclosure placed behind the red and gold bow of the *omamori* in figure 1. Rice is central in the healing rites of Kurozumi-kyō and it is used here to enhance the effectiveness of the *omamori*.

Rice is the basic staple in a Japanese diet. In the past, rice was even more essential than it is today when a vigorous economy makes a wide range of food abundant and easily available. In past

centuries it was so crucial to the maintenance of life that life and
rice were simply equated. Because rice possessed the power to
sustain life, it was believed able to fend off the negative events
which drain life of its joy. For example, keeping a few grains of rice
in a room where a person is confined for a birth or an illness would
assist recovery. In the past, sailors along the coast of eastern Japan
would scatter grains of rice on the waves to quiet their surging
threat, a practice which echoed a story from Shinto mythology in
which the kami Ninigi-no-mikoto scattered rice grains across the
sky as he descended from the floating bridge of heaven (the rain-
bow) to dispel the darkness covering the sky.[6] In the words of Kurozumi Nobuakira, "rice has within it the power of heaven and earth."[7]
Indeed, rice and the sacred were so closely related that the place
where rice is stored came to be called by the same word (*miyake*)
used for a shrine. Because of the simple and direct equation, rice
equals life equals the sacred power of existence, numerous amulets
and talismans offered by a broad range of Shinto shrines and Buddhist temples have rice enclosed.

## Worldview of *Omamori*

Correlative thinking undergirds and binds together the world
of *omamori*. That is, behind their construction and use lies a per-
ceptual pattern in which similarities suggest a sharing of properties.
If any object appears to correlate in shape, function, color, or sound
with any other object, then it shares characteristics with that object.
For example, if a horse sounds like thunder when it runs, then it
shares in the properties of thunder and storm. Or, if a frog disap-
pears and reappears like the moon, then the frog and the moon
have an affinity. If an object is colored red, then it will share in the
vitality of the animal world; if gold, the life color of the sun, it will
participate in the sun's abundant and ever-renewing energy. Thus
colors, objects, and sounds are not kept distinct from each other.
Rather, we see a process of reasoning which looks for likeness,
similarity, and correspondence; one could always share in the
other and often does. Attention does not focus upon the world as
merely objects to be analyzed, manipulated, and changed. Instead
the eyes are directed to the life force binding human beings and all
of nature together into a single contextual field. In the words of
Mircea Eliade, all is "bound together by harmonies, analogies, and
elements held in common ... a vast web in which every piece fits
and nothing is isolated from the rest."[8]

Miraculous stories (*engi*) are also important in the culture of *omamori*. Without them, amulets would have far less vitality than they do. Like other Japanese religious traditions, Kurozumi-kyō has many stories about its *omamori*. Some are old and others are more recent. For example, in 1983 the Nippon Broadcasting Corporation (NHK) televised a program featuring a Japanese couple, Mr. and Mrs. Takasuga, who had emigrated to Australia where, after many difficulties, they became the first successful rice growers in their new country. As NHK interviewed their now elderly granddaughter, she showed them cherished articles her grandparents had left behind. Among them was an *omamori* from Munetada Shrine. In the words of Kurozumi Nobuakira,

> The mere thinking of the fact that the Takasugas took their *omamori* wherever they went and prayed to Kami whenever they encountered a hardship or obstacle and of the fact that Kami extended her benevolence to them through the *omamori* and led them to success, fills our heart with great emotion and gratitude toward Kami.[9]

At the core of Kurozumi-kyō's *engi* heritage lie the stories of the miraculous healings of the founder Munetada. As one might expect, a relationship exists between the kinds of stories told in a tradition and the functions served by its *omamori*. The *omamori* function as tokens of the story, that is, they are perceived to encapsulate the redemptive moment when health was restored or success was achieved. In Kurozumi-kyō's case, because of the stories of the founder's acts of healing, many of its *omamori* are obtained for specific amuletic purposes, to ward off disease and prevent illness; or for a specific talismanic function, to attract health to someone already ill.

But the purposes served by *omamori* also reflect current social conditions. Close behind concern for health comes anxiety about traffic accidents and possible failure on school entrance examinations and academic tests.

## Distribution of *Omamori*

While amulets and talismans are available throughout the year, most people will obtain their *omamori* from Kurozumi-kyō during the festivals, especially at New Year's (*Saitan Sai*). Because the festivals are important times for their distribution, a list of its more important festivals with the estimated attendance figures at each is presented at the end of this chapter. The number of *omamori* distributed tends to approximate the number of people participating in a festival.

Prior to their distribution, special prayers are said over the *omamori* to empower them. Kurozumi-kyō teaches that with the prayer, the deity is welcomed and dwells in the object, ready to answer the individual's specific needs. Once the bearer's wishes are fulfilled, the *omamori* should be returned to the shrine where prayers will be offered first to give expressions of gratitude and then to invite the deity to leave them. At the New Year's festival and again at *Setsubun*, a special rite (*Karosai*) will be held in which all of the returned amulets and talismans will be burned. For this reason old examples cannot be found. We know that their forms have changed over the years and that the ones used today are somewhat different than those distributed by Kurozumi Munetada, but because earlier ones are no longer available we cannot specify what the differences are. It can be said with some degree of confidence, however, that because of more limited economic circumstances, silk brocade and wood were less commonly used in the past in the construction of *omamori* than today.

Whereas the lay members of Kurozumi-kyō once made the *omamori* by hand, this is no longer so. As in the case of so many other shrines and temples, lay people can still be found who vividly recall long hours of work making them during the weeks prior to a major festival. But now commercial firms, which in some cases have been supplying such liturgical materials for three hundred years, make them. This trend began in the early 1950s. Nevertheless, as an act of pastoral concern, a special *omamori* is occasionally made for a person with his or her name inscribed upon it, if it is felt that it will be beneficial to the recipient.

## Conclusion

Kurozumi-kyō shares with other Shinto and Buddhist traditions a common viewpoint. It understands *omamori* to be forms of divine epiphany which it distributes out of genuine pastoral concern. The *omamori* receive enhanced value through stories of miraculous events and through a correlative worldview which perceives the life force being shared through affinities. The importance of festivals to the *omamori* culture of Kurozumi-kyō, especially New Year's (*Oshogatsu*) and *Setsubun*, is also common to other Shinto and Buddhist traditions. In its understanding, construction, and use of *omamori*, Kurozumi-kyō is a genuine Japanese religious tradition.

More fundamentally, the *engi* and their tokens, the *omamori*, constitute a matrix of meanings and hopes which are therapeutic.

### Figure 2

Red and gold silk brocade *omamori*, 18.5 cm. long by 8.8 cm. wide. The shrine's emblem or *mon*, a flower (Oda-no-mokkou), appears at the top. Behind the silver and gold bow is a small triangular folded paper containing rice. The words *"osenmai"* (sacred rice) appear on the front. The two *kanji* at the bottom read *"inoru tokoro" (place of prayer)*, referring to Munetada Shrine as the place where through prayers this *omamori* was empowered. It will be placed on the *Kamidana* in the home.

### Figure 3

Like the *omamori* in figures 1 and 2, these three paper *ofuda*-style amulets and talismans are designed for the *Kamidana*, being 28.5 and 30 cm. long. Note the *kanji "inoru tokoro"* at the bottom of the *omamori* at the center.

Photos courtesy of Eugene Swanger.

They dispel the uneasiness common to all human beings caught in an opaque world where threats to a full and meaningful existence lurk unseen and potentially uncontrolled. They are an antidote to the anxieties and fears of people confronted by the monolithic forces of nature which can bring disease, accident, failure, and death. They make life more viable. In conveying promise and determination to not only endure but to overcome, they are a step toward freedom.

## Appendix

| Main festivals at Shintōzan | Date | Attendance |
|---|---|---|
| 1. New Year's Festival (*Saitan Sai*) | January 1 | 100,000 |
| 2. Voluntary Followers' Good Fortune Festival (*Tokushi Shinto Kaiun Sai*) | Second Sunday, January | 3,000 |
| 3. Founder's Festival (*Kyōso Taisai*) | First Saturday, April | (not available) |
| 4. Grand Purification Festival (*Ōharai Taisai*) | July 30 | 3,000 |
| 5. Transfer Memorial Festival (*Gosenza Kinen Sai*) | Fourth Sunday, October | 3,000 |
| 6. Grand Winter Solstice (*Toji Taisai*) | December 21-22 | 3,000 |
| **Main Festivals at Munetada Shrine** | | |
| 1. New Year's Festival (*Saitan Sai*) | January 1 | 50,000 |
| 2. Spring Welcoming Festival (*Setsubun*) | February 3 | 30,000 |
| 3. Grand Spring Festival (*Shunki Rei-Taisai*) | First Saturday, April | 2,000 |
| 4. Grand Parade (*Goshinkō*) | First Sunday, April | (not available) |
| 5. Grand Purification Festival | Fourth Sunday, July | 20,000 |
| 6. Winter Solstice Festival (*Toji Sai*) | December 1-2 | 2,000 |

From left to right, The Reverend Muneharu Kurozumi, Father Bertrand Buby, The Reverend Shinsel Kudo, and The Reverend Nobuakira Kurozumi, in front of Kennedy Union at the University of Dayton. Photo by Willis Stoesz.

# 12

# Shinto-Christian Comparison

edited by
Willis Stoesz

The parallel statements about world peace that appear in this chapter give us an important additional angle of vision on Kurozumi Shinto. By taking them as a point of departure we take the circumstance (and model) of dialogue into consideration as a condition by which we seek understanding. We should also observe that the presentations by the Reverend Muneharu Kurozumi given in previous chapters have an implicit dialogical character, since they are in formal terms self-disclosures rather than abstract scholarly discussions. Even those given first to Japanese audiences assume such a character in having been selected by him for the information of western audiences. This approach differs from the other chapters in this book which proceed from a point of view outside the Kurozumi circle of faith. The difference requires brief discussion.

An "outsider" in the study of religion, or "objectivist" as Ninian Smart puts it,[1] gains an advantage in breadth of perspective over the account of religion given by an insider. As Joseph Kitagawa indicates, the blind spots of those who explain religion "from the inside" must be corrected as we seek full understanding.[2] The outsider's advantage may, however, be purchased at the expense of turning religious subjects to be understood into objects, running the danger of introducing another sort of blind spot into the account given of them. The price to be paid may be minimized: Smart's suggestions about the scholar's practice of "structured empathy," and of self-disciplined use of his/her own subjective experience as a guide to understanding, explain how this may be done.[3] Still, the immediacy — the self-expressed intentionality — of the subject herself/himself tends to be obscured or omitted in the (necessary) treatment of the subject in relationship to more general historical or structural frameworks.

A rather different approach to understanding religion is set forth by Raimundo Panikkar, who holds an ideal of "dialogical dialogue" (as opposed to "dialectical dialogue," which, using adversarial reasoning, seeks to understand others in broad, impersonal frameworks). Here the method calls for dialogue partners to disclose their worldview-presuppositions to one another in depth and ultimacy;[4] the particularity of each dialogue participant receives central emphasis. The underlying myths by which each participating person is constituted as a "Thou" are to be opened to other dialogue participants, revealing him or her in distinctive wholeness. The advantage here is that nothing about the one remains (in principle) opaque to the other, and a kind of objectivity is achieved in that the inner intention of each participant is recognized and respected. The distinctive humanity of each comes into full relief within the dialogue. Yet this approach also has a shortcoming, in that what is distinctively disclosed in dialogical dialogue, however important for full understanding, does by definition not become available for general cultural discourse.

Some kind of middle ground is needed between scholarship governed by broad interpretive frameworks and the expressions of strictly confessional (or inter-confessional) points of view. The inclusion of dialogue material in this volume leads us to a model of such middle ground. We gain it by asking (as "outsider" scholar) what a Christian dialogue partner (who might have Panikkar's full dialogical understanding as a goal) needs to know about Kurozumi Shinto in order to move toward a fair and full understanding of those who speak in its name. Thus, we will in summarizing this book phrase issues to be clarified as they arise within western Christian standpoint (assuming, for purpose of inquiry, a Christian role) while making use of the broad interpretive frameworks employed in this volume to supply to someone in that standpoint the needed information and interpretation.[5]

Employing this model requires us to stretch both toward general frameworks of understanding and toward particularist understandings in which the unique character of the individual person is insisted upon. We make use of the broad terms of cultural discourse

while keeping in mind the distinctive persons we seek to understand. The goal is to delineate the underlying thought-patterns of
Kurozumi Shinto, needed by a dialogue partner to understand the
other distinctively, while leaving the actual pursuit of such dialogue to those who participate in the respective faiths. In the concluding chapter the outline of topics expresses this assumed interrogative point of view.

The following two talks are shortened versions of what was
said during the Conference on Kurozumi Shinto by The Reverend
Muneharu Kurozumi and Father Bertrand Buby. Father Buby
proved an ideal dialogue partner. Not only is he a New Testament
scholar and a veteran of many years' interfaith dialogue, but as
Provincial of the Cincinnati Province of the Society of Mary he
held rank in his religious institution that somewhat compares to
the Chief Patriarch's rank in his.

Both were asked to speak about their approach to the problem of world peace. They were asked to consider the following
outline in preparing these remarks:

> "1. The need for peace in the world;
>
> 2. What understanding of the nature of peace in the
>    world my own (Shinto, or Christian) religious faith
>    leads me to have;
>
> 3. What the most serious obstacles to world peace are,
>    and how religious faith helps overcome them."

It was specifically suggested that what they would say would
be taken as only the first word in a discussion that could be taken
up again subsequently: the talks should be exploratory and open-
ended rather than definitive in mood.

## The Idea of Peace in Shinto[6]

### The Reverend Muneharu Kurozumi

Because of Professor Martin's graceful help I was given an
opportunity to pray in a Shinto ceremony in such a solemn chapel
today.[7] This is a much esteemed opportunity for me and I want to
express my appreciation from my heart.

Also, I am deeply impressed to hear the pious prayer of Father
Buby. I am a Shintoist, but I am a human being just as he is. His
prayer has communicated with me.

Our Divine Founder Munetada read the following poems:

> The divine virtue
> of Amaterasu
> fills Heaven and Earth;
> Ah, in such abundance
> is this limitless grace.[2]

> For those who go forth
> together with the Kami
> Amaterasu,
> There will come day after day
> the feelings of gratitude.[49]

> In this world of ours
> we have all come together
> to form a circle;
> Let us pray to be joined
> by the Heart of all our hearts.[60]

**The idea of harmony**

Now I would like to talk particularly about "being circular" (*marukoto*).

The most important time of prayer in Kurozumi-kyō is the time of *nippai*, when we reverence the sunrise each morning. The oldest form of prayer in Shinto is part of it. The sun has a circular shape; and *marukoto* refers to things that are circular. There is a wish in Shinto that the human heart (*kokoro*) be circular. *Maru-koto* refers not only to circular shapes but also to functions that are circular. I might express this in the phrase "a well-balanced circulation."

For instance, a day becomes one day when the opposites of daytime and nighttime become one. A year becomes one when the opposites of summer and winter become united. The thought of Shinto is relativistic. Its approach is to value the condition in which opposing entities exist in a good balance.

A Japanese Shinto scholar named Ueda Kenji has said, "Shinto is originally a religion founded upon the world of relativistic entities," and, "recognition of relativity produces the concept of relation between strong and weak, and between big and small; it does not reject the existence of the other by making one's self absolute."

The Founder of Kurozumi-kyō has said, "In the Universe there is not one object or person that must be disposed of (*suteru*)," and, "The Universe is disordered (*fusoroi*)."[8] True harmony is found in each unique entity doing its own due task (*ninau*) and functioning cooperatively.

Here is an example from an experience familiar to us. One of the things I enjoy in this country is eating delicious beefsteak at inexpensive cost. Wherever I eat beefsteak it is always served with potatoes. When we eat meat, the acidity in our blood increases. By also eating alkaline food, potatoes, we keep a balance. If we were to eat only beefsteak we would become ill. Illness is a condition in which harmony within the body is being disturbed, and being healthy is a condition in which the inside of the body is at peace.

For another example, here is a story found in a Japanese junior high school textbook. In 1906 in the state of Arizona a reservation was established to protect about 4,000 deer from carnivorous animals such as puma and coyotes, out of concern for their survival. Of course the population of deer increased. In 1918 there were over 50,000 of them. However, at this time there occurred fighting among the deer, a thing which had never been seen before. Also, the deer began to die one after another from illness and starvation. The fact was that grass would no longer grow on the reservation. The reason for this was that before this, pumas and coyotes had eaten the deer and the feces of these carnivorous animals had become fertilizer and from this the grass had grown. The deer had been living on the grass. Therefore, in order for deer to survive, pumas and coyotes, which could be called the enemies of the deer, were necessary. Humans had disconnected the chain of food circulation.

This is only one example. The idea that "we are right and you are wrong, therefore we get rid of you," which is the same idea as "things get better if we remove the bad ones," seems to be the cause of destroying peace or of making a big mistake.

There are many people in this world who advocate that we should keep peace but we must fight for justice. For instance, think of some children who are fighting. Both would certainly insist that they were not wrong but the other was bad.

Rather, the person who considers himself or herself right should step back so as not to provoke fighting. This idea is an essential basis for peace. These are actually the words of the Japanese Emperor.

This year is the fortieth since the end of World War II. The misfortune four decades ago that the countries on the east and west sides of the Pacific Ocean, Japan and the United States, fought each other with that ocean between them, has connected the two countries tightly and has led to a peaceful and friendly relationship. This is an important fact not only for Japan and America, but also for world peace.

Now I would like to consider the way to achieve peace by using Japan as my theme. I am a Japanese, so I know the history of Japan in best detail, among the many countries in the world.

### The Emperor as symbol of peace

Many people seem to think the Japanese Emperor is a symbol of war, but actually he should be given just the opposite status. From ancient times he has been a symbol of peace. The relationship between him and his people is not that of authority and subordination or of a lord and his servants. According to Japanese history, the relationship is like that of parent and child. The spirit of the Emperor is a larger form of the spirit of parents toward their children.

In the year in which the war between Japan and America was over, in August of 1945, General MacArthur represented the United States, and he came to Japan. On September 27 of that year the Emperor visited General MacArthur. At first, General MacArthur seems to have thought he came to secure his own life. This would be understandable. According to the history of war in the past, this could be considered natural. But despite that expectation, the Emperor first said, "I come to you, General MacArthur, to offer myself to the judgment of the powers you represent as the one to bear sole responsibility for every political and military decision made and action taken by my people in the conduct of war." In fact, General MacArthur has written that his feeling at that moment was that he was deeply impressed.[9] The mutual trust established here was the first step to the relationship between Japan and the United States after the war. However, during the war many Japanese people fought with this country under the name of the Emperor, and they also began the war under his name.

Actually, the Pacific War was provoked by the Japanese attacking Pearl Harbor in 1941, well-remembered in this country by the phrase "Remember Pearl Harbor." On December 8th a declaration of war was submitted to the Emperor. Starting with the signature of the Prime Minister there followed the signatures of all the ministers. Even for the Emperor it was not possible to reject the declaration. This was because he is a constitutional monarch and not an absolute monarch. Moreover, when the declaration provoking the war was submitted to him the attack on Pearl Harbor had already taken place.

When my closest cousin was married, the Chief Priest of the Meiji Shrine, Kanroji Osanage, acted as go-between (nakōdo). During the war this man served as shōtencho, the person who acts in the Emperor's place in conducting a Shinto ceremony. Here is something I heard directly from this person.

When the Emperor was to sign the declaration of war between Japan and the United States, he signed it reciting a poem by the Meiji Emperor:

> It is our hope
> That all the world's oceans
> Be joined in peace,
> So why do the winds and waves
> Now rise up in angry rage?
> [trans. Wright 1984, 11]

I was told that his hand was shaking and that he was in tears.

A few days later, the commander of the air force unit which attacked Pearl Harbor came to the Emperor. He came proudly. Mr. Kanroji was at this time with the Emperor. The first words that the Emperor said, after listening silently to the report from the commander, were, "I hope you did not by accident bomb any private houses."

### Keeping balance in the world

The Meiji Emperor's poem was written in 1904. At this time Japan was fighting a war against Russia. As you know, Japan won this Japan-Russia war. Because President Roosevelt served for us, the peace treaty between Japan and Russia, the Portsmouth treaty, was established. Japan did not win even an acre of land in this war. This was because it was not an invasion but was fought to stop the Russians from advancing into China, the Korean peninsula, and Japan. However, it was still a war. The Meiji Emperor expressed his sorrow over the war by reading this poem. I also understand that the reason President Roosevelt gave his help was because he was deeply impressed by the poem. However, the majority of the Japanese people, especially the ones in the military, were proud of the victory over Russia.

And a few years later the Japanese military again stepped into the Korean peninsula and China with the excuse that the Russians were going to invade China and Korea again. It was when the present Emperor was still young. He strongly requested the Prime Minister and the members of the Diet to change the policy toward China. However, the powerful impetus to go into China had endless energy behind it. This was one of the causes of the Pacific War.

It is just as in the case of individuals. Although it is important to have self-confidence (*jishin*), being self-conceited can be the cause of big mistakes. Behind true self-confidence there is a humble spirit. Self-conceit when it is defeated is nothing but cynicism. When Japan lost the war against this country, many Japanese people believed everything Americans do is right. Their pride was turned into a cynical spirit. As an instance, right after the war I myself, not yet ten years old, was acquainted with a soldier of the American Army Occupation Force. He gave me a wonderful treasure: Hershey's chocolate and Wrigley's chewing gum. The soldier looked greater than any Japanese person. For us in the present time these things are not treasures or anything special at all. However, this matter of finding proper self-confidence is a problem.

As you know Japan revived very quickly because of the United States, and Japan has now developed greatly in economic terms. At first glance, Japanese people seem by the present time to have developed self-confidence and lost their meanness. This is the fortieth year since the Pacific War was over, and the eightieth year since the Japan-Russia War was over. Eighty years ago Japan won the war against the Russians and gained pride. And then forty years ago we lost the war and sank down to the depths. In order to prevent our present self-confidence from becoming the pride of eighty years ago, we religious practitioners and all the leaders of Japan have to put forth careful effort.

When we consider the example of the nation of Japan and its modern experience we can realize the importance of making efforts not to disturb the harmony of a country. We can understand it is important to an individual not to destroy harmony of spirit.

In a way, good may come even from unhappy events, as in the case of the deer in Arizona. For example, when energy under the earth's surface is distributed unevenly and gathers in one place, an earthquake occurs and restructures geological features and even the distribution of energy. I am not one to justify Japan in the Pacific

War. But I hesitate to say the Japanese people were all wrong and the countries of the Allied Powers represented by the United States were all correct. For instance, many Asian countries were until then colonized by European countries as you know. Vietnam was occupied by France, Indonesia by Holland, and Burma and the Malay Peninsula by England. In 1945 when the War was over each Asian country was liberated from colonization and became independent. I would like you to contemplate this fact carefully. Wasn't this a leveling off of uneven energy distribution by the cruel movement called war?

For world peace in the future, it is important for Japan and the United States, and of course for all countries, and not only politicians but also any kind of people, to consider how to keep balance in the world. In this sense, the fact that the income and outgo of Japanese trade with the United States has been in the black for Japan is truly a big problem between us.

Incidentally, a world map sold in Japan indicates the red-colored Japanese islands at the center; on the right, on the east side, is the United States, and England is at the west side. From the perspective of a Japanese world map the United States is the far east [with a laugh]. On a world map distributed in Australia and New Zealand the world is shown "upside-down" and these two countries are placed in the center, with Europe, Asia, and North America in the lower half. On the world map drawn on the floor in the airport of a city located on the way to Dayton, the United States was the center, China was the far east, and Japan the far west. From now on, we all should have world maps from all countries in addition to our own, in order to consider the balance of the world all the time, because the earth has a circular shape.

In conclusion, my wish for world peace is that we ask the Secretary of the Soviet Union and the President of this country to have regular discussions. In any aspect of the human world it is important that leaders have discussions and to establish relationships which are economically well-founded. Right now the Soviets cannot survive without grain from the United States. They should mutually enlarge this type of relationship.

I pray for the establishment of a strong relationship in this sense between this country and the Soviet Union. I believe this is the most important thing for world peace.

The Japanese people should also do our best as Japanese. Thank you very much.

Purification by waving the *haraigushi* during prayer at the
University of Dayton chapel. A small shrine for Amaterasu,
with an opened door, is on the altar. Photo by Willis Stoesz.

Offering a sacred branch (*tamagushi*). Photo by Willis Stoesz.

Professor Harold Wright interpreting the Chief Patriarch's
presentation. Photo by Willis Stoesz.

## World Peace: Shinto and Christianity
### Father Bertrand Buby

Today reminds us that we are joined by others of good will
who approach God in their own way and are just as concerned
about world peace as we are. Beyond what we can do as individuals, we are called to be interpersonal, international, and inter-
religious in order to bring about social peace, justice, and reconciliation.

Jesus inspires many of us through his "Sermon on the Mount," but it is especially the "Peace Churches"[10] who take Matthew 5:28-48 seriously:

> You have heard it said, 'An eye for an eye and a tooth for a tooth:' But I say to you, do not resist one who is evil.

> You have heard it said, 'You shall love your neighbor and hate your enemy.' But I say to you, love your enemies and pray for those who persecute you.

From such words of Jesus Christians are challenged to find ways to reconcile and bring about peace rather than being aggressively prepared to fight. As we see from this witness, more responses to any conflict are possible than either to fight or to capitulate.

The Sermon on the Mount is not an interior ethic nor an individual call. Jesus addresses all of his followers to bring about creative reconciliation and peace. They are to be happy and optimistic as peacemakers. "Blessed are the peacemakers." The admonition to "love your enemy" is directed to a group in relationship to other groups. Furthermore, all peoples are to be treated as our neighbors. There are no borders to our peacemaking ministry. The Sermon on the Mount calls us to think always in terms of reconciliation instead of redress.

In approaching this occasion and significant event, I was impressed with the wholesomeness and sensitivity of the Chief Patriarch in his correspondence with me. He had sent me an insightful book on *The Brilliant Life of Munetada Kurozumi*. In reading it I became more aware of the *peacefulness* and *hopefulness* that Shinto brings to the people of the world. As a Christian, I found myself at home with the reverence, joy, hope, and peace that permeate Shinto like the rays of the sun. What fascinated me was the first important word I learned in this religion: kami, referring to the sacred persons and places who, through having been here before, are still, after their death, persons alive. It's remarkably close to what I experience as the "communion of saints."

There is a great need for our world to share in the atmosphere of warmth and peace that Shinto has if we are to have a universal experience of peace. World peace depends on our being able to participate in an atmosphere of peace no matter where we are. There are kami in every religion who help us to search for, and be nourished in, meditation and prayer that brings inner peace and leads all who are of good will to effect world peace. I believe that Shinto brings the peaceful rays of the sun, the symbol of that country and its religion, to all of the countries of the world.

## The biblical concept of peace

As a Christian, I take my own notion of peace from the sacred revelation that God gives me in the Hebrew Scriptures and in the revelation of the New Testament which focuses on Jesus Christ. He is the Son of God who is called the Light of the World and who is the reflection of God's glory and the exact representation of God's being who sustains all things by the revelatory Word of God (Hebrews 1:3).

This peace or *shalom* in the Hebrew Scriptures is freely given as a gift of God as long as Israel — the People of God — chooses to obey the word of God. This word may be prophetic, challenging human shortcoming, or it may be the creating and sustaining promise of God. *Shalom* is found over 220 times in the Hebrew Scriptures. It is similar to the sun symbol in Shinto, in that it too is equated with bodily health and material prosperity while a more religious type of blessing, deliverance, and salvation is also portrayed by it. God's *shalom* is a universal and comprehensive word that appears in almost every book of the Torah, the Prophets, and the Writings. Just to show you how rich it is, fifteen words are used by a great Hebrew scholar to translate it (healthy, well, to be strong, to be complete, whole, sure, tranquil, cultivating peace, friendly, integrity, safety, salvation, peace, concord, friendship.)[11]

One can see how much of a challenge peace is. Each one of us can personalize aspects of its meaning, from the kiss of peace in our Eucharist to the friendly greeting we give to a student. Unlike in political language, peace is not just the absence of war but is a universal atmosphere of well-being and goodness extended to every person, community, and nation.

The word "peace" (*eirene*) occurs ninety-one times in the New Testament. Another remarkable fact is that it appears in every one of the 27 books of the Christian Scriptures. It is close in meaning to the rabbinic idea of greetings, well-being, salvation, and healing in Judaism. The inspired writers of the New Testament have transformed the original vernacular Greek word, merely meaning absence of war, to the Hebrew meaning of *shalom*. Its principal meaning is salvation in a deeper sense, so that it also designates our relationship to God, meaning our peace with God. *Eirene* is our entire eschatological salvation because it originates in the historical Christ-event and because Christ himself gives his peace as salvation for us. It is the state of final fulfillment of history, making fully present the normal state of the new creation in which we are restored as images of God. (cf. Hebrews 13:20; Romans 8:6-7, 16:2; Peter 3:14).

In the American Catholic Bishops Pastoral on Peace entitled *The Challenge of Peace*, paragraph 27 is the cornerstone of the biblical theology of peace. The latter part of it reads:

> For men and women of faith, peace will imply a right relationship with God, which entails forgiveness, reconciliation, and union. Finally, the Scriptures point to eschatological peace, a final, full realization of God's salvation when all creation will be made whole. Among these various meanings, the last two predominate in the Scriptures and provide direction to the other meanings of peace.[12]

The difficulty for anyone reading or interpreting the Scriptures is to live them out in the context of today's problems and possibilities. Paragraph 28 is the Bishops' statement of the method of interpretation needed to bring the message of the Scriptures to the *now* of today. The last sentence of that paragraph reads:

> Peace and war must always be seen in light of God's intervention in human affairs and our response to that intervention. Both are elements within the ongoing revelation of God's will for creation.[13]

The threat of nuclear war is the greatest obstacle that our world faces during the coming generation. Such a threat is real because of the fact and reality of Hiroshima. Since 1945 the weapons of nuclear war have so multiplied that many nations besides the superpowers possess them. Vatican Council II already in 1965 evaluated modern warfare with this statement:

> The whole human race faces a moment of supreme crisis in its advance towards maturity.[14]

I think all in this chapel would agree with that statement for we have seen and felt the effects of the crisis of the nuclear age in the lives of our people.

In the statement of the Bishops on peace we have been made aware that there is no satisfactory answer to the human problems of the nuclear age which fails to consider the moral and religious dimensions of the questions we face.

## Conclusion

The Christian is called to be like St. Francis of Assisi who in 1220 visited, dialogued, and dined with the Sultan of Islam and found him to be an intelligent, concerned person. Cardinal Pelagius wanted victory for the Church; Francis wanted peace. One was a Crusader; the other, a Christian.

Since World War II over 125 "small" wars have broken out in the Third World. Our task of establishing peace is monumental and difficult.

In order to prepare for world peace, nationalism must give way to universalism, which has always been an essential element of Christianity. The threat of nuclear war hangs over everyone today. We are "condemned" to unity, solidarity, neighborliness, whether we want it or not.

We can prepare for a world of peace for the future. We are like the Resurrected Jesus who is brilliant as the sun. Like Jesus we are to "shalomatize" the world.

In John 20:19-23 there are realities spoken of that can be present today: Jesus came and stood among his disciples and said to them *"Shalom lahem!"* Upon hearing this we are told the disciples had great joy. Jesus then said to them again, *"Shalom lahem!"* As the Father sent me so I send you."

We are all to be apostles of peace whether we are Shintoists, Muslims, Jewish, or Christian. May we have God's strength to "shalomatize" the world as the resurrected Jesus did.

# Part IV
# Conclusion

# 13

# Kurozumi-kyō in Western View

Willis Stoesz

We have seen that Kurozumi Shinto is part of a broad texture of Shinto in Japanese culture. As a sect it focuses Japanese religious concerns and themes in its own characteristic way. It both shapes the lives of ordinary people who are its members and wishes to make itself understood to a world audience. In presenting itself to this audience it invites our understanding. What is the inner attitude and way of thinking of Kurozumi Shinto, and in what sense is it a sect?

We may summarize our conclusions about Kurozumi Shinto under five headings. Here we draw on the Chief Patriarch's formal presentations, his informal presentation on the topic of peace, and on the other studies presented in this book. Immanentism, universality, pastoral intention, ritual focus, and the mediatorial role of the founder are issues that reward exploration. While these issues are phrased from within a western religious perspective and so presume a dialogical context of discussion, a more general descriptive category will be used in summarizing this conclusion. Partly we confirm familiar knowledge about Shinto, and partly we discern the distinctive character of this Japanese sect.

## Dialogical Context

### Immanentism

In Shinto view there is no transhistorical denouement for human actions as there is in Christian faith. Whereas in Christian faith the present is incomplete in comparison with the eschatological moments envisioned in scripture, celebrated in the Eucharist, and expected at the end of history, the Kurozumi founder's experience of unity with Amaterasu is a moment of fulfillment within present time and space. The ultimate reality of such an experience can be achieved in anyone's life; it needs only to be uncovered by purificatory practice and realized in one's immediate relationships with others.

Thus, peace is the harmony of all the parts of the cosmos-system with each other. It is a matter of keeping a balance of all with the all, as all the parts undergo the changes which time naturally brings. There is a natural alternation between opposites of all kinds, gauged by the *yin-yang* distinction. This is as true in the life of societies at the national and global levels as it is in the experience of the individual.

The way in which this balance can be maintained also takes its cues from within time and place, from Munetada's paradigmatic example. The way of sincerity illuminated by that example is the source of guidance for keeping all the factors of life — economic and material as well as social, emotional, and spiritual — in mutual supportiveness to (at peace with) one another.

It is in this perspective that The Reverend Kurozumi's comments about the Japanese emperor should be received. The emperor, he says, is one who only influences and does not direct the course of events, and his influence is small at the overt level.[1] As The Reverend Kurozumi also makes clear in his strong preference for the Yayoi period over the Jomon, those religious sensibilities that promote harmony rather than conflict should be recognized as typifying Japanese culture. That which makes for a harmonious way of relating within immediate moments is to be emphasized at all times. The kind of leadership role needed in order to maintain peace (one that for constitutional reasons is denied the emperor) is like a vigilant sea captain alert to natural alternations in the flow of events. Such a person because of his superior insight guides his ship among realities hidden to others that could disrupt or promote that harmony. No determinative vision of the goal of the voyage — no utopianism or messianism — is to be superimposed on decisions made in choosing a wise, harmonious style of proceeding through life. The emperor is presented as possessing the wisdom but not the power to lead in this way.

On the question of world peace The Reverend Kurozumi locates himself in Japanese society, however, in a way similar to how Father Buby locates himself in American society: on the side of those who would mitigate nationalistic egoism. Christian and Shinto, thus, are allies in a common cause even as their drastically different worldviews provide different perspectives for understanding the sources of peace.

## Universalism

We have shown the genesis of a universal attitude in the experience of Kurozumi Munetada. His ecstatic experience of the presence of Amaterasu, keyed as it was to an unbounded outer horizon, gave him flexibility about the inner form which any other experience could take. Other chapters broaden our view of the Neo-Confucian and Buddhist aspects of his thought-world, contributing to that universality. How do these particular sources of identity add up to a single point of view, such as might be disclosed to a partner in dialogical dialogue? Do not his roles as kami and as son of a Japanese family, so deeply distinctive to Japanese culture, mark him as ethnically particular rather than as universal? That a single point of view does emerge may be seen by a review of these elements in his experience. The perspective that emerges bears closer resemblance (in some respects) to a Christian outlook than one might expect from the general understanding of Shinto with which this present set of studies began.

Some of Munetada's basic worldview concepts derive from Neo-Confucianism. Especially important are the terms "Heaven" and "Heaven-and-Earth" which refer to the universal scene of human activity. Their original rootage in ancient Chinese culture established their unbounded horizon, with all existence to be under the purview of the emperor who was the mediating point in the comprehensive worldview known as Confucianism. The interaction of this worldview with subsequent Buddhist thinking confirmed its universal reference and made it more sophisticated. Especially, finding the presence of the macrocosm within each individual person as microcosm (*li* as principle; Japanese *ki*) was a decisive step toward a deepened Confucianism. Each person thus could find mediation with cosmic reality beyond himself/herself by drawing on personal subjective experience rather than referring only to the emperor. This Neo-Confucianism drew on Buddhist resources also in developing its own techniques of personal develment (including meditation), so as to bring out in the individual a macrocosmic horizon of awareness. The Confucian quest for sincerity became in Neo-Confucian hands a rich and varied search for self-fulfillment which could transcend immediate social horizons as it took its own basic worldview concepts seriously.

In Munetada's experience this kind of personal development took place in a way that was facilitated by the Ise cult devoted to Amaterasu and mobilized by his vow to become a living kami.

The Ise pilgrimage cult played a central role in Munetada's piety. He went to Ise six times, and throughout his career lectured on topics growing out of the cult of Amaterasu centered there. The first of his pilgrimages took place before his transformative experience of 1814; after retiring from priesthood in 1843 and devoting himself to full-time leadership of his group he began a series of lectures on Ise, based in his mature understanding of Amaterasu, that continued for seven years until his death.[2] The topic was much in the public eye at the time with the popularity of the Ise pilgrimage phenomenon, as Winston Davis has described.[3] Most significantly for Munetada, however, the practice of *nippai* was the central means of cultivation of inner spirit in his mature religious practice, in seeking union with Amaterasu by way of the sun as symbolic focus. When fully cultivated, the inner spirit displays sincerity (*makoto*) in that Amaterasu's presence is fully transparent in each moment. Gratitude to her means a constant wish to live harmoniously with all who live under the sun and under heaven.

It is important that after the founder's experience of union with Amaterasu in 1814 the side of Ise that emphasizes her as imperial ancestress has been largely ignored in Kurozumi practice. Amaterasu's character in Kurozumi piety also does not derive much from the stories about her in the *Kojiki*. The story of her combat with her brother Susanō-o does not seem to figure at all. It is more that Amaterasu is construed after the warm "heart of a Japanese parent," nourishing her dependents as rice nourishes life, rather than after such mythical sources. Fundamental also is the identification of Amaterasu with omnipresent Heaven and Heaven-and-Earth. In this way Neo-Confucian universal reference and ethical teaching, related to this fundamental terminology, are provided emotional force from the daily devotional cultus growing from the Ise tradition.

Munetada's vow to become a living kami, marking the distinctive turn in his development toward becoming the founder of

Kurozumi-kyō, displays both Shinto and Buddhist characteristics. According to the *Kyōsoden*, he was motivated in making his vow both by filial piety and by

> "... the disasters and suffering he saw around him. He felt deeply that this was the only way to offer a path of salvation to people who were suffering hardships around him."[4]

The strong compassion he felt for people suffering in the critical social and economic conditions of his day is a strain of feeling connecting with the Buddhist dimension of Japanese culture; his vow mobilized his intention to act in a way directed toward bringing aid to other people. Although the Confucian "mandate of heaven" surely lies in the background of Munetada's feeling for other people, his own vow-action, drawing on a bodhisattva model, is the central constituting factor of his attitude. The vow mobilized and gave shape to his basic sensitivities. Moreover, his intention in the vow, transformed as it was in the course of his experience, remains a central feature in Kurozumi-kyō appreciation of its founder. In classic Buddhist fashion, that intention was rooted in concern for suffering and directed toward giving universal aid. As the broad and general forces of economic and social change quickened the movement of people in late Edo society and raised their level of stress, the religious sensitivities of Munetada were attuned to the needs he perceived in them. The Kurozumi sense of mission to people outside the immediate social framework of family and parish (*uji*) is based in Buddhist themes and forms of expression.

Not only was his religious feeling given direction by his vow, but he also understood his experience of union with Amaterasu in terms of the familiar Buddhist teaching of nonduality. That experience enabled him to draw a distinction between form and spirit, with form (*sugata, katachi*) becoming both necessary and flexibly chosen. *Ikidōshi* ("eternal" or "abiding" life), results in not being preoccupied by outcomes of actions or by the external forms of things, but in enjoying those actions and forms by virtue of seeing their source in Amaterasu. This means an open-hearted release of compassion toward all kinds and levels of people. Though there is a quality of playfulness about Munetada, his fundamental ethical seriousness is always apparent.

The Buddhist aspect of his worldview thus provided him both flexibility in relation to received society and, impelled by his vow, impulse to move toward those he perceived to be in need without prior regard for their status in society. A universalizing direction of development, set in motion by his vow, was confirmed by his experience of Amaterasu within. His freedom from self-regard, rationalized by the concept of non-duality, enabled him to be open to others without needing first to insist upon the favor/return-of-favor moral framework of Japanese society.[5]

The Shinto side of Kurozumi thinking also must be examined in assessing the move toward universality. Here it is important to note the sort of kami Munetada aspired to be. He wished to be of benefit to all around him who might be in need, a living (*ikigami*) healing kami (*reijin*). The benefit deriving from him would not be available only to the members of a particular family or clan as would be the case with a kami (*ujikami*) honored only as a family ancestor, or to people relating to a particular parish or place. Thus, the kami cult centered on Munetada and responding to his vow could involve anyone, not only members of the Kurozumi family; and the social group nurtured by his worship could draw from wide-ranging societal sources. From the beginning of its history the Kurozumi religious movement included a notable good-news-spreading activity, showing up even in the way the wider organization of Kurozumi-kyō was set up by the leading disciples.

Fundamentally, of course, the universality of Kurozumi-kyō is based on the union of its founder with Amaterasu as universal Kami. Vow and ecstatic union are the two poles of his religious experience known as the Direct Acceptance of Divine Mission establishing Amaterasu as the impelling energy leading to sincere and compassionate action. Though filial piety and concepts of obligation (focusing religious concern within the specific social group) remain virtues at one level for Kurozumi-kyō, at the basic level of worldview-grasp Amaterasu transcends those values. Her presence as macrocosm within the microcosm — as it is put in Kurozumi terms, as "separated portion" (*bunshin*) within each spirit (*kokoro*) — occurs within everyone. Though myths of world-origin are part of the Shinto story, it is the power to generate sincerity, harmony, and well-being within everyone that displays the true creativity of Amaterasu.

On the one hand, the Kurozumi-kyō institutional matrix of its kami cult bears close resemblance to the kami cult practiced everywhere in Japan. In rituals, vestments, and shrine furnishings

Kurozumi-kyō is easily recognized as Shinto. In the main shrine at Shintozan are worshiped, along with Amaterasu and Munetada, the same myriads of kami (*yao-yorozu-no-kami*) worshiped everywhere else in Japan. These kami consist of all who in the past have been raised to kami status in Japan. To that company go those who after death are appropriately purified in Kurozumi-kyō ritual by their descendants. The Shinto idiom in which Munetada's religion is phrased, providing ritual access to divine power, is not only an idiom; as he lives his viewpoint it is a central medium of his message.

On the other hand, the distinctive character of this Kami is strongly emphasized. Stories (*engi*) about Munetada and repetitions of his poetry keep his personal character and presence alive in Kurozumi-kyō life. His worldview, with its Neo-Confucian and Buddhist constituent elements held in focus by devotion to Amaterasu, continues to animate the thinking of members of the group.

In sum, we can see the flexibility and sophistication — the strength of individual presence — with which a Kurozumi spokesperson can interact with others. That viewpoint possesses true universality, framed in the East Asian concepts of sincerity and harmony, in its ability to reach toward unbounded horizons of relationship. We remember that Kurozumi-kyō took its shape before the Meiji-era attempt was made to separate a national Shinto from the other aspects of this "seamless web."[6] In Munetada's religion we have an instance of an older and culturally richer Shinto than resulted from the experiment with State Shinto ending in 1945. Yet it is not only that web of concepts and attitudes that produces this universality, but Munetada's personal example that makes it a living attitude.

## Pastoral intention

Kurozumi concern to help people with their personal problems is shown in a number of ways. Pastoral guidance is a prominent feature of Kurozumi-kyō parish life.

Two points deserve mention in this connection. As Swanger has indicated, the use of *omamori* must be understood as an expression of Kurozumi religious teaching and not dismissed as superstition. The proper attitude of those using them is crucial to their proper use; and an underlying intent behind that use is transformation of inner attitude in those who receive them. While the proximate concerns of those who ask for *omamori* are not to go without satisfaction, ideally their horizon of aspiration should not remain at that level only but be broadened into a more encompassing sensitivity. This is a point Hepner overlooked in his criticism two generations ago. *Omamori* need not belong only to the realm of folk religion, at least not if the pastoral intention of Kurozumi leaders is understood. However, the point may be put more finely.

Thus, secondly, Kurozumi pastoral intent takes account of two levels of spiritual understanding. The Chief Patriarch contrasts a dependent spirituality (*tariki*), reliant on the authority of a priest, with a spirituality cultivated by one's own efforts (*jiriki*) and leading to a spirit that is as broad as the morning sun. He hopes, he says, that the latter will become increasingly common (see chapter 5). The presence of both levels within Kurozumi-kyō spirituality is recognized.

The lower of the two comprises the broad scene of Japanese interrelational attitudes as promoted under Kurozumi auspices. We see in the examples the Chief Patriarch cites, and in those cited by Hardacre, the warm, harmonious quality of life within the Japanese family or small group. Health and well-being are cultivated, using not only *omamori* but a wide variety of pastoral means such as healing sips of water, the practice of healing by touch, and such efforts at discussion as will bring about the desired results. Here the usual "core value" ideas of moral obligation hold and provide structure for interaction, as Hardacre has observed.[7] This-worldly benefits are anticipated by the one who follows the way of Munetada, at this level of Kurozumi religion.

Yet, as we have seen, that way finds its inspiration not only as self-cultivation but also as selflessness; and the expectation of benefit (including an obligation to return it) may be contrasted to Munetada's own example of nonchalance about personal benefit. The full power of Amaterasu's virtue becomes apparent to one who has attained the same non-dual character of experience as he did. In that form of experience, awareness of ensuing benefit is not lost, but such benefit is relativized in favor of the joy which one may know in the fullness of Amaterasu's presence within. The experience is valued for its own sake, not for the sake of specific consequences. The pastoral means ("skillfully" chosen, perhaps) that are employed to bring it about have value in leading to that result, and not for their own sake or only for proximate consequences. The joy that results, displayed in Munetada's poetry, is presented as a possibility for everyone. Those who have attained it are said to have attained the "heart of heaven".[8]

Thus, one may discern in The Chief Patriarch's pastoral guidance (especially in chapter 4) not only his concern that the satisfactions of harmonious relationship be available to all, but also that each person may experience the true sources of that generosity of spirit which makes those relationships possible. The prior presence of Amaterasu within is a principle of insight for Kuorzumi-kyō, by which the Chief Patriarch seeks to guide the religious life of its members. In pointing them toward the experience of *ikidōshi*, in urging them to remove self-concern (*ga*) so as to become kami who are one with Amaterasu, and in constantly pointing to the founder as example, he holds that higher goal before them while at the immediate level focussing attention on strengthing the interactive social framework of their lives.

## Ritual focus

The symbolic-ritual structure of Kurozumi religion centers in the practice of *nippai*. The worship of Amaterasu in this ritual functions as a sacrament, as the center of the experience of enabling power which within its worldview definitively serves to energize all aspects of life.

Its two main elements are the *Ōharai* prayer and the practice of *yoki*. Reciting *Ōharai* before sunrise serves to purify the inner spirit; the power of the words themselves of the ancient prayer (apart from their specific meaning) results in the removal of those impurities that have clouded and hemmed in the inner spirit (*bunshin*).

Once purified, the person is ready to welcome the rising sun. Being able actually to see the sun coming over the unbroken circle of the horizon reinforces the symbolism. Though the meaning of the ritual action remains the same if practiced under a cloudy sky or indoors, or even if it is done at another time of day, a richer experience results from timing one's intake of air to conincide with the very first rays of the sun coming over the horizon. An actual instance of harmony with nature is thus enacted, moving on the moment of the sun's first appearing. Coinciding with this experience is the perception of the whole circle of heaven-and-earth; the horizon visible to the eye, with the sun's first light just appearing, marks the unbounded ("circular") field of Amaterasu's presence. It is an instance of *ikidōshi*, of the microcosm experiencing union with the macrocosm, both as perceived directly by the senses and as moment of spiritual fulfillment.

To know Amaterasu aright thus involves one's whole self. This knowledge is attained in symbolic action in the ingestion of air at the moment of sunrise. As Hepner reports[9] the light of the sun and its warmth are understood to enter the body with the air taken in; yet Amaterasu is not identical to the sun but the sun is only the visible manifestation of her presence and power within. It is she herself that is received, and the air, light, and warmth are only the outward and sense-perceivable manifestations of her invisible power within.

Part of the action of *nippai* is the inner performance of an intention to greet Amaterasu. The Chief Patriarch urges Kurozumi-kyō members to "throw themselves" toward her as a child does in greeting its mother. That he uses this metaphor from ordinary experience, replete with dualistic implication, reflects ordinary pastoral strategy; the ritual may be relied upon fully, focused as it is on Amaterasu by way of Munetada. As Munetada's vow was confirmed and transformed in his chartering union with Amaterasu, so the Kurozumi-kyō worshiper may turn toward her and replicate in *nippai*, even if incompletely, that same pattern of experience. The heights of non-dualistic experience of Amaterasu loom in the person of Munetada Kami, whose complete unity with her represents the ideal experience which even the current Chief Patriarch attains in lesser degree.

## Munetada Kami as mediator

Finally, let us consider Munetada's mediatorial role. He is in fact regarded in Kurozumi piety as one who enables people to realize a proper relationship to Amaterasu the supreme deity, and to find ultimate fulfillment of their lives.

First, he is the one who has gone on before. He exemplifies the way others should live and show them how to do it. The role of supernatural guide through the difficulties of life is a familiar one in Japanese folklore. Figures such as Kobo Daishi, founder of Shingon Buddhism, and Jizo, the familiar roadside bodhisattva, are leading examples of this role. Here, in contrast to many such stories as they appear in folk religion, the role of guide is explicitly tied to a well-developed ethical teaching and to a universally-relevant worldview. The help that is given integrates the supplicant with family and community life through all the vicissitudes of that life. Specifically, he is the one (*sebumi*) who guides his followers across the stream of life to the "other shore" of union with Amaterasu.

The Buddhist "stream-crossing" metaphor is familiar in Japanese culture. The way of life taught by Munetada is well understood to be safe guidance to an ultimate, all-embracing goal.

He is not only guide but inner watcher. In a story told by the Chief Patriarch (see chapter 4) the woman who wished to be reconciled to her daughter-in-law felt that her sincerity was understood at first only by Munetada Kami, but that was enough to sustain her until full, explicit harmony with her daughter-in-law was attained. Inner awareness of the compassionate Munetada represents an interiorized kami-cult, as Miller has shown (see chapter 8). In this role Munetada Kami enables his devotees to attain sincerity and harmony beyond the limits of ordinary daily consciousness; their trust in his presence enables a deepened spirituality and a more confident base for interaction with others.

Further, Munetada is an enabler of health and well-being. In life he was a healer of disease and ailments, although it is important to bear in mind The Reverend Muneharu Kurozumi's point, that Munetada wished to be first a healer of the inner spirit, enabling removal of that self-concern that disrupts balanced, harmonious life. Fundamentally, each person's highest well-being derives from the inner presence of Amaterasu; Munetada's most important healing efforts were such as to enable the inner curative powers deriving from her to have their full effect. Yet, the various means Munetada used to bring that home to people established him in his own times as a mediator of Amaterasu. This aspect of his activity is still observed in the healing sips of water served where his presence as Kami is invoked (such as at his altar at the main shrine in Okayama) and in the distribution of *omamori*.

Mediation (*toritsugi*) of Amaterasu's presence in immediate social interaction is a responsibility of the Chief Patriarch, as well as of the priesthood of Kurozumi-kyō. It is significant that a hierarchy of mediative power is to be observed: The Reverend Kurozumi tells his people that it is important that he maintain a deeper relationship to Amaterasu than those he wishes to help. To attempt mediation without that deeper relationship is as self-defeating as trying to throw buckets of water upstairs. Mediation thus depends on the superior quality of persons in relation to each other rather than only on the power of mediative ritual. Munetada is the apex of the mediatorial hierarchy and continues to be available to any who call on him directly.

Ultimately, the way of Munetada is Amaterasu's Way. The founder of Kurozumi-kyō is the absolutely reliable guide to that Way since his union with her was so complete. The experience of receiving the Divine Mission in union with her gives him that status. In Kurozumi-kyō terms, anyone may enter that Way, since its sphere of reference extends to all mankind; his religion is the religion of humanity. It is not clear on present evidence how Kurozumi-kyō would explain the status of founders of other religions, although we mark a tolerant attitude accepting global pluralism in the Chief Patriarch's words. What is clear is that Munetada's mediation of Amaterasu's presence is intended to prepare those who follow that way to relate affirmatively and harmoniously with all others on a universal basis. He provides a personal point of contact for followers of his way which remains definitive for them until they gain their own full participation in Heaven's Way at the conclusion of the Kurozumi path.

In sum, when viewed in the context of dialogical self-disclosure, we see both a rich heritage of worldview concepts informing the thinking of Kurozumi Shinto and a universal attitude displayed in spite of the distinctive culture out of which Kurozumi religion comes. The impulse to universal mission generated in Kurozumi piety and articulated in terms of its own worldview strikes a responsive chord for Christians accustomed to ideas of apostleship and mission and of compassionate service to others. That Kurozumi-kyō differs from mainstream, conventional Shinto in these emphases, and that it is not one of the numerically dominant denominations of Japanese religion, do not alter that point.

## Dialogical Context: Summary

In this summary of Kurozumi-kyō we have considered its features in terms of issues that arise within a western and Christian point of view. The five categories examined are aspects of Kurozumi Shinto which a Christian dialogue partner — or simply someone whose ideas about religion come from acquaintance with Christian tradition and who seeks to know Shinto better — can use as basis of a search for understanding. Having met a person whose life is shaped by this Shinto tradition, who is he or she in full? It is reasonable to seek deeper understanding by asking questions that place the unfamiliar in context of the familiar in this way.

Having done so, a first reaction is that this examination produced useful information. Comparable characteristics emerge.

Setting aside for the moment its many characteristic Japanese features, we see that Kurozumi Shinto is a religion focusing on a deity who enables a universal point of view and way of thinking. Peace and harmony are emphasized and the religious-ethical life is cultivated. There is a ritual focus which can properly be called sacramental, and the founder continues to be relied on as a mediator between human and deity.

A second reaction soon carries one beyond such points of preliminary recognition of similarity. The pronounced immanental standpoint and absence of a transhistorical dimension are strong indications that a Christian-based examination will by itself provide less than complete understanding. The pronounced forward look in time which is part of Christian mass or eucharist is not visible in *nippai*. Absence of familiar Christian emphases on sin and guilt, on the shriving of the individual from such sins, and on a mediator who is co-equal with ultimate deity also indicate that if understanding is to be attained, further consideration is needed. The full reality does not become clear in response to strictly Christian interrogative categories, in spite of the useful comparisons that emerge from this procedure.

One way to move toward further understanding would be to continue the dialogical approach as phrased here through the medium of the scholar as go-between, and, with the help of a list of points familiar on the Kurozumi Shinto side of dialogue, make a responsive kind of examination. What points about the Christian dialogue partner's religion would be reasonable ones for a Japanese seeker of understanding to inquire about, who would from his or her side proceed from the familiar to the unfamiliar? However, we are not at the point of doing this; here a more limited procedure, using the scholar's go-between point of view as a device to introduce Kurozumi Shinto to a western audience, has been employed. Actual dialogue, however desirable that would be, must await further meetings of Shinto and Christian.

Another way to move toward understanding is to review how Kurozumi Shinto appears from a historical and descriptive point of view. Here too the present state of our information allows less than a full-scale exposition. However, there is a convenient way to take a step in this direction, enough to put the observations emerging within a dialogical context in broader perspective and to bring the present study to a conclusion.

## Comparative Context

We may do this by asking about the sectarian character of Kurozumi-kyō. The term "sect" (*kyōha*) has long been applied to the group, but is it a sect as that concept is understood in western scholarship? In sketching an answer we employ a general category that helps us see Kurozumi-kyō in broad comparative perspective. We will see that it shows some characteristics associated with sectarianism as understood in the west, but it does so in a distinctively Japanese manner.[10]

A first observation is that Kurozumi-kyō appears as a devotional cult. In emphasizing *nippai* it makes central to itself a practice that is otherwise generally available in popular religion. However, in adding to *nippai* the act of ingestion of air it does something that may seem strange to those who are not members; and in investing *nippai* with its own framework of meanings it gives a distinctive and more extended interpretation of this practice than is ordinarily given it in popular religion. Doing *yōki* thus becomes an emblem of participation in Kurozumi-kyō as well the group's central occasion of symbolic interaction with its ultimate reality. *Nippai* is a distinctive ritual nucleus setting the group apart from other forms of Japanese religion.

Kurozumi-kyō also appears sectarian in that membership is elective, at least in principle, and not simply natural. While most if not all its members are born into Kurozumi-kyō families, each must promise by personal letter of intent (*shinmon*) to follow the way of Munetada. Progress toward an elite level of experience depends on devotedness in personal practice.[11] A system of degrees of spiritual advancement is recognized by which the organization has expressed its character ideal. Those who achieve the Way of Heaven completely may display the same complete joy and steadiness of character the founder exemplified.

This distinctive ideal is, as we have seen, definitively embodied in the memory of its founder. Since Kurozumi Munetada set forth a distinctive reformulation of Japanese religion based on his own ecstatic experience he deserves to be acknowledged as a founder and not simply as one who selectively emphasized some aspect of the common tradition.[12] He was more than a sage. As one who paradigmatically experienced union with Amaterasu he gave a fresh formulation of Amaterasu's way for others. Kurozumi-kyō has its own store of inspired insight and example on which to base its guidance of personal character development toward a transcendent ideal.

Thus, in relying on its founder, in institutionalizing the process of development toward elite spiritual status, and in using a distinctive cultus, Kurozumi-kyō may be described as a sect as that term is generally understood.

In other ways Kurozumi-kyō does not correspond to characteristics of sectarianism as conceived in western scholarship. For instance, in seeking better behavior in its ordinary members it does not concern itself primarily with a rigorously correct set of beliefs or behaviors. Preconceived models of correct behavior or belief are less important than the achievement of fully harmonious relationships. In seeking solutions to problems, attention is paid to "making use of" the immediate details of familial or group life to bring about the desired harmony. Western models of sectarian radical perfectionism — sometimes utopian in character — do not apply in this Japanese context. Although an elite level of personal experience is held as an ideal, Kurozumi practice relies on the "skillful means" tradition (the Buddhist concept of *upaya*) in accepting lower levels of attainment for the relative good they represent. Those who do not measure up to the ideal are by no means mustered out. Kurozumi-kyō is not phrased dialectically or oppositionally as many western sects are, but comprehensively, in catholic fashion.[13]

This attitude, emphasizing acceptance and compassion toward those of lower levels of attainment rather than setting exclusionary high standards of action or belief, extends also to people outside the group. Its attitude is that all should be sharers of the goodness of Amaterasu; indeed, it draws on the concept, well understood by its leaders, that all human beings are part of her universal circle. All are already sharers of her universal goodness and need only become aware of this truth in order to make good on their own inner potential. From the beginning Kurozumi-kyō was concerned for the wider society.

In this connection the subordinate role of ancestors must be appreciated. On the one hand, ancestors supply a momentum of character and identity that carries living people forward through their lives. Tendencies toward good fortune must be traced to their continuing influence. Those who after death become kami, as all should, join the myriads of kami of the Japanese people. Such assumptions are fundamental in Japanese culture. On the other hand, Amaterasu provides, at an ultimate but attainable level, a power and sanction that supersede the power and sanction of family and household (*uchi, ie*). Her presence sets an implicit universal horizon of social interaction (which may become explicit) transcending the horizon set by family and country. Even the myriads of kami find their home in her. The inner development of Kurozumi Munetada, rooted in her, traces a spiritual grammar which guides Kurozumi-kyō's articulation of its goals toward such universal perspective. That many of its members have not attained this level of expression of their religion, in spite of the emotional power of the *nippai* cultus which includes that as part of its horizon of aspiration, does not negate its presence as an ideal for all.

In this aspect of its attitude toward ancestors Kurozumi-kyō is set apart from Japanese religion generally as a sect might be set apart. Yet, from the beginning it has had the renewal of society as a whole as its goal. Its purpose was never merely to perfect the few but rather to renew the world as a whole. Its universalizing thrust thus had the paradoxical effect of supporting its sectarian character within Japanese society, however much that thrust was blocked or blunted during the rise of State Shinto and until 1945.

## Conclusion

The character of Munetada is the direct source of self-understanding and self-definition for Kurozumi-kyō. Its memory of him is of one who both fulfilled and transcended accepted moral conventions in exercise of his compassionate vow. In abstract description he appears to us as an instance of syncretistic reintegration of diverse cultural materials; in his living presence as perceived in Kurozumi faith he is a powerful figure who understands in deep detail how life appears as viewed from within the worldview to which Japanese people continue to be heir. In affirming the values of that worldview Munetada Kami is thus for members of Kurozumi-kyō a powerful guide to ultimate sources of goodness, enabling Shinto to be a living, vital tradition. In presenting an example of transcension of those values he also opens to them the possibility of relating to others without having to insist on replication in those others of that same pattern.

The sect which stems from him carries forward the same potential. An outward-facing attitude is typical of many other of the post-World War II "new religions" of Japan. However, we see that the universal attitude of Kurozumi-kyō, informing the manner in which its representatives come into contact with people of other cultures, derives from the inner resources of its own tradition. The inner dynamic of Kurozumi-kyō is both deeply Japanese and deeply universal.

# Appendixes

# Appendix I

## *Michi no Kotowari*
### *["Concerning the Way"]*

The origin of all living things in Heaven or on earth is Amaterasu
Ōmikami. She is the parent deity of all beings, and her bright, shining essence pervades Heaven and Earth. All living things without
exception are nurtured in her light and warmth, ceaselessly. Truly,
this is a great blessing. The warmth in our bodies is the heart which
we receive from the Kami of the Sun. When we abandon selfish
desire and become upright in honesty, then our hearts become one
with the heart of the Kami of the Sun.

The heart is the master and the body the servant. When we are
enlightened, the heart commands the body; but when we are con-
fused, the body commands the heart. Forget the body and entrust
everything to the Kami of the Sun, every day. Make your heart
one which savors every sight and sound, joyous and grateful day
and night.

Breathe in the sun's vital essence and store it in your lower
abdomen. Cultivate your essence as do Heaven and Earth, with
pleasure and joyously, so that no dullness remains in your heart.
When the heart is vital, so is the whole human being. To live thus is
the way of the great deity. Joy is the heart of the great deity.

The teaching has come down from Heaven, and the Way is
manifest in Heaven and in nature. Never depart from sincerity. Entrust everything to Heaven. Abandon selfish desire. Manifest the
vital essence of the sun. Grasp vitality firmly. The heart of the an-
cients had no form, and neither does ours today.

When we dwell in the heart and forget the body, now is the
age of kami, the age of kami is today, and this moment is the age of
kami. Everything in life depends entirely upon the heart. When the
heart becomes one with Kami, then we become one with Kami.

*[Translated by Helen Hardacre]*

# Appendix II
# Establishing Peace

The Reverend Muneharu Kurozumi
Chief Patriarch, Kurozumi-kyō

*[This is a presentation given by the Reverend Muneharu Kurozumi on August 4, 1987. The occasion was a "Religious Summit Meeting on Mt. Hiei," for the purpose of "Prayer for World Peace." The sponsoring group was the Japan Conference of Religious Representatives, a committee of the Japan Federation of Religion. This Federation includes the Japan Buddhist Federation, the Sectarian Shinto Federation, the Christian Church of Japan Federation, the United Association of Shinto Shrines and the Union of New Religious Organizations of Japan. The occasion was intended to carry forward the spirit of the "Day of Prayer for Peace" by world religious leaders held in Assisi, Italy at the invitation of Pope John Paul II in October, 1986. The site of the 1987 meeting was the Enryaku-ji on Mt. Hiei northeast of Kyoto, chosen in recognition of the 1200th anniversary of the founding by Saichō of that temple so important in Japanese history. A number of Japanese religious leaders spoke and offered prayer.]*

I am much honored and privileged to have this opportunity to present my views on World Peace at this auspicious Religious Summit Meeting.

First, I would like to offer our gratitude to our own Holy God Almighty to whom we owe our very existence, and also our sincere reverence to the Holy Priest Saichō who founded the Tendai-shu headquarters monastery of Enryaku-ji on Mt. Hiei. The fact that Enryaku-ji is hosting the Religious Summit on its 1,200th anniversary makes the meeting very meaningful.

As one of the religious leaders of Japan, I fully realize that in order to establish peace between countries and people we need to give up the common belief that one side is always right and the others are wrong. There is no person or country that is superior to others or that has more rights. Just as there is no individual and no life of absolute perfection, there is not an indefectible country nor is there a country with a faultless history.

On the one hand, to have people hold pride in their country and culture may be necessary for governing and uniting the country and for maintaining their identity. A self-respecting nationalism, however, can easily lead people to hold the narrow view that their country is the best one and the only one that is right. This would eventually and unfortunately bring self-destruction to the people and to their country as well as hurt others. Of course, everyone has the right to take pride in their own country but one must be constantly aware that others have the same right to be proud of their country and cultural background.

This thought, that one country is the only one that is right and the others are wrong, and that it has the right to correct others, is the very cause of the misstep that leads to the disturbance of peace.

Once I had the opportunity to discuss religion with a Muslim friend of mine. Through his explanation I came to know that the word *Islam* essentially means "peace." My friend told me of a passage in the Holy Qur'an, "Unto you your religion, and unto me my religion" (CIX, the Disbelievers, 6). This doubtlessly teaches us the importance of showing our sincere respect to others' being, along with a mutual and profound recognition of the differences between ourselves and others.

A friendship based on this kind of recognition of differences, and on a constant search for things we share in common, binds and ties us together. Eventually it establishes a friendly peace among individuals as well as between countries.

From ancient days and through the centuries Shinto followers have used round polished metal mirrors as their divine object of worship. The Mirror, of course, symbolizes the Sun, the very source of all creatures and of existence and the embodiment of our Almighty God. In addition, since a mirror reflects a worshiper back to himself or herself, when one is worshiping God one is also at the same time worshiping or praying to one's self. This brings out the fact that we are all sacred beings, because in our hearts or souls abides God. In other words, to prostrate oneself at a shrine or before God will have the additional meaning that one is praying to the inner god, the sacred deity who resides within our hearts and souls.

According to Buddhism, a temple is dedicated in order to enshrine Buddha. What I learned from a Buddhist is that the gentle, amiable, and peaceful countenance of Buddha is understood to manifest and reflect the heart that is ideal in the view of Buddhism. We may say that this demonstrates the fact that Buddha resides in every heart and soul. This is why we can be enlightened through the inner Buddha on worshiping the outer Buddha.

This is what a Christian taught me. Needless to say, the Christian Cross is where Jesus Christ was crucified; moreover it is said that the Cross manifests self-sacrifice and love, the underlying teachings of Christianity. While the crosspiece severs our ego, the vertical piece symbolizes the love extending from Heaven to Earth. The Cross teaches us self-sacrifice and the love that binds us to Heaven.

The Mirror, the Buddha, and the Cross, regardless of the religion they come from, each lead us in our efforts to establish peace, the sacred goal of mankind.

Nevertheless, the endeavor to give up the thought that one is superior to others, to extend love, mercy, and benevolence to others, and to live with sincerity, all helps glorify Allah, God, and Buddha residing within us. We may say that Mercy is Buddha, Love is Allah and the Christian God, and Sincerity is the Shinto God.

Fortunately, we religious people understand the virtue of prayer. Praying for the well-being of all people on earth is a daily observance for all of us. Although each prayer by itself may not be of much help, praying together as we are today, along with our own separate consistent and daily prayers, surely will purify the world and ever glorify our inner Buddha, God, and Allah. I do hope that our daily prayers will ever purify our hearts and enlighten us and that we religious people will on our own initiative set vivid examples of dedication for others to follow. This will spread love, mercy, and sincerity to others. May we religious people all combine our resources and efforts in realizing the divine mission equally entrusted to us by Allah, Buddha, and God: the prevalence of Peace on Earth.

I want to take advantage of this opportunity to propose that we all hang in our offices different world maps published in different parts of the world. This would be a step toward understanding the pride everyone feels in their own culture and toward accepting differences in world cultures. It may sound strange, but looking at a world globe would not help much. In some world maps distributed in Australia and New Zealand the world is shown upside-down and the two countries are placed in the center, with Europe, Asia, and North America in the lower half. On world maps available in Europe, Japan is located in the far east, whereas on those sold in this country Japan stands out in the center in brilliant red. In this case the United States is in the far east and the United Kingdom is in the far west. Just gazing at different world maps all at one time has the effect of reminding us that no person or country is superior to others.

Before closing, I would like to introduce to you a poem by the Founder of Kurozumi-kyō Shinto, the Reverend Munetada Kurozumi. It might be more meaningful if I add that the poem was composed in the Edo era when Japan was closed to the outside world.

> True Sincerity
> > is the one thing we should
> > > cherish above all;
> With Sincerity alone
> > the Earth can be a Family.

[*Translated at Kurozumi-kyō headquarters and edited by Willis Stoesz.*]

# Notes and References

## Preface

1. *Kyō* means "teaching" and, by extension, a sect or denomination. In this case, it refers to those who follow the teaching of Kurozumi Munetada.

2. Kami is a term that eludes precise definition in any language. It refers to the powers or presences that are objects of awe and worship in Japanese culture, and that generate harmony, purity, material well-being, and willingness to act in the group interest. See chapters 5 and 8; and Sokyo Ono, *Shinto; The Kami Way* (Rutland, Vt.: Charles E. Tuttle Company, 1962).

I will leave "kami" unitalicized in the belief that it has become a familiar term in English along with such other words as "samurai" and "Zen." It will be capitalized when an individual Kami such as Amaterasu or Munetada is being referred to. Similarly, the terms "founder" and "emperor" will be capitalized when used as a term of respect from within Kurozumi faith. Also, Japanese order of names (e.g., "Kurozumi Muneharu") will be observed unless used as part of English phraseology (e.g., "The Reverend Muneharu Kurozumi").

3. The most recent study is by Helen Hardacre, *Kurozumikyō and the New Religions of Japan* (Princeton: Princeton University Press, 1986). Much of the information in the following paragraphs is drawn from this source and from Professor Hardacre's conference presentation. Other sources in English are Charles W. Hepner, *The Kurozumi Sect of Shinto* (Tokyo: Meiji Japan Society, 1935) and Taisen Nobuhara, *The Brilliant Life of Munetada Kurozumi*, trans. Tsukasa Sakai and Kazuko Sasage (Tokyo: PMC Publications, 1980). Hepner's work is objective enough that its Christian categories of interpretation do not obscure the valuable information he presents. Nobuhara's work provides no scholarly apparatus, but is thorough enough to allow us to be engaged in the inner intention of the Kurozumi tradition. There is a body of scholarly work on Kurozumi-kyō in Japanese, as Professor Hardacre's chapter shows. See also the convenient summary of the history of this ancient area (known as Kibi) given by Richard Beardsley *et al.*, *Village Japan* (Chicago: University of Chicago Press, 1959).

4. See Hardacre, *Kurozumikyō and the New Religions of Japan*, p. 104 for justification of the use of the term *church* to refer to the local groups (*kyōkai*) of Kurozumi-kyō members.

5. A word about translation should be added. In each case these chapters were given initial translation by Japanese students attending Earlham College, kindly introduced to me by Professor Jackson Bailey of that institution. I turned the resulting rough English into smoother-reading prose. Lists of basic terms in English and of usages which seemed awkward were sent to Kurozumi headquarters. In return, lists of the corresponding original terms were furnished me in *kana* and in *kanji* characters, so that numerous clarifications became possible. I also secured

the help of others, both American scholars and Japanese exchange professors at Wright State, in clarifying particular expressions. Finally, the draft translation of each chapter was sent to the Reverend Muneharu Kurozumi for his approval. Comments from him resulted in still further clarifications. The result is that we have texts of his chapters which say in English what he, the author, wanted to have said. For any misunderstandings and errors on my part I assume full responsibility.

6. Many of the *dōka* are cited in the text, especially in chapters 3, 4, and 5. Numbers in square brackets at those points indicate their numbers in chapter six, where the original is given in *romaji*. In this way it is possible to compare those that are translated by more than one contributor.

7. President Tsutomu Kake of the Kake Institute, the parent organization of the Okayama University of Science, has been honored by the Japanese government for his contributions to international education. Vice President Elenore Koch of Wright State, serving with Robert J. Kegerreis, President at the time, has also received national recognition in this area.

8. Accompanying the Reverend Muneharu Kurozumi, Chief Patriarch (*kyōshu*) of Kurozumi kyō, were The Reverend Nobuakira Kurozumi and The Reverend Shinsei Kudo of the Kurozumi-kyō headquarters staff. The three performed *nippai* each morning at the Wright Brothers Memorial hill near the Wright State campus, attended by numbers of students and interested community members. On the way to Dayton the Chief Patriarch performed a service in Utah for the pacification of the spirits of Japanese laborers who had died there before World War I while engaged in railway construction.

9. H. Byron Earhart, *Religions of Japan: Many Traditions Within One Sacred Way* (San Francisco: Harper and Row, 1984), p. 120; Harold Wright, trans., *Ten Thousand Leaves* (Woodstock: Overlook Press, 1986), pp. 33, 35; Carmen Blacker, *The Catalpa Bow* (London: George Allen and Unwin, 1975), pp. 21ff. The kindness of the Meiji Shrine in Tokyo in making translations of the poetry of the Meiji Emperor and Empress available is appreciated by its visitors.

## 1. The Modern Vitality of Shinto

1. Edward Albert Shils, *Tradition* (Chicago: University of Chicago, 1981); Jaroslav Pelikan, *The Vindication of Tradition* (New Haven: Yale University Press, 1984).

2. Pelikan, *The Vindication of Tradition*, p. 65.

3. Kiyomi Morioka, "Folk Religion and Shinto," in *Religion in Changing Japanese Society* (Tokyo: University of Tokyo, 1975), p. 70.

4. H. Byron Earhart, *Religions of Japan: Many Traditions Within One Sacred Way* (San Francisco: Harper and Row, 1984), p. 120.

## 2. Kurozumi Munetada, Founder of Kurozumi-kyō

1. William G. Beasley, *The Meiji Restoration* (Stanford: Stanford University Press, 1972), pp. 15-16.

2. Ibid., pp. 14-15.

3. On the political structure of Kurozumi's domain, Okayama, during the Tokugawa period, see John W. Hall, *Government and Local Power in Japan* (Princeton: Princeton University Press, 1966), chapters 12 and 13; see also Nagayama Usaburo, *Okayama-ken tsushi.* 2 vols. (Okayama: Seibundo, 1930) and Taniguchi Sumio, *Okayama-han seishi no kenkyu* (Tokyo: Koshobo, 1964).

4. Beasley, *Meiji Restoration,* p. 51.

5. Ibid., pp. 63-68.

6. Hayashiya Tatsusaburō, ed., *Bakumatsu bunka no kenkyū* (Tokyo: Iwanami shoten, 1978), p. 10.

7. Ibid., p. 29. These persons are called *sōmō* in contemporary accounts.

8. Beasley, *Meiji Restoration,* p. 57.

9. Ibid., pp. 57-59.

10. Kamata Michitaka, "Ara-mura fukko no nomin undo," in Hayashiya, *Bakumatsu bunka no kenkyū,* pp. 321-324.

11. Indispensable conditions for the spread of pilgrimage were improved transportation and safety on the roads, and the spread of currency (Shinjō Tsunezō, *Shaji to kōtsū,* Nihon rekishi shinsho (Tokyo: Chibundō, 1960), pp. 112-113). In the Tokugawa period transportation facilities such as rental horses, palanquins, and porters came within the economic reach of commoners.

12. Shinjō, *Shaji to kōtsū,* pp. 120-123.

13. Ibid., pp. 72-78.

14. See Robert Bellah, *Tokugawa Religion* (New York: Free Press, 1956), on which the characterization in this paragraph relies heavily, especially chapter 3.

15. W. T. deBary, "Sagehood as a Secular and Spiritual Ideal in Tokugawa Neo-Confucianism," in W. T. deBary and Irene Bloom, eds. *Principle and Practicality* (New York: Columbia University Press, 1979), pp. 127-188. See also Rodney L. Taylor, "The Cultivation of Sagehood as a Religious Goal in Neo-Confucianism: A Study of Selected Writings of Kao P'an-lung (1562-1626)" (Ph.D. dissertation, Columbia University, 1974.)

16. Though Confucians would not like the comparison, the idea is similar to the "aspiration for enlightenment" (*bodhicitta*) of Buddhist tradition and signals the moment when the aspirant becomes deeply serious about the quest.

17. deBary "Sagehood as a Secular and Spiritual Ideal," *passim.*

18. On Ansai's view of the unity of Shinto and Confucianism, see Okada Takehiko , "Practical Learning in the Chu Shi School: Yamazaki Ansai and Kaibara Ekken," in W. T. deBary and Irene Bloom, eds. *Principle and Practicality* (New York: Columbia University Press, 1979), p. 248.

19. On Kaibara Ekken's view of the unity of Shinto and Confucianism, see Okada, "Practical Learning in the Chu Shi School," p. 248.

20. On the religious thought of Nakae Toju, see Yamashita, Ryuji "Nakae Tōju's Religious Thought and Its Relation to Jitsugaku" in W. T. deBary and Irene Bloom, eds. *Principle and Practicality* (New York: Columbia University Press, 1979).

21. Ibid., p. 315.

22. See Bellah, *Tokugawa Religion*, chapter 6.

23. W. T. deBary, *Neo-Confucian Orthodoxy and the Learning of the Mind-and-Heart* (New York: Columbia University Press, 1981), pp. 206-210.

24. Jennifer Robertson, "Rooting the Pine: *Shingaku* Methods of Organization," *Monumenta Nipponica* 34 (Autumn 1979): 313.

25. Ibid., p. 320.

26. Kurozumi's father's rank was *negi*. A *negi* is an assistant in ritual, and the term may be used in addition to designate any priest of any shrine but Ise, where several grades of *negi* serve. When used as a term of rank, a *negi* falls below *kannushi* and above *hafuri* (Shimonaku Yasaburō, *Shinto daijiten*, 3 vols. [Tokyo: Heibonsha, 1940], 3:99).

27. He and his father held the rank of *kachi*. *Kachi* were low-ranking samurai who were originally in charge of security matters and supervision of the route of march on their alternate years' journeys to Edo.

28. Kurozumi Tadaaki, *Kurozumikyō kyōsoden*, 5th ed. (Okayama: Kurozumikyo Nisshinsha, 1976), pp. 20-21; 24-27.

29. Charles Hepner, *The Kurozumi Sect of Shinto* (Tokyo: The Meiji Japan Society, 1935), p. 96. Hepner says Kurozumi did not know of *kokugaku*, but even if he had no direct acquaintance with works of Motoori and Hirata, their disciples were so active in Okayama that it is impossible that Kurozumi would not have known their views. On the general characteristics of the education of the Shinto priest in the Tokugawa period, see Kishimoto Yoshio, *Kinsei Shintō kyōikushi*. (Tokyo: Ōbunsha, 1962) pp. 31, 148ff. On the theistic religious-ethical strain of Neo-Confucian thought which most likely influenced Kurozumi, see deBary, *Neo-Confucian Orthodoxy*, p. 66ff.

30. *Reijin* designates a kami believed to excel in communication between kami and human beings.

31. *Nippai*, the custom of sun worship, was common in Okayama folk religion and was not an invention by Kurozumi (Kōmoto Kazushi, *Kurozumikyō tokuhon* (Okayama: Kurozumikyo Nisshinsha, 1961), p. 126.

32. Traditional calculation counted a newborn baby as one year old. Thus, by this method Kurozumi was reckoned thirty-five in 1814, though by western custom he would be thirty-four.

33. Kōmoto, *Kurozumikyō tokuhon*, pp. 5-7. The term *tenmei* is of course the Mandate of Heaven in Confucian terms, and such a translation would not be entirely out of place in Kurozumi's case save for his lack of any political concern.

34. Ibid., p. 43. He also used the terms *ten* and *tenchi*, "Heaven" and "Heaven and Earth," interchangeably with the above terms of deity. However, he sometimes used the term *ten* in the sense of "divine will," particularly when he spoke of entrusting all things to divine will (*ten ni makase*) (*Kyōtenshō*, Kurozumikyō kyōhanhensan iinkai. *Kurozumikyō kyōtenshō* (Okayama: Kurozumikyō Nisshinsha, 1981), pp. 60-61, 98, 110, 120, 129, 131, 134, 145).

35. Needless to say, Kurozumi was not the first to speak of Amaterasu. She stands at the head of the Yamato pantheon in the Kojiki and Nihon Shoki, and her cult at Ise received steadily increasing popular devotion during Kurozumi's lifetime. Contemporary Shinto scholars were intent on clarifying the significance of this deity to secular rule (Kōmoto, *Kurozumikyō tokuhon*, pp. 24-48.).

36. Ibid., pp. 24-48. Kurozumi's most characteristic statement along these lines is the short poem still used as a grace before meals: "How blessed it is that the grace of Amaterasu pervades all the universe, omitting nothing." (Amaterasu, kami no mitoku wa, ametsuchi ni michite, kakenaki megumi naru ka na.) (*Kyōtenshō*, p. 6) [*see also chapter 6, Dōka 2 — ed. note*]

37. Both Buddhism and Shinto tended to accord high positions in parish organizations to people in positions of local authority, such as village headmen. In other ways also they accepted the prevailing status order of society as inviolable.

38. "Amaterasu, kami no miya ni sumu hito wa, kagiri shirarenu inochi naruran," and "Amaterasu, kami no migokoro waga kokoro; Futatsu nakereba, shi suru mono nashi" (*Kyōtenshō*, p. 5).

39. Kōmoto, *Kurozumikyō tokuhon*, pp. 8-80, *passim*; Hepner, *The Kurozumi Sect of Shinto*, pp. 105ff.

40. Hara Keigo, *Kurozumi Munetada* Jimbutsu Yosho 42 (Tokyo: Yoshikawa kōbunkan, 1960), p. 12. Kurozumi also practiced curing by holy water and holy rice, and he developed a means of administering *majinai* by proxy to those too ill to visit him personally. The last means was called *kage no majinai*.

41. Kōmoto Kazushi, *Kyōsosama no oitsuwa* [*Tales of the Founder*] (Okayama: Kurozumikyō Nisshinsha, 1976), pp. 1-4.

42. Murakami Shigeyoshi, *Seimei no oshie*. Tōyōbunko 319. (Tokyo: Heibonsha, 1977), p. 338.

43. Those Buddhist priests who practiced healing customarily enjoyed more or less exclusive right to cure parishioners, while secular physicians mainly practiced among samurai. *Yamabushi* also had parish-like territories to which they could buy or sell title.

44. Hara, *Kurozumi Munetada*, chapter 5.

45. For a historical survey of Japanese religious techniques of healing see Helen Hardacre, "The Transformation of Healing in the New Religions of Japan," *Journal of the History of Religions* 20 (May, 1982): 45-60.

46. This verse is found in the Founder's prayer, "Michi no Kotowari": "Kokoro wa shujin nari. Katachi wa kerai nari. Satoreba, kokoro ga mi o tsukai; mayoeba, mi ga kokoro o tsukau." [*see Appendix I — ed. note.*]

47. *Kyōtenshō*, p. 3: "Amaterasu, kami no migokoro, hitogokoro. Hitotsu ni nareba, ikidōshi nari." [*See also Chapter 6, dōka 13 — ed. note.*]

48. From the prayer, "Michi no Kotowari": "Inishie no kokoro mo katachi nashi; ima no kokoro mo katachi nashi. Kokoro nomi ni shite, katachi o wasururu toki wa, ima mo kamiyo; jindai konnichi; konnichi jindai." [*See Appendix I — ed. note.*]

49. Taniguchi Sumio, "Bakumatsu ni okeru Kurozumikyō no ichikōsatsu," *Okayama daigaku kyōikubu kenkyū shūroku* 6 (1968): 70.

50. Ibid., p. 72. Kurozumi's correspondence has been edited and compiled in a critical edition by Murakami Shigeyoshi in *Minshū shūkyō no shisō*. Nihon shisō taikei 67. (Tokyo: Iwanami shoten, 1977). In roughly half of the approximately 200 letters the addressee is known, and most of these are to samurai followers. In his letters, Kurozumi commented on the health of family left behind, and in many cases he tendered spiritual counsel, sometimes in poetic form.

51. *Daimyō* were required to spend half their time in Edo; thus they alternated between Edo and their home domains.

52. Kurozumi Tadaaki, *Kurozumikyō kyōsoden*, pp. 67-68. The shrine's complaint is reproduced in full on these pages.

53. Hepner, *Kurozumi Sect of Shinto*, p. 75; Taniguchi, "Bakumatsu ni okeru Kurozumikyō," p. 66. Unfortunately no texts of these lectures remain.

54. Seclusion was practiced by other founders of new religions at the end of the Tokugawa period. For example, Kawate Bunjirō, founder of Konkōkyō, remained in seclusion for most of his life. See Murakami Shigeyoshi, *Konkō daijin no shōgai* (Tokyo: Kōdansha, 1972) and Delwin B. Schneider, *Konkōkyō: a Japanese Religion* (Tokyo: ISR Press, 1962).

55. His solicitous treatment of merchant followers may have been prompted by his own financial circumstances, which were bad. A poor manager of money, Kurozumi was often hounded by creditors. As often as not, he secured loans for a third party and then had to bear the money-lender's wrath when that person failed to repay (see Hepner, *Kurozumi Sect of Shinto*, pp. 80f. and Kōmoto, *Kyōsosama no oitsuwa*, pp. 7-12).

56. Taniguchi, "Bakumatsu ni okeru Kurozumikyō," p. 75.

57. Hepner, *Kurozumi Sect of Shinto*, p. 65-71 discusses recorded instances of Kurozumi's divinations.

58. Hellmut Wilhelm, *Change; Eight Lectures on the I Ching*, trans. Cary F. Baynes (Princeton: Princeton University Press, 1960), p. 19. Wilhelm discusses non-deterministic uses of hexagram divination.

59. Once a month is a figure that appears frequently, but we do not know whether this was an invariable standard.

60. Kurozumi Tadaaki, *Kurozumikyō kyōsoden*, pp. 65-66. For example, a predominantly samurai confraternity in the castle town was called Kometsukikai, while a merchant assembly was called Shichijima-ya, after the main convenor's place of business (see also Kōmoto, *Kyōsosama no oitsuwa*, pp. 215-216.).

61. Headmen attended meetings and contributed to the group under the rubric of *hatsuhō*, "first fruits" (Taniguchi, "Bakumatsu ni okeru Kurozumikyō," p. 79).

62. Marius Jansen, *Sakamoto Ryōma and the Meiji Restoration* (Princeton: Princeton University Press, 1961), pp. 30-31.

63. Kurozumi Tadaaki, *Kurozumikyō kyōsoden*, p. 66. *The Tales of the Founder* describes a meeting held in a temple, much to the displeasure of the priest, who was not informed in advance (see Kōmoto, *Kyōsosama no oitsuwa*, pp. 61-63).

64. Sasaki Junnosuke, *Bakamatsu shakairon* (Tokyo: Kōshobō, 1969), p. 147-148.

65. Ibid., p. 263. While new agricultural technologies spread to rural areas in the seventeenth century production increased, and village headmen became wealthy peasants: *gōnō*.

66. Shibata Hajime, *Kinsei gōnō no gakumon shisō*, ed. Negishi Yoichi (Tokyo: Shinseisha, 1966), pp. 150 ff.

67. The Tenshinkō was established for ordinary peasants (*komae byakushō*).

68. R. P. Dore, *Education in Tokugawa Japan* (Berkeley: University of California Press, 1965), pp. 237-241. Dore shows how preachers of a variety of creeds were adapted to promote core values and maintenance of the status quo, and how these harmonized with Confucian orthodoxy.

69. Murakami, *Seimei no oshie*, pp. 47, 338. Furuta had a stipend of 550 *koku*. As late as the mid 1840's Furuta is recorded as a regular at *kōshaku*.

70. Kurozumi Tadaaki, *Kurozumikyō kyōsoden*, p. 72. Ishio's stipend was 140 *koku*. His correspondence with Kurozumi is one of the richest sources on early practices of Kurozumi's followers. Ishio apparently proselytized in Edo using calligraphic scrolls (*sansha taku sen*) in Kurozumi's hand. These bore the names of Tenshō Daijin, Hachiman, and Kasuga Myōjin. While Ishio was in Edo, his father housed the *kōseki* back in Okayama. These activities were known to the *han*.

71. Ibid.

72. Ibid., pp. 53-72. (See also Hepner, *Kurozumi Sect of Shinto*, p. 186)

73. Ibid. Apparently there were no female ministers until the Meiji period.

74. Ibid., p. 101. The Principles are known as the *Shichi-ka-jō*, or as *Nichi-nichi kanai kokoroe no koto*. The original is as follows:

  1. Shinkoku no hito ni umare, tsune ni shinshin naki koko.
  2. Hara o tate, mono o ku suru koto.
  3. Ono ga manshin ni te, hito o mikudasu koto.
  4. Hito no aku o mite, onore ni akushin o masu koto.
  5. Mubyō no toki, kagyō okotari no koto.
  6. Makoto no michi ni irinagara, kokoro ni makoto naki koto.
  7. Nichi-nichi arigataki koto o torihazusu koto.

  > Migi no jōjō sune ni wasurubekarazu.
  > Osorubeshi, osorubeshi.
  > Tachi mukō hito no kokoro wa kagami nari.
  > Onore ga sugata o utsushite yamin.

75. Kodera Motonoko, "Kurozumikyō no rekishiteki seikaku," *Okayama shigaku* 24 (September 1971): 46-50.

76. Kurozumi Tadaaki, *Kurozumikyō kyōsoden*, p. 126.

77. Ibid., pp. 125-127.

78. Taniguchi, "Bakumatsu ni okeru Kurozumikyō," p. 77. In addition to village headmen, there was a great variety among Kurozumi's commoner followers. *The Tales of the Founder* includes stories about the following sorts of people: *ōjōya*, of Akasaka in Bizen (25,66); the *ōjōya* of Oku county, Nakayama Tsunejirō

(160ff.); a Bitchu doctor (41); a Mimasaka Shinto priest (136); a Mimasaka doctor (151); an Oku cotton merchant (140); a drug manufacturer (47); a dyer (155); a stone mason (194); a tile maker (196); and a Bizen potter (205). The presence of a significant number of artisans is notable.

79. Ibid., p. 75; Kodera, "Kurozumikyō no rekishiteki seikaku," pp. 46-49.

80. Kodera, "Kurozumikyō no rekishiteki seikaku," p. 46.

81. Not applause, but a *kashiwade*, a clap indicating agreement, as someone in a Christian church might say "amen" in the middle of a sermon.

82. Kurozumi Tadaaki, *Kurozumikyō kyōsoden*, pp. 62-64. In ordinary etiquette a commoner should not pass a samurai on the road.

83. Kōmoto, *Kyōsosama no oitsuwa*, pp. 63-66; [*see, chapter 5.* Ed. note]

## 3. The Teaching of Kurozumi-kyō

[*Editorial notes and subtitles have been supplied by the editor.*]

[*Translated by Takeda Akihiro and edited by Willis Stoesz. Both the translation and the editing were assisted by Helen Hardacre, with additional contributions by Harold Wright and The Reverend Nobuakira Kurozumi. All the poetry was translated by Harold Wright.*]

1. *Tenmei jikiju.* This term, central for Kurozumi-kyō, is subject to varying translation. "Direct Receipt of Heavenly Mission" is Hardacre's choice (see chapter 2). Kurozumi-kyō leaders suggest leaving it untranslated, or using the choice given here (letter from Kurozumi Nobuakira, March 8, 1986). The Reverend Kurozumi paraphrases "Direct Acceptance of Divine Mission" as "the mystic experience of Munetada; being appointed directly by Amaterasu to spread her blessings." The "charter" of the group's tradition in the founder's experience of Kami Amaterasu (or as the *kanji* of her name may alternatively be read, Tenshō Daijin) is thereby underlined, a point that is not so clear when the linguistically more straightforward reading "heaven" (*Ten*) is used in this key phrase.

2. The date here given follows contemporary usage. The subject of dates of events in Japanese history before the calendar reform of 1873 is a complex one (Gen Iasaka *et al., Kōdansha Encyclopedia of Japan* [Tokyo: Yoshikawa kobunkan, 1960] 1:229-232). However, the connection of the dates of the founder's birth and of his enlightenment experience with the winter solstice is very clear in Kurozumi tradition. See chapter 2.

3. The spirit of Munetada was first enshrined at the Kaguraoka Shrine in Kyoto in March, 1862 as Munetada Daimyōjin. This shrine is thus the older of the two main shrines of Kurozumi-kyō. The spirit of the founder was also enshrined at Imamura near Okayama in 1885. The delay arose because of the Meiji government's gradual development of a national policy about religion (Charles Hepner, *The Kurozumi Sect of Shinto* (Tokyo: The Meiji Japan Society, 1935), p. 190.

4. Yoshida Kanetomo (1435-1511) was a major founder of the revival of Shinto, in reaction to then-regnant Buddhism. His work in the ranking of shrines and of kami and his formulation of a syncretic Shinto was carried forward by the important Yoshida Shrine in Kyoto. See Tsunoda Ryusaku *et al.*, eds., *Sources of*

*Japanese Tradition.* 2 vols. (New York and London: Columbia University Press, 1964) 1:265 ff.

5. That is, *sebumi* plus the honorific *Mi,* as a title of the Kami Munetada.

6. I.e., humans may realize their kami nature through bringing the prior presence of Kami into overt expression.

7. *Issai shintoku kami no hakarai..*

8. Natsume Sōseki (1867-1916) is usually regarded as the leading novelist of modern Japan. For a discussion of his concept of *sokuten kyoshi,* "leaving it to Heaven," see Beongcheon Yu, *Natsume Soseki* (New York: Twayne Publishers, 1969).

9. See chapter 2, p. 42.

## 4. Following the Way

*[Editorial notes have been supplied by the editor.]*

*[Translated by Murano Aiyumu and edited by Willis Stoesz. The assistance of Naoki Shiwaku, Helen Hardacre, and The Reverend Muneharu Kurozumi is gratefully acknowledged. Poetry and prayer are translated by Harold Wright.]*

1. The term *"michizure"* referring to ordinary members of Kurozumi-kyō is frequently employed in these lectures. A literal rendering, "way-companion," is used in this chapter when implied in context. For further explanation of categories of church membership see Helen Hardacre, *Kurozumikyō and the New Religions of Japan* (Princeton: Princeton University Press, 1986), p. 106.

2. *Kyōsoshin,* the site of Kurozumi-kyō headquarters in Omoto-cho (also known as Imamura and as Kaminakano), now in the southwest outskirts of Okayama city. The founder's house dedicated in 1848 is in the precincts, together with what was the main shrine until the removal of the enshrined Kami to Shintōzan, several miles to the northwest, in 1974.

3. The Reverend Muneharu Kurozumi explains that one may see the rising sun on the horizon from the place for *nippai* on the high hilltop under the open sky at Shintōzan. The sun's rising is anticipated (one may say, "waited upon") while *Ōharai* is prayed; just at sunrise *yōki* is taken in; and then in the next few moments hymns of praise to Amaterasu are sung. This is *"nippai* of *ohimachi."* At Omoto the horizon is obscured by houses and other buildings (letter from The Reverend Muneharu Kurozumi, September 16, 1987). For the text of the Great Purification Prayer see Hardacre, *Kurozumikyō and the New Religions of Japan,* pp. 196-198; and *Norito; a New Translation of the Ancient Japanese Ritual Prayers,* trans. Donald Philippi (Tokyo: Institute of Japanese Culture and Classics, Kokugakuin University, 1959), pp. 45-49.

4. *Okage.* As will become evident in this chapter, *virtue* refers to divine empowerment, as well as to the benefit or blessing (of various sorts) which results. The related term *shintoku* refers to divine initiative in producing *okage,* implying the divine virtue and power of Kami. See also Johannes Laube, "Zur Bedeutungsgeschichte des Konfuzianistischen Begriffs "Makoto" ("Wahrhaftigkeit")," *Fernöstliche Kultur,* ed. Helga Wormit (Marburg: N. G. Elwert Verlag, 1975), pp. 100-157.

5. See Konishi Jin'ichi, *A History of Japanese Literature*, Vol. 1, trans. Eileen Gatten and Nicholas Teele, ed. Earl Miner (Princeton: Princeton University Press, 1984), pp. 107 ff., 203 ff, 393 ff. Konishi sees *ga* (Japanese self-identity) as the successor in modern society to the *kotodama* concept. The Kurozumi approach is to overcome the egoism implied in *ga*. See the concluding pages of this chapter.

6. For details of local Kurozumi-kyō congregational organization and leadership see Hardacre, *Kurozumikyō and the New Religions of Japan*, chapters 4 and 5.

7. See chapter 2.

8. See the discussion of the "August-Sun-Spirit-Theory" (Go-Yō-Ki-Setsu) in Charles Hepner, *The Kurozumi Sect of Shinto* (Tokyo: The Meiji Japan Society, 1935), pp. 138 ff. The divine virtue is communicated by the rays of the sun's light, by the warmth of the sun, and by the air itself. The present explanation minimizes the role of air. *Nippai* may be considered comparable to Christian Mass or Eucharist in enabling divine presence and power to become effective in the life of the believer.

9. The idea that kami may be enshrined both in some central shrine and in a subordinate "separated" location is familiar in Shinto. At the same time, Kurozumi-kyō's thinking is fundamentally informed by the macrocosm-microcosm analogy: Amaterasu Ōmikami is both universally present and "separately" present in each human being. She is both universal deity and the divine inner spirit linking each person with universal reality. The interplay of these ways of understanding divine presence informs Kurozumi-kyō spirituality. Here, "inner spirit" or "divine inner spirit" will be used to translate *bunshin* (or *gobunshin*).

10. *Ikidōshi*. See the closing pages of this chapter; see also chapter 7 and Hepner, *The Kurozumi Sect of Shinto*, p. 141.

11. *Toritsugi*, implying mediation. The goal of *toritsugi* is inner union with Kami.

12. The quotation about *deku* was taken from a painting by a man named Nakagawa which had been presented to the Chief Patriarch. The painter had commented that he did not paint by his own volition but could paint well only when the presence of deity replaced his self-sense as the agent of the work. Just so, says the Chief Patriarch, the act of trust leads to being protected by Kami and having a wonderful life (letter of The Reverend Muneharu Kurozumi, October 1, 1987). For theories of inspiration in the art of painting see Makoto Ueda, *Literary and Art Theories in Japan* (Cleveland: The Press of Western Reserve University, 1967).

13. *Kokoro* includes much of what is meant both by "mind" and by "heart," implying both thought and feeling. Context affects which way it is translated, but something is inevitably missing in either case. See notes in Chapters 6, 8, and 9.

14. A kind of wood.

15. The analogy to the transmission of divine virtue at *nippai* is clear (see note 8).

16. A familiar designation for Kurozumi Munekazu, the Fifth Patriarch.

17. A similar account of religious conversion is cited by Hardacre, *Kurozumi-kyō and the New Religions of Japan*, pp. 90 ff.

18. Akagi Tadaharu, a leading member of the Seven High Disciples (*kōtei*), active in promoting the teaching in Kyoto after the founder's death (see chapter 2).

19. Located in the northern part of Okayama prefecture.

20. Cp. Hepner, *The Kurozumi Sect of Shinto*, p. 216.

21. See also Hardacre, *Kurozumikyō and the New Religions of Japan*, pp. 173 ff. For general information on this topic see Robert J. Smith, *Ancestor Worship in Contemporary Japan* (Stanford: Stanford University Press, 1974).

22. The national shrine in Tokyo for all those who have died in the service of their country, comparable to Arlington Cemetery in the U.S.A. The Reverend Kurozumi comments that at Yasukuni Shrine there are many *mitama*, who undoubtedly have become kami, and that he goes there to express gratitude to them (letter from The Reverend Muneharu Kurozumi, September 16, 1987).

23. A Shinto-style ancestors' memorial tablet; *shintai* or physical indication of a kami's presence (Smith, *Ancestor Worship*, p. 74).

24. In the *mitama-nagome* festival the people and the *mitama*/kami jointly celebrated the tenth anniversary of the move to Shintōzan.

25. See note 10.

26. A traditional dumpling made of rice and seasonal herbs; in this case, spring herbs.

27. Ken-chan is his playmate. "Chan" is a diminutive term for rather small boys.

28. "*Arigatō-gozaimasu* movement" refers to a campaign to support, by financial contribution and by voluntary service, a hospital in Okayama city, the Asahigawa-So. Contributions go to a foundation which supports medical staff. The hospital serves handicapped children from many Asian countries. More generally, Kurozumi members repeat the phrase constantly in daily life as a prayer of thanks to Amaterasu Ōmikami and to Munetada Kami (letter from The Reverend Muneharu Kurozumi, September 16, 1987). "Thank you very much" is also a most familiar phrase in Japanese everyday polite conversation.

## 5. Kurozumi-kyō in Japanese Culture

[*Editorial notes, title, and subtitles have been supplied by the editor*]

[*This translation was prepared in rough draft by Hashida Hiromi from a written version of the talk as subsequently edited by The Reverend Muneharu Kurozumi. The translation, edited by Willis Stoesz, includes much phraseology given in Helen Hardacre's on-the-spot interpretation as video taped.*]

1. It should be added that a "Conference on Shinto Since 1945" was held at the Blaisdell Institute at Claremont Graduate School in California in September, 1965, including distinguished scholars and priests from Japan and the U.S.A. (letter from Ms. Tania Rizzo, Special Collections Librarian, Honnold Library, Claremont Colleges, September 17, 1987). More recently, a series of exchange worship occasions has been held at the Cathedral of St. John the Divine in New York and at the

Headquarters of the Ōmoto sect of Shinto in Kyoto, and this has involved some presentations about Shinto by its leaders in New York (interview with The Reverend James P. Morton, Dean of the Cathedral Church of St. John the Divine, New York, July 1986).

2. The Yayoi period, in which rice culture took hold and a fresh development of culture took place in Japan, is put between 300 B.C. and 300 A.D. For discussion of early Japan see Richard J. Pearson, *et al.*, eds. *Windows on the Japanese Past: Studies in Archaeology and Prehistory* (Ann Arbor: Center for Japanese Studies, University of Michigan, 1986); see also Joseph Kitagawa, *On Understanding Japanese History* (Princeton: Princeton University Press, 1987), chapter 1 *et passim.*

3. In this myth Amaterasu had retired to a rock cave, rejecting the boisterousness of Susanō no-mikoto, her brother. The whole world was plunged into darkness as a result, until, her curiosity aroused by some happy singing and dancing, she again came out. A straw rope was then tied across the mouth of the cave, implying that the world could from then on count on her continuing presence. *Kojiki,* trans. Donald Philippi (Princeton: Princeton University Press, 1969), pp. 81-86.

4. The same argument is made also to Kurozumi members, underlining its universal intent (see chapter 4).

5. On "rounded thing," *marugoto,* see chapter 7.

6. *Shin shukyō.* The reference is to the wave of Japanese post-war religions marked by a number of common features including faith healing and concern for physical health. Two general discussions, in some ways dated but still useful, are H. Neill McFarland, *The Rush Hour of the Gods* (New York: Macmillan, 1967) and Harry Thomsen, *The New Religions of Japan* (Rutland, Vt.: Charles E. Tuttle Co., 1963).

7. The Reverend Kurozumi read this passage to the audience in English. The quotation is from a thesis published by Cardinal Karol Wojtyla (Tommas D'Aquino Nel Sus VII Centenario, Congresso Internazionale. Roma, 1974), p. 389. See Cardinal Karol Wojtyla, *The Acting Person,* trans. from Polish by Andrzej Potocki (Dordrecht: D. Reidel, 1979) for Pope John Paul II's definitive philosophical work.

### 6. Kurozumi Munetada's Poetry: The Dokā

[*Ed. note:* The dokā — *296 of them — are authoritatively collected in* Kyōkyōsho *1926 (see Charles W. Hepner, The Kurozumi Sect of Shinto. Tokyo: Meiji Japan Society, 1935, p. 94f., 241). The* Kyōkyōsho *also contains the founder's letters and other records; some of this material has been separately edited (see Helen Hardacre,* Kurozumikyō and the New Religions of Japan. Princeton: Princeton University Press, 1986, for details). See also The Reverend Muneharu Kurozumi's comments on Kurozumi-kyō's understanding of "canon" (chapter 3). The* dokā *are listed alphabetically in the* Kyōkyōsho; *the editor is responsible for their arrangement here.*]

1. The poems selected here have been translated for the text of a number of the articles which make up the body of this present book. I have added a number of

others that I have found to be representative of important themes or imagery. I believe that this short collection of 62 poems represents well the *dokā* of Kurozumi Munetada.

I have attempted to approximate the 5, 7, 5, 7, 7 syllable phrases of the original. I hope not too much has been lost and little added. One of the major difficulties encountered in translating this type of didactic poetry is the rendering of such important words as *makoto* (sincerity, true heart, faithfulness, honesty, "Truth," etc. I have used "True Sincerity.") and *kokoro* (heart, mind, spirit, mentality, mind-heart, and even at times, "thought" etc. I have used "heart.")

2. [*Ed. note: According to ancient mythology Awaji Island (in the Inland Sea opposite present-day Osaka) was the first of the islands of Japan (Yamato) to be brought into being by the primal pair of kami, Izanagi and Izanami. See Kojiki, trans. Donald Philippi (Princeton: Princeton University Press, 1969), p. 53.*]

## 7. The Universal Attitude of Kurozumi Munetada

1. See chapters 2 and 3 for "outsider's" and "insider's" accounts of Kurozumi Munetada's life.

2. The concept of intention is well suited to characterize Munetada's inner life, and to draw attention to the emerging focus of his experience. Miller's discussion in this volume shows the Buddhist character of Munetada's *ikigami* vow. Until now this important concept has lacked clear analysis: note Carmen Blacker, *The Catalpa Bow* (London: Allen and Unwin, 1975) and Susumu Shimazono, "The Living Kami Idea in the New Religions of Japan," *Japanese Journal of Religious Studies* 6 (1979): 389-312. It appears on present study that Munetada's vow was itself an important innovative, syncretic act, bringing together Shinto, Buddhist, and Confucian themes and giving the *ikigami* concept distinctive definition. For a characterization of the genesis of Munetada's vow see Kurozumi Tadaaki, "Kurozumikyō Kyōsoden," trans. Harold Wright and Julie Iezzo (unpublished manuscript, 1987), chap. 2. This chapter and the next dwell on inner and outer aspects of Munetada's experience respectively.

3. Munetada's experience of unity with Amaterasu by way of the sun invested this familiar practice with distinctive meaning so that it became the central ritual of the Kurozumi-kyō cultus.

4. As an official biography of Munetada (Kurozumi Tadaaki , *Kurozumikyō Kyōsoden*, 5th ed. (Okayama: Kurozumikyō Nisshinsha, 1976.) shows, the original five were the present rules 1, 3, 4, 5 and 6. I am grateful to Professor (D.C. Holtom, *The National Faith of Japan* (New York: Paragon, 1965), p. 255) Wright and Julie Iezzo, trans., *Kurozumikyō Kyōsoden*, (unpublished manuscript, 1987). See *infra* and note 6. They are to be distinguished from a set of Five Teachings (*Oshie no Goji*) set forth by an immediate disciple, Hoshijima Ryohei (D.C. Holtom, *The National Faith of Japan* [New York: Paragon, 1965], p. 255) and from a modern set formulated by the present Chief Patriarch (see chapter 3).

5. See Dore's description of the instruction typically given in the kind of school Gonkichi attended (R. P. Dore, *Education in Tokugawa Japan* (Berkeley: University of California Press, 1965), pp. 271ff, 323ff.). See also chapter 2. One of young

Munetada's teachers, who instructed him in Confucian classics, was one Uchimura Sanzi who also served as a private secretary to the Ikeda family, rulers of Bizen. See Wright, "*Kurozumikyō Kyōsoden*," chapter 2.

6. Munetada's changes in revising the five rules to become the Seven Rules may be seen by comparing:

| The Original Five Rules (Wright 1987, chapter 2) | The Seven Rules (see chapter 2, note 74) |
|---|---|
| 1. Shinjin no ie ni umare tsune ni shinjin naki koto. | 1. Shinkoku no hito ni umare, tsune ni shinshin naki koto. |
| | 2. Hara o tate, mono o ku ni suru koto. |
| 2. Ono ga manshin ni te hito o mikudasu koto. | 3. Ono ga manshin ni te, hito o |
| 3. Hito no aku o mite ga ni akushin o masu koto. | 4. Hito no aku o mite, onore ni akushin o masu koto. |
| 4. Mubyō no toki kagyō okotari no koto. | 5. Mubyō no toki, kagyō okotari |
| 5. Makoto no michi ni irinagara makoto naki koto. | 6. Makoto no michi ni irinagara, kokoro ni makoto naki koto. |
| | 7. Nichi-nichi arigataki koto o tori-hazusu koto. |
| Tachi muko<br>    hito no kokoro zo<br>        kagami nari<br>Ono ga kokoro o<br>    utsushite ya min.<br><br>Migi no jōjō makoto ni osoroshiki koto nari. Tsune ni ai kokoroe shugyō itasubeki mono nari. | Migi no jōjō tsune ni wasurubekarazu.<br>Osorubeshi, osorubeshi.<br>Tachi mukō hito no kokoro wa kagami nari.<br>Onore ga sugata o utsushite yamin. |

It should be noted that "Divine Land," or "Land of the Gods," (*shin koku*) replaces the more intimate "home (or, house) of faith" (*shinjin no ie*) in rule 1 of the Seven, befitting the broader social context for which they were intended. Along with this broadened field of reference goes greater emphasis on interiority: the need for sincerity in the inner spirit is emphasized in the new rule six (*kokoro ni*).

It should be noted also that a number of translations suggest a prescriptive mood. However, Hepner's translation of the Seven Rules preserves the original diagnostic mood of the rules (Charles Hepner, *The Kurozumi Sect of Shinto* (Tokyo: The Meiji Japan Society, 1935), pp. 159ff.; see also Holtom, *The National Faith of Japan*, p. 254; chapter 2; Johannes Laube, "Zur Bedeutungsgeschichte des Konfuzianistischen Begriffs 'Makoto' ('Wahrhaftigkeit') in Fernöstliche Kultur, ed. Helga Wormit (Marburg: N. G. Elwert Verlag, 1975), p. 143; Nobuhara Taisen, *The Brilliant Life of Munetada Kurozumi, a Philosopher and Worshipper of the Sun*, 2nd ed. (Tokyo: PMC Publications, 1982), p. 104.

1. "Born in the Land of the Gods, and yet constantly without faith.

2. "The matter of getting Angry, and causing Pain to things.

3. "The matter of Self-Pride, which looks down on other people.

4. "The matter of strengthening one's Evil Purposes, by observing the Evil of others.

5. "The matter of neglecting one's Occupation when not ill.

6. "The matter of being in the True Way, without having Truth in the Heart.

7. "The matter of failing to realize the things for which we should be daily Thankful."

7. Compare Hepner, *The Kurozumi Sect of Shinto*, pp. 159ff.

8. See Okada Takehiko, "Neo Confucian Thinkers in Nineteenth-Century Japan," in *Confucianism and Tokugawa Culture*, ed. Peter Nosco (Princeton: Princeton University Press, 1984) for an overview of what Confucians in western Japan were teaching. For more general orientation in Japanese Confucian emphases in mind-and-heart cultures see W. T. deBary, "Sagehood as a Secular and Spiritual Ideal in Tokugawa Neo-Confucianism," in *Principle and Practicality*, ed. W. T. deBary and Irene Bloom (New York: Columbia University Press, 1979) and Robert Bellah, *Tokugawa Religion* (New York: Free Press, 1985).

9. The psychologist Robert Lifton provides an analysis of "ecstatic transcendence," showing how the inner psychic process is decentered in this kind of experience and then attains a recentered new conformation of its constitutive images and forms (Robert Jay Lifton, *The Broken Connection* (New York: Simon and Schuster, 1979), pp. 24-35). The role of such experience in Munetada's case may be noted, resulting in terms and concepts (including ethical norms and self-concepts) associated with non-dualist experience becoming more prominent than before; as Lifton says, gaining fresh emotional valence. Such terms would have been familiar to the founder before his "charter experience" but would not before then have "come to life" so as to center his inner self-understanding.

From a different (but converging) angle of explanation, Ninian Smart points out that a "noumenal outreach" present in the "focus" of a religious person's experience enables fresh "pictures" held within the consciousness-process to emerge as constitutive of the religious understanding (Ninian Smart, *The Phenomenon of Religion* (New York: Seabury Press, 1973), pp. 66ff.)

Munetada's experience represents a rich source of insight into these matters and well rewards study. For instance, while the Confucian Heaven-Earth terminology enables a universal perspective that is linked with ethical considerations, that terminology is complemented by Amaterasu pietism and cultus, and by Buddhist conceptual valences that radically diagnose egoistic inner horizons. All this engenders no sense of contradiction but is held in focus by the encounter with the sun given ritual constancy in *nippai* practice, and ethical constancy in rules for daily living (See chapter 4).

10. Hepner, *The Kurozumi Sect of Shinto*, pp. 119, 146, 164, 184.

11. Ibid. p. 147.

12. Nobuhara regards Munetada's unconcern with conceptual consistency a strength; "clear virtue" consists in receiving the fresh presence of Amaterasu in each moment and not in conformity to received ideas however venerable or consistent with one another (Nobuhara, *The Brilliant Life*, pp. 12ff.) However, compare Nakamura's general comment on this characteristic of Japanese culture (Nakamura Hajime, *Ways of Thinking of Eastern Peoples*, rev. trans., ed. Philip Wiener (Honolulu: East-West Center Press, 1964), pp. 531ff.)

13. Joachim Wach, *Sociology of Religion* (Chicago: University of Chicago Press, 1962), pp. 17ff.

14. See Nakamura, *Ways of Thinking*, pp. 407ff.; Robert J. Smith, *Ancestor Worship in Contemporary Japan* (Stanford: Stanford University Press, 1974), pp. 37ff.; Chie Nakane, *Japanese Society* (Berkeley, University of California Press, 1972), pp. 120ff.; Sokyo Ono, *Shinto: The Kami Way*, in collaboration with William P. Woodard (Rutland, Vt.: Charles E. Tuttle Co., 1962), pp. 6ff. Using Ninian Smart's term, we can put it this way: Amaterasu as the "focus" of ritual religious attention is experienced as relevant first of all to interpersonal relationship; belief and action draw on that context of manifestation as their paradigm (Smart, *The Phenomenon of Religion*, pp. 28, 64ff.).

15. Of a number of relevant *dokā*, see especially nos. 11 and 21 (chapter 6).

16. The term is used in several senses. Here the founder refers to the presence of Amaterasu perceived from within in relation to his imperfect "separated" self. Cp. Hepner, *The Kurozumi Sect of Shinto*, p. 111; and Nobuhara, *The Brilliant Life*, p. 42, citing a sermon of Munetada; note also Kurozumi Muneharu's account of his own similiar experience (chapter 4).

17. Hepner, *The Kurozumi Sect of Shinto*, pp. 120f.

18. In the conclusion of the Seven Rules the word *sugata* replaces the word *kokoro* used in the parallel passage as given in the five rules, emphasizing "the face you have presented" (see note 6) to others and not simply the hearts of each. Munetada's appreciation of the importance of a stable and constant mind was expressed by personal example. The story of his crossing a swollen stream on a narrow footbridge, stumbling, and being momentarily startled is an example (see chapter 5). His reaction was to apologize to Amaterasu for injuring her presence within himself by his momentary loss of equanimity. A frequently cited incident is his confronting a drunken samurai near the Okayama castle who was threatening passersby. His shouted remonstrance to the samurai was to remember who and where he was at that moment, and into what danger he had placed himself by his behavior. This helped the man return to his proper attitude-set (Nobuhara, *The Brilliant Life*, pp. 94ff.). Munetada's point is a subtle one. *Makoto* draws on strong, *yōki*-supported energy for relationship; reliance on form (*sugata*) would by itself be a source of illusoriness. Hepner, *The Kurozumi Sect of Shinto*, p. 134 misjudges Munetada on this point, attributing to him the view that form (*sugata*, *katachi*) is in itself a source of evil. It is rather *attitude toward* form that is for Munetada the source of good or ill.

19. Hepner, *The Kurozumi Sect of Shinto*, p. 126.

20. Laube, "Zur Bedeutungsgeschichte des Konfuzianistischen," p. 142.

21. "Michi wa Ten no Michi nari. Waga toku Michi ni arazu. Ten no Michi nara, Ten ni makase mireba sugu ni Ware nashi. Ware nakereba, Ten no Kokoro bakari nari. Sono Ten no Kokoro ga Waga Michi nari. Sono Michi ga Ike-mono nari. Kono Ikimono mina Mu nari. Sono Mu koso Ichi-Dai-Ji nari" (Hepner, *The Kurozumi Sect of Shinto*, p. 120.)

22. Nobuhara, *The Brilliant Life*, p. 54.

23. The method is discussed more fully in Willis Stoesz, *Search for Unity* (unpublished manuscript).

24. Ruth Benedict, *The Chrysanthemum and the Sword* (Rutland, Vt.: Charles E. Tuttle Co., 1954); Takie Sugiyama Lebra, "Reciprocity and the Asymmetric Principle: An Analytic Reappraisal of the Japanese Concept of *On*," in *Japanese Culture and Behavior*," ed. Takie Sugiyama Lebra and William P. Lebra (Honolulu: University of Hawaii Press, 1974); Takie Sugiyama Lebra, *Japanese Patterns of Behavior* (Honolulu: University of Hawaii Press, 1976); Nakane, *Japanese Society*; Ichiro Hori, "The Appearance of Individual Self-consciousness in Japanese Religion and Its Historical Transformations," in *The Japanese Mind*, ed. Charles Moore (Honolulu: University of Hawaii Press, 1967), pp. 202ff.

25. Hori, "The Appearance of Individual Self-consciousness," pp. 202ff; cp. Nakane, *Japanese Society*, pp. 42ff.

26. Bellah, *Tokugawa Religion*, pp. 70ff.

27. Lebra, "Reciprocity and the Asymmetric Principle."

28. Hardacre points out the importance of self-cultivation in Kurozumi-kyō life, expressed as a "... pattern of gratitude and repayment of benefice" (Helen Hardacre, *Kurozumikyō and the New Religions of Japan* [Princeton: Princeton University, 1986] p. 185). No doubt the pattern of *on-hōon* continues to shape Kurozumi-kyō social interaction. Even Munetada's help could be construed as conferring benefit to be repaid. However, the Chief Patriarch emphasizes that union with Kami should (at least for some people) come through self-effort (*jiriki*), rather than through mediation such as that given by a minister (see chapter 5). At any rate, Munetada's ability to give reliable mediation rests on his non-dual identification with Amaterasu; and that way to live (e.g., living like a *deku*; cp. chapter 4) is the ideal for everyone, no matter how slow some may be to follow that way in its fullness. Two levels of religious experience thus must be recognized within the life of Kurozumi-kyō.

29. A parallel may be drawn to Ishida Baigan's universal attitude (Bellah, *Tokugawa Religion*, pp. 73, 154ff.). However, Baigan's concerns remain culture-specific insofar as he emphasizes the importance of specific economic goals. Munetada's universal attitude more thoroughly relativizes such specific goals, though it must be said his nonchalance about money sometimes frustrated his creditors. It is suggestive that the socio-economic context of Munetada's life in Okayama was that of a group experiencing rising prosperity in an urban setting. Cf. Susan Hanley and Kozo Yamamura, *Economic and Demographic Change in Preindustrial Japan* (Princeton: Princeton University Press, 1977), pp. 161-198; and Tetsuo Najita, "Method and Analysis in the Conceptual Portrayal of Tokugawa Intellectual History," in Tetsuo Najita and Irwin Scheiner, eds., *Japanese Thought in the Tokugawa Period 1600-1867: Methods and Metaphors* (Chicago: University of

Chicago Press, 1978), pp. 3-38, cf. 24. Munetada's influence, in Scheiner's terms, paralleled the aspirations of *yonaoshi* type of peasant revolts which sought renewal of the whole world order and did not simply appeal to the existing web of social obligations for redress of grievances (Irwin Scheiner, "Benevolent Lords and Honorable Peasants: Rebellion and Peasant Consciousness in Tokugawa Japan," in Najita and Scheiner, *Japanese Thought in the Tokugawa Period*, pp. 39-62; cp. 56 f.; cp. see chapter 2).

## 8. The Internalization of Kami

1. By a conventional historical account I mean an attempt to establish a clear cause-and-effect relationship between the doctrines, experiences, and practices of specific Buddhist figures and those of Kurozumi Munetada. Strictly such an account would need not only to demonstrate similarity but also establish that Munetada had studied with or otherwise interacted with such figures. So far as I know, no investigator has yet uncovered anything like the detailed evidence such a study would require.

The surviving historical documents are almost entirely silent concerning the early influences upon Munetada; even his education can only be guessed at.

2. Thus, I do not give much space to the comparisons of Neo-Confucian writings to those of Munetada and his followers, work already done elsewhere. And while something must be said about the parallels between the language of Munetada and that of Mahayana Buddhist metaphysics and psychology, especially that associated with the Zen school, I have resisted the temptation to dwell upon this aspect of the problem. As was noted above, Munetada was not a philosopher and it does not serve the cause of understanding to ignore this fact.

3. I have consciously avoided this rendering in this paper. In my view to render *hsin* as "heart" unnecessarily narrows the term and obscures more than it reveals. I suspect that this translation is as much an attempt to exempt these traditions from the embarrassment of acknowledging any debt to Buddhism as it is an attempt to render the true sense of the term, that is, its meaning within a given context.

4. Charles Hepner, *The Kurozumi Sect of Shinto* (Tokyo: The Meiji Japan Society, 1935), p. 101.

5. *Kyōkyōsho*. Kurozumi Muneyasu, ed., *Kurozumi Kyōkyōsho*, 2 vols. (Okayama: San yo shin po insatsu bu, 1926-1927), 2: 292; Hepner, *The Kurozumi Sect of Shinto*, p. 79.

6. Toshio Kuroda, "Shinto in the History of Japanese Religion," *Journal of Japanese Studies* 7 (1981): 1-21.

7. Ibid., p. 3.

8. *Kyōkyōsho*, 1:33.

9. See chapter 6, *Dokā* no. 9.

10. Something of the breadth of the changes in Shinto can be seen from an article by Willis Stoesz (Willis Stoesz, "The Universal Attitude of Konkō Daijin," *Japanese Journal of Religious Studies* 13 (1986): 6, 11). In his category of "universalization" Stoesz has described more fully the new attitude toward deity in the kami cults of the Tokugawa period, only one aspect of which I call internalization.

11. My category of internalization also overlaps somewhat with the term "rationalization" in the sense established in the Weberian school of sociology. This thesis is basically that modernity begets a new attitude toward the sacred, one which is more "rational" because analyzable in means-and-end terms. What I call internalization in Shinto may or may not be a part of this historical tendency; but if so then the processes of rationalization must be reckoned to have begun in Japan long before the modern period. Further, rationalization theory gives primacy to the ethical dimension of religion, whereas I will focus upon the psychological, and, for want of a better word, the phenomenological. As Rudolf Otto might put it, experience is logically prior to morality. For a detailed application of the category of rationalization to Japanese religion, see Robert Bellah, *Tokugawa Religion* (New York: Free Press, 1985).

12. Cf. *nippai* (sun worship) and use of *Ōharai*. Note also that the Jodo rituals of chanting *Nembutsu* still retain a residual meditative quality.

13. Genchi Kato, *A Study of Shinto* (New York: Barnes and Noble, 1926), p. 160.

14. A. L. Sadler, trans., *The Ise Daijingu or Diary of a Pilgrimage to Ise* (Tokyo: Meiji Japan Society, 1940), pp. 10-11.

15. Kato, *A Study of Shinto*, p. 161, citing "Shinto gobusho,": in *Kokushi taikei*, 1st series, 7:457.

16. Interestingly, we can trace in the history of the Chinese *te* (*toku*) much the same change.

17. Even the rice fields which Susanō-o disordered were "heavenly rice fields" and thus are probably a reference to ritual, archetypal cultivation; see Alan L. Miller, "Ame no miso-ori me (The Heavenly Weaving Maiden): The Cosmic Weaver in Early Shinto Myth and Ritual," *History of Religions* 24 (1984): 27-48.

18. See Alan L. Miller, "Of Weavers and Birds: Structure and Symbol in Japanese Myth and Folktale," *History of Religions* 26 (1987): 209-327.

19. *Kojiki*, trans. Donald Philippi (Princeton: Princeton University Press, 1969), p. 79.

20. See chapter 4.

21. *Kyōkyōsho*, 1:40.

22. Ibid., 1:33.

23. I have argued elsewhere that the living Buddha idea is, strictly speaking, really a misnomer for bodhisattva if structure and function are considered (see Alan Miller, "Altruism by Accident? Thomas Nagel's 'rational altruism' juxtaposed to Pseudo-Asvaghosha's 'spontaneous compassion.'" (Paper delivered at the American Academy of Religion Annual Meeting, 1984); see also Alan Miller, "The Bodhisattva Ideal from the Point of View of Karma." (Paper delivered at the Ohio Academy of Religion Annual Meeting, 1986).

24. Hepner, *The Kurozumi Sect of Shinto*, p. 63.

25. Ibid.

26. Ibid., p. 59.

27. Helen Hardacre, *Kurozumikyō and the New Religions of Japan* (Princeton: Princeton University Press, 1986), cp. W. T. deBary and Irene Bloom, eds., *Principal and Practicality* (New York: Columbia University Press, 1979).

28. See Anthony Wallace, *Religion: An Anthropological View* (New York: Random House, 1966).

29. Ichiro Hori, *Folk Religion in Japan*, ed. Joseph M. Kitagawa and Alan Miller (Chicago: University of Chicago Press, 1968).

30. Susumu Shimazono, "The Living Kami Idea in the New Religions of Japan," *Japanese Journal of Religious Studies* 6 (1979): 389-412.

31. See Mircea Eliade, *Shamanism: Archaic Techniques of Ecstasy* (New York: Bollingen Foundation, 1964).

32. Hepner, *The Kurozumi Sect of Shinto*, p. 61.

33. Even some Neo-Confucian scholars had largely given up this aspect of their own tradition. This we might suppose to be a result of the Japanization of Neo-Confucian thought, a dimension of Tokugawa Confucianism little explored by modern scholars. But see Ryuji Yamashita, "Nakae Tōju's Religious Thought and Its Relation to 'Jitsugaku'," in *Principle and Practicality*, ed. W. T. deBary and Irene Bloom (New York: Columbia University Press, 1979).

34. *Kyōkyōsho*, 1:85-86.

35. Ibid., 2:288.

36. Hajime Nakamura, *Ways of Thinking of Eastern Peoples*, rev. trans., ed. Philip Wiener (Honolulu: East-West Center Press, 1964), p. 467. This tendency may be simply an aspect of a deeper tendency connected to the possible etymology of the word kami itself. There still exists in modern Japanese the usage of kami as high in elevation, status, and power, suggesting that kami (deity) may have once been but an adjective meaning extraordinary and awesome. Yet the explicit claim to kami-hood is not attested to in the case of the Japanese emperors before the period of the Taika Reforms (c. 645 A.D.).

37. One scholar attributed it to the jealousy of Buddhists who were imitating the Shinto ancestral cult which assumed that the dead became kami. See Sir Charles Eliot, *Japanese Buddhism* (London: Edward Arnold Co., 1959), quoted in Ichiro Hori, "The Appearance of Individual Self-consciousness in Japanese Religion and Its Historical Transformation," in *The Japanese Mind*, ed. Charles Moore (Honolulu: University of Hawaii Press, 1967), p. 203.

23. Toshio Kuroda, "Shinto in the History of Japanese Religion."

39. Ichiro Hori, *Folk Religion in Japan*, pp. 43ff.

40. Cf. the history of the conception of the deity in Konkōkyō, from malevolent to benevolent deity. See Delwin B. Schneider, *Konkōkyō: A Japanese Religion* (Tokyo: ISR Press, 1962) and Willis Stoesz, "The Universal Attitude of Konkō Daijin," *Japanese Journal of Religion* 13 (1986). Concerning Sugawara Michizane, it is perhaps not surprising that he was one of Munetada's heroes. Note that the *Tenmangu ryaku yurai* ("abridged history of the Kitano shrine") along with the "Popular Sermons" of Ikkyū and several others, was among the works which the founder is known to have copied in his own hand. See *Kyōkyōsho*, 2: 281-297, cited Hepner, *The Kurozumi Sect of Shinto*, p. 98.

41. Eliot, *Japanese Buddhism*, p. 306.

42. Munetada frequently celebrated the mystery of the fullness of emptiness in his poems: "By calling Nothing nothing, people are deluded: / Nothing is indeed the source of Everything." *Kyōkyōsho*, 1:10.

43. In Pure Land the vow of Amida was also a power at work in the world but in a different way. Amida as a bodhisattva vowed to become not a perfect bodhisattva but a Buddha whose merits could provide a means of salvation to those unable by their own efforts to tread the bodhisattva path. As such Amida becomes essentially inactive, although he has bodhisattvas such as Avalokitesvara to act for him. Yet, once one had been born into the Pure Land, the bodhisattva ideal again came into play. One could be perfected in the benign environment of the Pure Land, thence to return to the world of suffering to lead others to perfection as a bodhisattva.

Having ceased to be a bodhisattva, Amida logically had to become what he did become in popular Buddhism in Japan, namely, a god of the afterlife rather than an active force in this life. On the level of personal piety in Pure Land Buddhism the vow is retained in attenuated form: it reappears as the felt determination to be born in the Pure Land. But, especially in Shin Buddhism, it is not interpreted as a power of the self, one's own power, but is seen as recognition of Amida's grace. The very impulse itself comes from Amida. This is the concept of the faith-mind (*shinjin*) in the thought of Shinran, a notion which is interpreted as both intensity (*shinshin*) and sincerity (*seishin*). This understanding of sincerity wants further study for its influence on Munetada. That is, if one considers the Shin-shu materials, sincerity is no longer the exclusive province of Neo-Confucianism.

44. To the three modes already discussed one might consider adding a fourth, the ascetic model. This is a model which has been articulated especially by Blacker. It is more problematic in its application to our data and presents difficulties when one attempts to differentiate it from the other three. Indeed we might venture to say that some form of asceticism is endemic to all religious activity. Moreover I would also argue that asceticism is a pan-human activity rooted (it must be) in the most basic structures of human nature. Carmen Blacker, *The Catalpa Bow* (London: Allen and Unwin, 1975), pp. 21-22 describes it as follows:

> He is primarily a healer, one who is capable of banishing the malevolent spirits responsible for sickness and madness and transforming them into powers for good. To acquire the powers necessary for this feat he must accomplish a severe regimen of ascetic practice, which should properly include, besides fasting, standing under a waterfall and reciting sacred texts, a journey to the other world.... This journey he may accomplish in ecstatic, visionary form; his soul alone travels, his body left behind meanwhile in a state of suspended animation. Or he may accomplish the journey by means of symbolic mimesis; the other world projected by means of powerful symbolism on to the geography of our own, he can make the journey through the barrier in body as well as soul.

In my view the documentation of soul-travel in Japan is problematic; nonetheless, the description of symbolic mimesis well fits the Shugendo adepts which form the main prototype for Ms. Blacker's typology.

Munetada exhibits some aspects of the ascetic in two ways: his practices of what Shinto calls *komori* or seclusion; and his role as a healer, as a practicer of *majinai*.

Originally the practice of *komori* was an aspect of *imi*, or abstinence. As such it was for specific purposes in Shinto: to bring about a desired effect (protect a ship at sea because it contained an especially pure person, an abstainer) or to purify a priest immediately prior to his participation in a ritual. Munetada's practice of what is called *imi* is not of this kind; it is rather like the Zen *sesshin* or extended period of intense meditation, or like the more general monastic practice of establishing a hermitage for intense meditation by one already an adept at the art.

As for the art of healing, this is so much a pan-Japanese practice and at the same time such an emphasis of all the New Religions from late Tokugawa to the present that it is difficult to see what use can be made of the practice in the present essay.

## 9. The Dōka in Historical Perspective

1. *Kojiki*, trans. Donald Philippi (Princeton: Princeton University Press, 1969), p. 91. For the original see the *Nihon koten bungaku taikei* (hereafter NKBT), Vol. 1 *Kojiki, Norito* (Tokyo: Iwanami Shoten, 1958), pp. 88-89. For another translation, see Robert Brower and Earl Miner, *Japanese Court Poetry* (Stanford: Stanford University Press, 1961), p. 58. The tale is also found in the *Nihon Shoki* (cf. NKBT 67:122-23; *Nihongi*, trans. W. G. Aston [Rutland, Vt: Charles E. Tuttle Co., 1972], pp. 53-54).

2. Cf. Takeda Yukichi, *Kiki kayōshū zenkō* (Tokyo: Meiji Shoin, 1956), p. 28.

3. Cf. NKBT 3:34, note 1.

4. For the relevant passage see *Kojiki*, pp. 41-41. NKBT 1:46-47. Konishi Jin'-chi has some interesting things to say on this topic. See Jin'ichi Konishi, *A History of Japanese Literature*, Volume 1, trans., Eileen Gatten and Nicholas Teele, ed. Earl Miner (Princeton: Princeton University Press, 1984), pp. 254-260.

5. See especially Tsuchihashi Yutaka, *Kodai kayō to girei no kenkyū* (Tokyo: Iwanami Shoten, 1965); *Kodai kayō senchushaku — Nihonshoki-hen* (Tokyo: Kadokawa Shoten, 1976); and *Kodai kayō zenchushaku — Kojiki-hen* (Tokyo: Kadokawa Shoten, 1983).

6. On *kotodama shinko* the reader will find Ito Haku, "Man'yōjin to kotō-dama" in Hisamatsu Senichi, ed., *Man'yōshū koza*, 3 vols. (Tokyo: Yuseidō, 1973) 3:46-63, especially useful. In English the best source is Konishi, *A History of Japanese Literature*, Chapter 1 and 203-212, 253-54, 327ff., *passim*.

7. Note that the terms "primary orality" and "secondary orality" are taken from Walter J. Ong, *Orality and Literacy: The Technologizing of the Word* (London and New York: Methuen, 1982). One of the few English-language sources to address the important issues of the implications of the introduction of writing in Early Japan is David Pollack, *The Fracture of Meaning: Japan's Synthesis of China from the Eighth through the Eighteenth Centuries* (Princeton: Princeton University Press, 1986), Chapter 1.

8. For a somewhat critical study of how the concept of *Yamato-damashi* has continued to be used for ideological purposes, see Roy Andrew Miller, "The 'Spirit' of the Japanese Language," *Journal of Japanese Studies* 3 (Summer, 1977): 251-98; and *Japan's Modern Myth: The Language and Beyond* (New York and Tokyo: Weatherhill, 1982).

9. NKBT 1:216-17; *Kojiki*, pp. 242-43.

10. Paul Friedrich, an anthropologist, linguist, and poet, has noted that everyday conversation today is no different in this, although we generally do not pay any attention to this aspect of metaphorical language. Among other examples he cites American black rap and the speech of children, and even creates a poem out of snatches of taped interviews with people about Joe DiMaggio. See Paul Friedrich, *The Language Parallax: Linguistic Relativism and Poetic Indeterminancy* (Austin: University of Texas Press, 1986).

Note that in the original Japanese the old man (*okina*) is referred to with the honorific particle *mi-*. While this may represent a retrospective recognition of his relationship to the imperial prince Yamato-takeru, in light of the medieval No play, *Okina*, where an old man is revealed actually to be a kami in disguise, this servant may also be more than meets the eye. Yamatotakeru, after all, was anything but adept at recognizing such kami, a failing which led to his death.

11. All of these varieties of ritual poetry are treated in Gary L. Ebersole, *Myth, Ritual Poetry and the Politics of Death in Early Japan* (Princeton: Princeton University Press, 1989).

12. Among western language sources dealing with ritual poetry in the Heian and subsequent periods, see especially Gary L. Ebersole, "The Buddhist Ritual Use of Linked Poetry in Medieval Japan," *The Eastern Buddhist*, n.s., 16 (Autumn, 1983): 50-71; Bernand Frank, *"Kata-imi et kata-tagae: etude sur les interdits de direction à l'époque Heian," Bulletin de la Maison Franco-japonaise*, n.s., 5 (1958); Dennis Hirota, trans., "'In Practice of the Way' *Sasamegoto*, An Instruction Book in Linked Verse," *Chanoyu Quarterly* 19 (1977); 23-46; Harmut O. Rotermund, *Majinai-Uta. Mitteilungen die Deutschen Gesellschaft fur Batur und Völkerkunde Ostasiens* 59 (1973); Harmut O. Rotermund, "Quelques aspects de la magie verbale dans les croyances populaires au Japan," in Bernard Frank, ed., *Mélanges Offerts à M. Charles Haguenauer* (Paris: College de France, 1980), pp. 425-42; and M.C. Haguenauer, "La danse rituelle dans la cérémonie du chinkonsai," *Journal asiatique* (avril-juin, 1930): 299-350.

13. For an introduction to the thought of Kūkai, see Yoshito S. Hakeda, *Kūkai: Major Works* (New York: Columbia University Press, 1972), especially "The Meanings of Sound, Word, and Reality (*Shoji jissō gi*), pp. 234-246.

14. Cf. Yamada Shōsen, "Gachirin-kan to chūsei waka" in *Bukkyō to girei*, ed. Bukkyō minzoku-gakkai (Tokyo: Kokusho-kankōkai, 1977), pp. 301-314; and Manabu Watanabe, "Religious Symbolism in Saigyo's Verses: A Contribution to Discussions of His Views on Nature and Religion," (*History of Religions* 26 (May 1987): 382-400.

15. Shitateru-hime (also called Taka-hime no mikoto), a daughter of the earthly kami Okuni-nushi, is found in the myth of the descent of the imperial family from

Amaterasu, the Sun Goddess. When Ame-no-waka-hiko was sent down from the High Heavens to pacify the land and prepare the way for the descent of Amaterasu's son, who was to rule there, he instead took Shitateru-hime as his wife and plotted to gain the land for himself. He was eventually slain by a sacred arrow cast down from heaven. At his funeral the widowed Shitateru-hime sang two *uta*. It is these that are alluded to by Ki no Tsurayuki as the first poems/songs on earth. For the complete myth, see *Kojiki*, pp. 120-128; NKBT 1:113-119.

16. Translation from *Kokinshū*, ed., trans. Laurel Rasplica Rodd. *Kokinshū: A Collection of Poems Ancient and Modern* (Princeton: Princeton University Press, 1984), p. 35.

17. On the "seamless world," see especially Joseph M. Kitagawa, "Reality and Illusion: Some Characteristics of the Early Japanese World of Meaning," *Journal of the Oriental Society of Australia* 11 (1976): 3-18; and "'A Past of Things Present': Notes on Major Motifs in Early Japanese Religions," *History of Religions* 20 (August-November, 1980): 27-42.

18. I have translated the difficult term *makoto* here as "ultimate reality." More literally it means "sincerity," "fidelity," or "truth," but in Munetada's usage *makoto* seems to refer to an unchanging eternal truth that is ever-present in this world, although often obscured, unrecognized, and uncultivated by people. It also indicates the identity of the pure human mind-heart (*kokoro*) with Heaven and Earth. [*Ed. note: Cp. Chapter 6, dōka 10. Ikimono, "living-thing(s)," may be translated either in the singular or in the plural. Both readings fall within Munetada's frame of reference, referring either to the omnipresent Amaterasu or to the "many things" given unity by her.*]

Unless otherwise noted, citations of Munetada's *dōka* are from Taisen Nobuhara, *The Brilliant Life of Munetada Kurozumi, a Philosopher and Worshipper of the Sun*, 2nd ed. (Tokyo: PMC Publications, 1982), pp. 140ff.

19. Kuroda Toshio has cogently argued that there is no distinct religion which can properly be labelled Shinto until perhaps the establishment of State Shinto in the 19th century. For a summary presentation of his argument see Toshio Kuroda, "Shinto in the History of Japanese Religion," *Journal of Japanese Religion* 7 (1981): 1-21.

20. On this, see especially Watase Masatada, "Hitomaro hinkyū banka no tōjō: sono uta no ba megutte," *Kokubungaku: kaishaku to kanshō* 35 (July, 1970): 32-41; and *Kakinomoto Hitomaro kenkyū*, 3 vols. (Tokyo: ōfusha, 1976), vol. 3.

21. Cf. William LaFleur, "Saigyō and the Buddhist Value of Nature," Pt. 1, *History of Religions* 13 (November, 1973): 93-128; and Pt. 2, *ibid.* 13 (February, 1974): 227-248. An important corrective to certain assertions made by LaFleur is Manabu Watanabe, "Religious Symbolism in Saigyō's Verses: A Contribution to Discussions of His Views on Nature and Religion," *History of Religions* 26 (May 1987): 382-400.

22. See chapter 2.

23. NKBT 5:64-65. For other translations on this verse, see Brower and Miner, *Japanese Court Poetry*, p. 135 and Ian Hideo Levy, trans. *The Ten Thousand Leaves*, Vol. I. (Princeton: Princeton University Press, 1981), p. 352.

24. For other translations of this verse, see Brower and Miner, *Japanese Court Poetry*, p. 190 and *Kokinshū*, p. 289. I have translated *ma* as "spacetime" because it has both spatial and temporal dimensions. In the former it can mean "space between" two points or objects, "empty space," "void," "gap," etc; in the latter it can mean "period of time," "interval," etc.

25. The translations here are Hardacre's (see chapter 2), although I have arranged them into five lines.

26. *Kokinshū*. p. 64. For another rendering of this see Brower and Miner, *Japanese Court Poetry*, p. 199.

27. See also William R. LaFleur, *Mirror for the Moon: Selection of Poems by Saigyō 1110-1190* (New York: New Directions Books, 1978), p. 6.

28. LaFleur has rendered this differently (see Ibid.).

29. See also Ibid., p. 71.

30. Translation adapted from Ibid., p. 77.

31. [*Dōka* 32]. See also the following verses on this point:

| | |
|---|---|
| ari to mite | Seeing it as existing |
| naki koso onoga | nothing takes on the form |
| sugata nari | of ourselves. |
| arite mayowanu | Not being deluded by "existence" |
| mi koso yasukere | only can comfort the body.[35] |
| | |
| ari to mite | Seeing it as existing |
| naki koso onoga | nothing becomes |
| sumika nari | our dwelling. |
| naki o tanoshimu | Enjoy nothingness |
| kokoro yasusayo | and comfort your heart-mind. |

32. Munetada's use of the term *marugoto*, which I have rendered "the cosmic circle," recalls the esoteric Buddhist practice of mandala meditation using, among other things, pictures of the moon. Some scholars have suggested that medieval monk-poets such as Saigyō may have used the actual moon, as well as paintings, in their meditative praxis. In that form of meditation the mind was identified with the moon and the moon with the mind, so that all distinction of subject and object was overcome. Cf. the following verse of Saigyō (*Sankashu* 1784):

| | |
|---|---|
| yatsuba byakuren | [Headnote: "A verse on the |
| ichū-kan no kokoro o | essence of the white lotus |
| | flower put in a circle an |
| | elbow's length across."] |
| | |
| kumo ōu | The light of the moon |
| Futakami-yama no | on Mount Futakami, |
| tsukikage wa | covered with clouds, |
| kokoro ni sumu ya | could be seen residing |
| miru ni aru ramu | in the mind in its purity. |

Trans. Manabu Watanabe, "Religious Symbolism in Saigyo's Verses: A Contribution to Discussions of His Views on Nature and Religion," *History of Religions* 26 (May 1987): 392-393.

33. For an example of how *dōka* are used in sermons today, see Helen Hardacre, *Kurozumikyō and the New Religions of Japan* (Princeton: Princeton University Press, 1986), pp. 77-78.

## 10. Kurozumi Munetada's Use of the Tanka Form

1. *Kojiki*, trans. Donald Philippi (Princeton: Princeton University Press, 1969), p. 91.

2. *The Manyōshū; The Nippon Gakujutsu Shinkokai Translation of One Thousand Poems* (New York: Columbia University Press, 1965).

3. Collections of individual poets reaching tens of thousands of poems are not unknown. The Emperor Meiji (r. 1868-1912) is said to have written some 100,000 himself.

4. Earl Miner et al., *The Princeton Companion to Classical Japanese Literature (Princeton: Princeton University Press, 1985), pp. 6ff.*

5. Harold Wright, *Ten Thousand Leaves: Love Poems from the Manyōshū* (Woodstock, N.Y.: The Overlook Press, 1986), p. 35.

6. Harold Wright, *The Waka Poetry of the Emperor Meiji* (Tokyo: Meiji Jingu Office, 1984), p. 21.

7. Harold Wright, "The Poetry of Japan," *Asia* No. 16 (Autumn, 1969): 69.

8. Wright, *The Waka Poetry of the Emperor Meiji*, p. 18.

9. Edward G. Seidensticker, trans., *Tale of Genji*, 2 vols. (New York: Alfred A. Knopf, 1976). See Chapter 51, "A Boat Upon the Waters," 2:972-1012.

10. Wright, *Ten Thousand Leaves*, p. 33.

11. Names and location have been changed for publication.

12. Wright, "The Poetry of Japan," p. 74. As a Buddhist priest Saigyō should not have felt the slightest attachment to the things of the world. Yet, such deep beauty moves him. This is a confessional poem.

13. Wright, *The Waka Poetry of the Emperor Meiji*, p. 24.

14. Harold Wright and Julie Iezzo, trans., Kurozumi Tadaaki, "*Kurozumikyō Kyōsoden*" (manuscript, 1987), chapter 6.

## 11. Omamori *in Kurozumi-kyō*

1. Erich Neumann, *The Great Mother* (New York: Bollingen, 1963), pp. 42-43. Carl Jung provides numerous examples of this same thought pattern. E.g., "A Zulu myth tells a woman to catch a drop of blood in a pot, then close the pot, put it aside for eight months, and open it again in the ninth month. She follows this advice, opens the pot in the ninth month, and finds a child inside it." Carl Jung, *Symbols of Transformation* (New York: Pantheon, 1956), p. 203.

2. Yanagida Kunio, *Utsobo Bune No Hanashi* (Tokyo: Imoto no Chikara, 1927), pp. 307-342. For other helpful discussions of vessel symbolism see: Carmen Blacker, *The Catalpa Bow* (London: Allen Unwin, 1975), pp. 98-99; Cornelius Ouwehand, *Namazue and Their Themes* (Leiden: Brill, 1964), pp. 122, 186-87, 190: Naomi Miller, *Heavenly Caves: Reflections on the Garden Grotto* (New York: Braziller, 1982), p. 119; Mariel von Franz, *Interpretation of Fairy Tales* (Zurich: Spring, 1973), pp. 88-91.

3. Egerton Ryerson, *The Netsuke of Japan: Legend, History, Folklore and Customs* (New York: Castle, 1958), p. 45.

4. W. H. Desmonde, *Myth, Magic and Money: The Origin of Money in Religious Ritual* (Glencoe, N.Y.: Free Press, 1962), p. 123; Von Franz, *Interpretation of Fairy Tales*, p. 60.

5. Joya Moku, *Things Japanese (Tokyo: Tokyo News Service, 1960)*, pp. 72-73; W. G. Aston, *Shinto* (Tokyo: Logos, 1968), pp. 193-194.

6. W. L. Hildburth, "Some Japanese Minor Magical or Religious Practices Connected With Traveling," *Japan Society Transaction and Proceedings*, 14 (1915-1916): 86-124. For the use of rice in Kurozumi-kyō healing rites see Helen Hardacre, *Kurozumikyō and the New Religions of Japan* (Princeton: Princeton University Press, 1986), p. 95.

7. Letter from Kurozumi Nobuakira, November 21, 1985.

8. Mircea Eliade, *Patterns in Comparative Religion* (New York: World, 1958), p. 157.

9. Letter from Kurozumi Nobuakira, November 21, 1985.

## 12. Shinto-Christian Comparisons

1. Ninian Smart, "Scientific Phenomenology and Wilfred Cantwell Smith's Misgivings," in Frank Whaling, ed., *The World's Religious Traditions; Current Perspectives in Religious Studies* (New York: Crossroad, 1986), p. 268.

2. Joseph Kitagawa, *On Understanding Japanese Religion* (Princeton: Princeton University Press, 1987), p. 296.

3. Smart, "Scientific Phenomenology," pp. 268ff.

4. Raimundo Panikkar, "The Dialogical Dialogue," in Whaling, ed., *The World's Religious Traditions*, p. 218f.

5. The question of the role of the academic study of religion in promoting this dialogue requires brief discussion. Under what metaphor might this role be understood?

In part we acted in the role of *nakōdo*, the "go-between" or matchmaker familiar in Japanese society who plays a part in many kinds of social negotiation, especially in arranging marriages. Yet, we had no thought of suggesting any preordained outcomes. We assumed the interaction might well open insights unsuspected in advance. The role of the Socratic midwife, whose contribution is to bring about learning by bringing to light presuppositions embedded in the minds of interlocutors, also is suggestive. Yet, again, prior presuppositions from either camp were not to structure any projected outcomes definitively, in the sense in which Socrates uncovered Platonic ideas. To some extent, we sought to act as an "honest broker," making it possible for "clients" to carry out transactions in their own interest in a manner beyond their ordinary wont, informed in some part by discoveries made in the course of dialogue. The objectivity or professional character of the academic enterprise comes into view under this metaphor, in that the personal faith commitment of the academic scholar is not being advanced through the negotiations.

Though the academic student of religion does not here act in the role of the research scientist carrying out an experiment, neither is he/she a technician carrying out a piece of social engineering. We assumed we were setting up a situation in which the inner spirit of each dialogue participant might, in unpredicted ways, lead to the discovery of fresh understanding of the religious faith of both sides. Better global religious understanding is a moral desideratum entirely appropriate to the academic study of religion.

Whatever the mix of metaphors that best illuminates this or other instances in which the academic study of religion becomes involved in the dialogue of representatives of religious traditions with each other, it is clear that those who profess that study need not live in ivory towers; that, on the other hand, they should not in carrying out that enterprise presume to speak for the traditions; that their independent point of view enables them to make a definite contribution; and that real understanding may emerge both among the participants and among the onlooking inquirers who wish better to understand each tradition.

6. Translated in rough draft by Hashida Hiromi and edited by Willis Stoesz. Subtitles have been supplied by the editor. Poetry is translated by Harold Wright; his comments helped clarify the quotations. Notes 7-9 are supplied by the editor.

7. Professor Judith Martin of the University of Dayton assisted in the service of *norito*, offering the *sakaki* (yew). Brother David Herbold of the Marianist Order assisted in translation.

8. I.e., "No object or person is not part of things"; "It is the [whole] Universe (*Ametsuchi*) that [must be considered when something] is disordered."

9. See Douglas MacArthur, *Reminiscences* (New York: McGraw-Hill, 1964), p. 288. MacArthur added: "This courageous assumption of a responsibility implicit with death, a responsibility clearly belied by facts of which I was fully aware, moved me to the very marrow of my bones. He was an Emperor by inherent birth, but in that instant I knew I faced the First Gentleman of Japan in his own right." See also the account provided by Matsudaira Yasumasa, a close associate of the Emperor at war's end, printed as part of General MacArthur's war reports. Matsudaira Yasumasa, "Appendix: The Japanese Emperor and the War," *Reports of General MacArthur*. Volume II, Part II. *Japanese Operations in the Southwest Pacific Area* (Washington: U.S. Government Printing Office, 1966), pp. 762-771.

10. I.e., the Church of the Brethren, the Mennonites, and the Society of Friends, known as the historic Peace Churches.

11. Solomon Mandelkern, ed., *Veteris Testamenti, Concordantiae* (Jerusalem: Schocken, 1964), p. 1180, col. 1.

12. *The Challenge of Peace: God's Promise and Our Response. A Pastoral Letter on War and Peace.* May 3, 1983 (Washington D.C.: United States Catholic Conference, 1983), p. 9.

13. Ibid., pp. 9ff.

14. "Constitution on the Church in the Modern World," proclaimed by Pope Paul VI, December 7, 1965. *The Teachings of the Second Vatican Council; Complete Texts of the Constitutions, Decrees, and Declarations,* introd. Gregory Baum. (Westminster, MD: The Newman Press, 1966), pp.   439-556, cp. 538.

## 13. Kurozumi-kyō in Western View

1. Note Doi's argument that the emperor, as the symbolic apex of the deference/dependence system structuring Japanese society, is as powerless as a babe in arms. He can generate action in others as the object of obligation and reverence, but not through commands. Takeo, Doi, *The Anatomy of Dependence*, trans. John Bester (Tokyo: Kodansha, 1981), pp. 58f. The question of the role of the emperor in Japanese culture and society is complex, going far beyond present context.

2. Charles Hepner, *The Kurozumi Sect of Shinto* (Tokyo: The Meiji Japan Society, 1935), p. 85.

3. Winston Davis, "Pilgrimage and World Revewal: A Study of Religion and Social Values in Tokugawa Japan" Parts 1 and 2 *History of Religions* 23, Nos. 2 and 3 (1983-4). Munetada's message was perceived by his followers as resulting in the fresh vitality of the "age of the gods" (see chapter 3), but the reckless behavior of many Ise pilgrimage participants must have concerned him a great deal.

4. Harold Wright and Julie Iezzo, trans., Kurozumi Tadaaki, "Kurozumikyō Kyōsoden" (manuscript, 1987), chapter 2.

5. Whether his conceptual knowledge of nondualism was mediated to him by way of Neo-Confucianism, or whether he derived it directly from Buddhist sources such as the writing of Ikkyū, is a question we need not pursue here. The former is likely in view of the prominence of Neo-Confucianism in Okayama; but then it appears his experience of unity with Amaterasu led him to a stronger appreciation of the same emphasis in Buddhist sources. He drew from various sources; and we should not overlook his independence as a religious virtuoso in adapting his conceptual resources to his experiential needs. On Buddhist dimensions of Neo-Confucianism note the discussion by Tu Wei-ming, *Humanity and Self-Cultivation; Essays in Confucian Thought* (Berkeley: Asian Humanities Press, 1979), p. 174.

6. Helen Hardacre, "Creating State Shinto: The Great Promulgation Campaign and the New Religions," *Journal of Japanese Studies* 12 (Winter, 1986), 29-64. Kurozumi-kyō participation in State Shinto educational efforts was contrary to its fundamental vision of things (cp. 57f.), to which present Kurozumi-kyō leadership has returned.

7. See chapter 2; Helen Hardacre, *Kurozumikyō and the New Religions of Japan* (Princeton: Princeton University Press, 1986), p. 188.

8. Hepner, *The Kurozumi Sect of Shinto*, p. 212.

9. Ibid., p. 138ff.

10. See Yanagawa Kei'ichi and Abe Yoshiya, "Some Observations on the Sociology of Religion in Japan," *Japanese Journal of Religious Studies* 5 (March, 1978): 5-27, for a discussion of some of the issues involved in such comparison. See also Joachim Wach, *Sociology of Religion* (Chicago: University of Chicago Press, 1962), pp. 196-205 and Bryan Wilson, *Religious Sects; a Sociological Study* (New York: McGraw-Hill, 1970), pp. 23-35.

11. See Hepner, *The Kurozumi Sect of Shinto*, pp. 211ff., 221 for a description of these degrees as adopted in the 1927 edition of the Constitution. Personal recourse to *shinmon*, initiating the process of development, is thus analogous to adult baptism in Christian churches (originating as sects) that reject infant baptism.

12. Wach's comment to the contrary was made without apparent familiarity with Hepner's work (Wach, *Sociology of Religion*, p. 130). Not nearly so great a shift in direction of cultural development was set by Munetada as founder as in the case of Gotama or Christ as founders. However, his example is definitive as a source of ultimacy for Kurozumi-kyō members, and the universal sphere of reference is undeniable.

13. In this respect a metaphor derived from holography — in which each part of a picture expresses the picture as a whole — would describe the relation of Kurozumi-kyō to Japanese culture as a whole better than metaphors derived from the Christian church-sect distinction. See for instance the provocative discussion by Henri Bortoft, "Counterfeit and Authentic Wholes: Finding a Means for Dwelling in Nature," in David Seamon and Robert Mugerauer, eds., *Dwelling, Place and Environment; Toward a Phenomenology of Person and World* (Dordrecht: Martinus Nijhoff Publishers, 1985), pp. 281-302. Bryan Wilson's concept of the modern religious movement as a mediating institution between the individual and society as a whole is a step in this direction as well. Bryan Wilson, *Religion in Sociological Perspective* (Oxford: Oxford University Press, 1982), p. 135.

# Bibliography

Ashton, W. G. *Shinto*. Tokyo: Logos, 1968.

Beardsley, Richard K., *et al. Village Japan*. Chicago: University of Chicago Press, 1959.

Beasley, William G. *The Meiji Restoration*. Stanford University Press, 1972.

Bellah, Robert. *Tokugawa Religion*. 1957: reprint ed., New York: Free Press, 1985.

Benedict, Ruth. *The Chrysanthemum and the Sword*. 1946: reprint ed., Rutland, Vt.: Charles E. Tuttle Co., 1954.

Blacker, Carmen. "Millenarian Aspects of the New Religions in Japan." In *Tradition and Modernization in Japanese Culture*, edited by Donald Shively. Princeton: Princeton University Press, 1971.

_____. *The Catalpa Bow*. London: Allen and Unwin, 1975.

Brower, Robert, and Miner, Earl. *Japanese Court Poetry*. Stanford: Stanford University Press, 1961.

*The Challenge of Peace: God's Promise and Our Response. A Pastoral Letter on War and Peace. May 3, 1983*. Washington, D.C.: United States Catholic Conference, 1983.

Davis, Winston. "Pilgrimage and World Renewal: A Study of Religion and Social Values in Tokugawa Japan." Parts 1 and 2. *History of Religions*. 23, nos. 2 and 3 (1983-84).

deBary, W. T. "Sagehood as a Secular and Spiritual Ideal in Tokugawa Neo-Confucianism." In *Principle and Practicality*, edited by W. T. deBary and Irene Bloom. New York: Columbia University Press, 1979.

_____. *Neo-Confucian Orthodoxy and the Learning of the Mind-and-Heart*. New York: Columbia University Press, 1981.

DeBary, W. T. and Bloom, Irene, eds. *Principle and Practicality*. New York: Columbia University Press, 1979.

Desmonde, W. H. *Magic, Myth and Money: The Origin of Money in Religious Ritual*. New York: Free Press of Glencoe, 1962.

Dore, R. P. *Education in Tokugawa Japan*. Berkeley: University of California Press, 1965.

Earhart, H. Byron. *Japanese Religion*. 3rd. ed. Belmont, CA: Wadsworth Publishing Co., 1982.

_____. *Religions of Japan: Many Traditions Within One Sacred Way*. San Francisco: Harper and Row, 1984.

Eliade, Mircea. *Patterns in Comparative Religion*. New York: World, 1958.

Eliot, Sir Charles. *Japanese Buddhism*. 1935: reprint ed., London: Edward Arnold and Co., 1959.

Hara, Keigo. *Kurozumi Munetada*. Jimbutsu Yosho 42. Tokyo: Yoshikawa kobunkan, 1960.

Hardacre, Helen. "Creating State Shinto: The Great Promulgation Campaign and the New Religions." *Journal of Japanese Studies*. 12 (Winter 1986): 29-64.

_____. *Kurozumikyō and the New Religions of Japan*. Princeton: Princeton University Press, 1986.

Hayashiya, Tatsusaburō, ed. *Bakumatsu bunka no kenkyū*. Tokyo: Iwanami shoten, 1978.

Hepner, Charles. *The Kurozumi Sect of Shinto*. Tokyo: The Meiji Japan Society, 1935.

Hildburth, W. L. "Some Japanese Minor Magical or Religious Practices Connected With Traveling." *Japan Society Transactions and Proceedings*. 14 (1915-1916): 86-124.

Holtom, D. C. *The National Faith of Japan*. 1938: reprint ed., New York: Paragon, 1965.

Hori, Ichiro. *Waga kuni minkan shinko-shi no kenkyu*. (Study of the history of Japanese folk beliefs.) 2 volumes. Tokyo: Sogenshinja, 1953-1955.

_____. "The Appearance of Individual Self-consciousness in Japanese Religion and Its Historical Transformation." In *The Japanese Mind*, edited by Charles Moore. Honolulu: University of Hawaii Press, 1967.

_____. *Folk Religion in Japan*. Edited by Joseph M. Kitagawa and Alan Miller. Chicago: University of Chicago Press, 1968.

Itasaka, Gen, *et al.*, eds., *Kodansha Encyclopedia of Japan*. Tokyo: Kodansha International Ltd., 1983.

Jansen, Marius. *Sakamoto Ryōma and the Meiji Restoration*. Princeton: Princeton University Press, 1961.

Joya, Moku. *Things Japanese*. Tokyo: Tokyo News Service, 1960.

Kamata, Michitaka. "Ara-mura fukko no nomin undo." In *Bakumatsu bunka no kenkyū*, edited by Hayashiya Tatsusaburō. Tokyo: Iwanami shoten, 1978.

Kato, Genchi. *A Study of Shinto*. New York: Barnes and Noble, 1926.

Kitagawa, Joseph. *Religion in Japanese History*. New York: Columbia University Press, 1966.

_____. *On Understanding Japanese Religion*. Princeton: Princeton University Press, 1987.

Kiyota, Minoru. *Gedatsukai: Its Theory and Practice*. Los Angeles and Tokyo: Buddhist Books International, 1982.

Kodera, Motonoko. "Kurozumikyō no rekishiteki seikaku." *Okayama shigaku* 24 (September 1971): 39-64.

*Kojiki*. Translated by Donald Philipi. Tokyo: University of Tokyo Press, 1968; Princeton: Princeton University Press, 1969.

*Kokinshū: A Collection of Poems Ancient and Modern.* Edited by Laurel Rasplica Rodd. Princeton: Princeton University Press, 1984.

Kōmoto, Kazushi. *Kurozumikyō tokuhon.* Okayama: Kurozumikyō Nisshinsha, 1961.

_____. *Kyōsosama no oitsuwa* [*Tales of the Founder*]. Okayama: Kurozumikyō Nisshinsha, 1976.

Konishi, Jin'ichi. *A History of Japanese Literature.* Volume 1. Translated by Eileen Gatten and Nicholas Teele. Edited by Earl Miner. Princeton: Princeton University Press, 1984.

Kuroda, Toshio. "Shinto in the History of Japanese Religion." *Journal of Japanese Studies* 7 (1981): 1-21.

Kurozumi, Tadaaki. *Kurozumikyō kyōsoden.* 5th. ed. Okayama: Kurozumikyō Nisshinsha, 1976.

*Kyōkyōsho. Kurozumi Kyōkyōsho* [The Official Texts of the Kurozumi Sect]. Edited under the direction of Kurozumi Muneyasu (Third Patriarch). Vols. 1-2. 1909-1914 reprint ed. Okayama: San yo shin po insatsu bu, 1926-27.

*Kyōtenshō.* Kurozumikyō kyōhanhensan iinkai. *Kurozumikyō kyōtenshō.* Okayama: Kurozumikyō Nisshinsha, 1981.

LaFleur, William R. *Mirror for the Moon: A Selection of Poems by Saigyo 1110-1190.* New York: New Directions Books, 1978.

Laube, Johannes. "Zur Bedeutungsgeschichte des Konfuzianistischen Begriffs 'Makoto' ('Wahrhaftigkeit')." In *Fernöstliche Kultur.* Edited by Helga Wormit. Marburg: N. G. Elwert Verlag, 1975.

Lebra, Takie Sugiyama. "Reciprocity and the Asymmetric Principle: An Analytic Reappraisal of the Japanese Concept of *On.*" In *Japanese Culture and Behavior.* Edited by Takie Sugiyama Lebra and William P. Lebra. 1969: reprint ed., Honolulu: University of Hawaii Press, 1974.

_____. *Japanese Patterns of Behavior.* Honolulu: University of Hawaii Press, 1976.

Lee, Robert. "The Individuation of the Self in Japanese History." *Japanese Journal of Religious Studies* 4 (1977): 5-39.

*Manyōshū; The Nippon Gakujutsu Shinkōkai: Translation of One Thousand Poems.* New York: Columbia University Press, 1965.

Miner, Earl, *et al. The Princeton Companion to Classical Japanese Literature.* Princeton: Princeton University Press, 1985.

Morioka, Kiyomi. "Folk Religion and Shinto." In *Religion and Changing Japanese Society.* Tokyo: University of Tokyo, 1975.

Murakami, Shigeyoshi. *Seimei no oshie.* Toyobunko 319. Tokyo: Heibonsha, 1977.

_____. *Japanese Religion in the Modern Century.* Translated by H. Byron Earhart. Tokyo: University of Tokyo Press, 1980.

Najita, Tetsuo and Scheiner, Irwin, eds. *Japanese Thought in the Tokugawa Period 1600-1867: Methods and Metaphors.* Chicago: University of Chicago Press, 1978.

Nakamura, Hajime. *Ways of Thinking of Eastern Peoples.* Revised, translated, and edited by Philip Wiener. Honolulu: East-West Center Press, 1964.

Nakane, Chie. *Japanese Society.* 1970: reprint ed., Berkeley and Los Angeles: University of California Press, 1972.

Neumann, Erich. *The Great Mother.* New York: Bollingen, 1963.

*Nihongi [Nihon Shoki].* Translated by W. G. Aston. Rutland, Vt. and Tokyo: Charles E. Tuttle Co., 1972.

Nobuhara, Taisen. *The Brilliant Life of Munetada Kurozumi, a Philosopher and Worshipper of the Sun,* translated by Tsukasa Sakai and Kazuko Sasage. 2nd ed. Tokyo: PMC Publications, 1982.

Okada, Takehiko. "Practical Learning in the Chu Hsi School: Yamazaki Ansai and Kaibara Ekken." In *Principle and Practicality,* edited by W. T. deBary and Irene Bloom. New York: Columbia University Press, 1979.

_____. "Neo-Confucian Thinkers in Nineteenth-Century Japan." In *Confucianism and Tokugawa Culture,* edited by Peter Nosco. Princeton: Princeton University Press, 1984.

Ono, Sokyo. *Shinto: The Kami Way.* In collaboration with William P. Woodard. Rutland, Vt. and Tokyo: Charles E. Tuttle Co., 1962.

Panikkar, Raimundo. "The Dialogical Dialogue." in *The World's Religious Traditions; Current Perspectives in Religious Studies,* edited by Frank Whaling. New York: Crossroad, 1986.

Pelikan, Jaroslav. *The Vindication of Tradition.* New Haven: Yale University Press, 1984.

Robertson, Jennifer. "Rooting the Pine: *Shingaku* Methods of Organization." *Monumenta Nipponica* 34 (Autumn 1979): 311-332.

Ryerson, Egerton. *The Netsuke of Japan: Legend, History, Folklore and Customs.* New York: Castle, 1958.

Sadler, A. L., trans. *The Ise Daijingu or Diary of a Pilgrimage to Ise.* Tokyo: Meiji Japan Society, 1940.

Sansom, George B. *Japan; A Short Cultural History.* 2nd rev. ed. Stanford: Stanford University Press, 1952.

Sasaki, Junnosuke. *Bakamatsu shakairon.* Tokyo: Kōshobō, 1969.

Schneider, Delwin B. *Konkōkyō: A Japanese Religion.* Tokyo: ISR Press, 1962.

Seidensticker, Edward G., trans. *Tale of Genji.* 2 vols. New York: Alfred A. Knopf, 1976.

Shibata, Hajime. *Kinsei gōnō no gakumon shisō.* Edited by Negishi Yoichi. Tokyo: Shinseisha, 1966.

Shils, Edward Albert. *Tradition.* Chicago: University of Chicago Press, 1981.

Shimazono, Susumu. "The Living Kami Idea in the New Religions of Japan." *Japanese Journal of Religious Studies* 6 (1979): 389-412.

Shimonaku, Yasaburō. *Shinto daijiten.* 3 vols. Tokyo: Heibonsha, 1940.

Shinjō, Tsuenezō. *Shaji to kōtsū.* Nihon rekishi shinsho. Tokyo: Chibundō, 1960.

Smart, Ninian. *The Phenomenon of Religion*. New York: Seabury Press, 1973.

_____. "Scientific Phenomenology and Wilfred Cantwell Smith's Misgivings." In *The World's Religious Traditions; Current Perspectives in Religious Studies*, edited by Frank Whaling. New York: Crossroad, 1986.

Smith, Robert J. *Ancestor Worship in Contemporary Japan*. Stanford: Stanford University Press, 1974.

Stoesz, Willis. "The Universal Attitude of Konkō Daijin." *Japanese Journal of Religious Studies* 13 (1986): 3-29.

Taniguchi, Sumio. "Bakumatsu ni okeru Kurozumikyō no ichikōsatsu." *Okayama daigaku kyōikubu kenkyū shureku* 6 (1968): 65-81.

von Franz, Mariel L. *Interpretation of Fairy Tales*. Zurich: Spring, 1973.

Wach, Joachim. *Sociology of Religion*. Chicago: University of Chicago Press, 1962.

Watanabe, Manabu. "Religious Symbolism in Saigyō's Verses: A Contribution to Discussions of His Views on Nature and Religion." *History of Religions* 26 (May, 1987): 382-400.

Whaling, Frank, ed. *The World's Religious Traditions; Current Perspectives in Religious Studies*. New York: Crossroad, 1986.

Wilhelm, Hellmut. *Change; Eight Lectures on the I Ching*. Translated by Cary F. Baynes. Princeton: Princeton University Press, 1960.

Wright, Harold. "The Poetry of Japan." *Asia* No. 16 (Autumn, 1969): 61-90.

_____. *The Waka Poetry of the Emperor Meiji*. Tokyo: Meiji Jingu Office, 1984.

_____. *Ten Thousand Leaves: Love Poems from the Manyōshū*. Woodstock, N.Y.: The Overlook Press, 1986.

Wright, Harold and Iezzo, Julie, trans. *Kurozumikyō Kyōsoden*. Unpublished manuscript.

Yamashita, Ryuji. "Nakae Tōju's Religious Thought and Its Relation to Jitsugaku." In *Principle and Practicality*, edited by W. T. deBary and Irene Bloom. New York, Columbia University Press, 1979.

Yanagida, Kunio. *Utsobo Bune No Hanashi*. Tokyo: Imoto no Chikara, 1927.

# Index

# Contributors

**Father Bertrand Buby** was the Provincial of the Cincinnati Province of the Society of Mary (Marianists), with his office at Bergamo near Dayton, Ohio. In his role as Provincial, he also oversaw the work of his Province as it extends to Japan and to Africa. He is a New Testament scholar, and the author of *Mary; the Faithful Disciple* (New York: Paulist Press, 1985). He has been for some years a leader in Jewish-Christian dialogue activities.

**H. Byron Earhart** is Professor of Religion at Western Michigan University in Kalamazoo, Michigan. He is author of a number of books and monographs on Japanese religion, including *Japanese Religion* (Belmont: Wadsworth Publishing Co., 1982), a widely used textbook now in its third edition. His *Gedatsukai and Religion in Contemporary Japan* has been published by the Indiana University Press (1989).

**Gary L. Ebersole** is Assistant Professor of East Asian Languages and Literatures and Associate in the Center for Comparative Studies in the Humanities, as well as Director of the Religious Studies Program, at Ohio State University. His *Myth, Ritual Poetry and the Politics of Death in Early Japan* is forthcoming at the Princeton University Press.

**Helen Hardacre** is Associate Professor of Religion and of East Asian Studies at Princeton University. In addition to her book on Kurozumi-kyō she has published *Lay Buddhism in Contemporary Japan: Reiyūkai Kyōdan* (Princeton: Princeton University Press, 1984) as well as other studies. Her current research concerns the development of State Shinto.

**The Reverend Muneharu Kurozumi** is the Chief Patriarch (*Kyōshū*) of Kurozumi-kyō, with headquarters near the city of Okayama. He is a direct descendant of the Founder, the sixth member of his family to lead his denomination. In 1979 he took part in a symposium of world religious leaders at Princeton and spoke at Saint Patrick's Cathedral in New York. He has led his denomination into its new headquarters buildings at Shintozan, has spoken throughout Japan, and has travelled to New Zealand, Australia, and the United States.

**Alan Miller** is Associate Professor of Religion at Miami University. He is the author of the section on East Asian Religions in the textbook *Religions of the World* edited by John Y. Fenton and others (New York: St. Martin's Press, 1984; also published separately in paperback as *Asian Religions*, edited by Niels Nielsen). He co-edited Ichiro Hori, *Folk Religion in Japan* (Chicago: University of Chicago Press, 1968) and has published recent articles on early Japanese religious history in *History of Religions*.

**Willis Stoesz** is Associate Professor of Religion at Wright State University and Chair of the Department of Religion. While engaged in research in Japanese religion at

Okayama University of Science he became acquainted with the leaders of Kurozumi-kyo. His recent article in the *Japanese Journal of Religious Studies* dealt with the founder of Konkō-kyō, another Shinto sect with headquarters near Okayama.

**Eugene Swanger** is Professor of Religion and of East Asian Studies at Wittenberg University. He founded the Program in East Asian Studies there and directed it for some years, and serves as Chairman of the Department of Religion. He teaches in the East Asia Seminar at the Foreign Studies Institute of the U. S. State Department. His manuscript *Omamori; A Handbook on Japanese Amulets and Talismans* is nearing completion.

**Harold Wright** is Professor of Japanese Language and Literature at Antioch College. During one of his periods of work in Japan he translated poetry of the Meiji Emperor and Empress. Recently he has been in Japan on a National Endowment for the Arts fellowship to work on a translation project with Tanikawa Shuntaro. He has translated *The Selected Poems of Shuntaro Tanikawa* (San Francisco: North Point Press, 1983) and also published poetry from the Man'yōshū as *Ten Thousand Leaves; Love Poems from the Man'yōshū* (Woodstock, N.Y.: Overlook Press, 1986).